CHINA IN THE INTERNATIONAL SYSTEM, 1918–20

China in the International System, 1918–20

The Middle Kingdom at the Periphery

Zhang Yongjin
Junior Research Fellow in Chinese Studies
Wolfson College, Oxford

St. Martin's Press   New York

First published in the United States of America in 1991

Printed in Hong Kong

ISBN 0–312–05341–X

Library of Congress Cataloging-in-Publication Data
Zhang, Yongjin.
China in the international system, 1918–20: the middle kingdom at
the periphery/Zhang Yongjin.
p.   cm.
Includes bibliographical references and index.
ISBN 0–312–05341–X
1. China—Foreign relations—1912–1949.   I. Title
DS775.8.Z43   1991
327.51′009′041—dc20   90–43360
                                                       CIP

To the memory of my mother

Contents

Acknowledgements   ix

Note on Transliteration   x

List of Abbreviations   xi

Introduction   **1**

1   An Empire Contracted in a World Expanded   **6**
Two 'Families of Nations', East and West   6
Problems of Communication between Two Civilizations,
East and West   12
The Collapse of Sinocentrism   I   15
The Collapse of Sinocentrism   II   21
The 'Core' and 'Periphery' in the International System   26
A Nation among the Nations   33

2   A Disappointed Nation at Paris, 1919   **39**
Getting Prepared   41
A Bone of Contention   51
An Unrewarding Supplication   59
An 'Even Break'?   65
Nationalism and the May Fourth Movement   74
The Issue of Signature   78
Absence from the Hall of Mirrors   88

3   Whither China in East Asian International Order   **100**
The British Perspective   102
The American Perspective   115
The Japanese Perspective   127
The Chinese Perspective   138

"]

4 Russian Breakthrough **148**
Opportunities Undreamed of 149
Along the Borderlands 155
A Special Mission 165
The Break 175

Conclusion **187**

Notes and References 197
Glossary 240
Bibliography 244
Index 255

Acknowledgements

In the course of preparing and completing this book, I have accumulated a number of intellectual and personal debts. I would like to take this opportunity to thank all the people who have encouraged and assisted my studies in Oxford. I owe a special debt to Mr Don Markwell, Professor Adam Roberts and Mr Christopher Seton-Watson for their patience, stimulus and guidance over the last five years. I would also like to acknowledge the assistance of a number of libraries around the globe, in particular the National Library of China in Beijing, the Second National Archive Library in Nanjing; Library of Congress and the National Archives in Washington, the Butler Library of Columbia University, the Firestone and Mudd Libraries of Princeton University, and Sterling Memorial Library of Yale University; and the Public Record Office and the British Library in London and the Bodleian Library in Oxford. I am grateful to Wolfson College, Oxford, for offering this research fellowship so that I can put the final touch to the manuscript. Finally, I would like to thank my wife and my daughter for their love, tolerance and encouragement and for the five years during most of which we have lived in two parts of the world, the East and the West.

ZHANG YONGJIN

Note on Transliteration

In transliterating Chinese characters, the *pinyin* system has been used throughout the text, except in the quotes, where the original spelling stands unchanged. A glossary is appended at the end of the book (pp. 240–3).

List of Abbreviations

CA	Chinese archives deposited in the Second National Archive Library in Nanjing, China
CAB	Cabinet Documents (Public Record Office, London)
CER	Chinese Eastern Railway
CHC	*Cambridge History of China*
CSPSR	*Chinese Social and Political Science Review*
DBFP	*Documents on British Foreign Policy, 1919–1939, First Series*
FO	Foreign Office Documents (Public Record Office, London)
FRUS	*Papers Relating to the Foreign Relations of the United States*
JFMA	*Japanese Foreign Ministry Archives*
ML	*Miji Lucun* (A Record of Secret Correspondence)
NCH	*North China Herald*
NGB	*Nihon gaikō bunshō* (Documents on Japanese Foreign Policy)
WAYDZ	*Wusi Aiguo Yundong Dangan Ziliao* (Source Materials about The May Fourth Patriotic Movement)
ZEGS	*Zhong E Guanxi Shiliao* (Archival Materials on Sino-Russian Relations
ZEGS – EDHWS	*Zhong E Guanxi Shiliao – E Dui Hua Waijiao Shitan* (Soviet Preliminary Diplomatic Feelers to China)
ZEGS – EZB	*Zhong E Guanxi Shiliao – E Zhengbian* (Russian Revolution)
ZEGS – EZYYI	*Zhong E Guanxi Shiliao – E Zhengbian Yu Yiban Jiaoshe* (Russian Revolution and General Contact)
ZEGS – TESD	*Zhong E Guanxi Shiliao – Tingzhi E Shiling Daiyu* (Discontinuation of Recognition of Russian Minister and Consuls)
ZEGS – XB	*Zhong E Guanxi Shiliao – Xinjiang Bianfang* (Xinjiang Frontier Defence)
ZEGS – YJ	*Zhong E Guanxi Shiliao – Yiban Jiaoshe* (General Contact)
ZEGS – ZT	*Zhong E Guanxi Shiliao – Zhongdong Tielu* (Chinese Eastern Railway)

Introduction

China's integration into the contemporary international society looks today, at the end of 1989, increasingly like a process incomplete. One hundred and fifty years after the so-called 'Opium War' of 1839–1840 when the British first 'opened' China for Western commerce, China's strenuous efforts in search of a creative answer to foreign challenges seem to be still going on. More than a hundred years's modernization of China is today more of a failure than a success. Like their predecessors, contemporary Chinese intellectuals are still grappling with the incompatabilities between the Chinese and the Western cultures. The economic reforms in the 1980s bear striking similarities to the Self-Strengthening Movement in the 1860s and the 1870s. The trauma of China's modernization is far from over. It is seventy years since the Paris Peace Conference, when the present-day international society was taking shape with its global institutions and democratic principles, and when China was for the first time accepted into the Family of Nations, as reflected, for example, in its membership of the League of Nations. The year 1919 of course also witnessed the coming to maturity of Chinese nationalism, with its strongest yet manifestation during the May Fourth Movement. Yet, then as now, China had to adjust itself to the changing values and principles of the international society so as to take its rightful place in that society. Then, as now, China's place in the international system posed a 'China problem' for the Western powers in their perception of a global international order. Then, as now, the international society was faced with the problem of how to respond to the ups and downs of China's adaptations and adjustments to the values and institutions of the changing international system. From the vantage point of 1989, one may indeed ask: What is, after all, behind such a sequence as 1839, 1919, 1949 and 1989?

The analogy must not be stretched too far, however. Historical events are never affected by analogies but determined by the combinations of circumstances. Historical circumstances may indeed vary. Nevertheless, the theme–China's integration into the international society–seems perpetual. It is likely to remain with us, not only as a matter of historical interest, but more probably as a matter of future importance.

1

This book is a study of that perpetual theme: China's integration into the present-day international society. It concentrates on China's diplomatic efforts in the three years immediately after World War I (1918–1920) to win for itself an equal place in the international order under reconstruction. It aims at, first, providing a systematic account of the assertive diplomacy of China, then a 'probationary' member of the emerging international society, to claim its full membership in that society; and secondly, evaluating those efforts in the historical and theoretical framework of China's gradual integration into the global international system and the emergence of a universal international society.

Although this study is not intended to be a definitive history of China's diplomacy in the period, it must be noted that this subject matter has been little studied, if not totally neglected, in both Chinese and Western scholarship. Detailed studies are still lacking of such principal events of the period as China's preparation for and participation in the Paris Peace Conference, and decision-making in Beijing on the issue of China's signature of the Versailles Treaty. Besides, the few existing monographs and relevant works on China's foreign relations in the period tend to jump from a casual mention of the Shandong question at the Paris Peace Conference to China's attendance at the Washington Conference of 1921–1922. These few works are overshadowed by the large volume of literature, both in Chinese and in English, on China's domestic transformations, political, intellectual and social, as embodied in the so-called 'May Fourth Movement' and on the birth of the Communist movement in China. The contrast is striking.

Some reasons for this neglect may be suggested. The years fall within one of the most chaotic periods of the early Republic of China, beset with every dissension, confusion and complication of warlord politics. The question was not irrelevant as to whether, without a stable central government but with foreign omnipresence, China could possibly develop any positive diplomacy. On the other hand, the intellectual revolution and social transformation in China initiated by the New Culture Movement in 1915 was reaching its peak in 1919, particularly in the broadly defined 'May Fourth Movement'. This singularly important transformation of China seems to have fascinated most scholars of the period to the exclusion of anything else.

Scholars interested in the issues were further hampered by two daunting obstacles: inaccessibility of the Chinese archives which have survived years of havoc of warlord politics and civil wars, and lack of an analytical framework within which fresh and meaningful intepretations of this part of the history of modern China's external relations can be sought. Until recently, the Second National Archive Library at Nanjing which houses most Chinese archives of the Nationalist period (1911–1949) remained closed to the general public. On the other hand, the inadequacy of 'China's response to the West' as an overall single paradigm to account for political, economic and social changes of modern China has long been recognized and criticized. The alternatives, however, are very limited indeed.

The theoretical studies on the states systems and the expansion of international society started mainly by Martin Wight and Hedley Bull have provided an alternative and illuminating approach to the historical study of relations between Europe and non-European states originally belonging to different international systems.[1] The history of modern international relations is seen as 'the expansion of the international society of European states across the rest of the globe, and its transformation from a society fashioned in Europe and dominated by Europeans into the global international society of today'.[2] In particular, this approach examines the problem of relations between Europe and non-European states from the point of view of the latter's entry into international society. In the study of modern China's external relations, this furnishes a new and alternative analytical framework for new interpretations of the history of Sino-foreign relations. Of equal importance is the fact that, thanks to the changes in China in the last few years, official Chinese diplomatic record are now available for consultation, although they are at best incomplete and access to them is still contingent.

Three general points must be made clear at the outset. First, my attempt to adopt the theoretical or quasi-theoretical approach particularly suggested by Bull for a historical study of modern China's external relations presupposes my adoption of the concepts of 'states system' and 'international society' defined by Hedley Bull. In his words,

> Where states are in regular contact with one another, and where in addition there is interaction between them sufficient to make the behaviour of each a necessary element in the calculations of the other, then we may speak of their forming a system.[3]

What, then, is an international society? And what is the correlation between an international system and an international society? Bull and

Watson later carefully made the definition and the distinction in the following words:

> By an international society we mean a group of states (or, more generally, a group of independent political communities) which not merely form a system, in the sense that the behaviour of each is a necessary factor in the calculations of the others, but also have established by dialogue and consent common rules and institutions for the conduct of their relations, and recognize their common interest in maintaining these arrangements.[4]

Secondly, this is not a theoretical inquiry. It is a case study of diplomatic history conducted in the theoretical framework of the expansion of international society. Transformations and changes have long been recognized as characterizing the 'May Fourth' era in Chinese history. What is not well recognized is China's changing attitude in conducting its foreign relations manifested most unequivocally in the same period. The intensity of Chinese diplomacy and the consistency of its aim have not received due attention either in the study of Chinese history or in that of international relations. Inquiries into the problem of reconstruction of the East Asian international system after World War I have always centred on issues such as the end of the Anglo-Japanese Alliance, the American–Japanese confrontation, and compromise in the Pacific and naval disarmament. China has been neglected as if international politics are entirely the 'Great Powers' politics'. One purpose of this study is, among other things, to approach in an unconventional way the problem of reconstructing the international order in East Asia from the perspective of a weak state–China. This being so, archival materials have been widely used to describe the main events of China's diplomacy in the period. Special attention is given to the interpretation of those events to see (1) how China's place in the post-war East Asian international system under reconstruction is the central theme of conflict between China and the Great Powers, and (2) how, while the Powers still intended to deny China full sovereignty, China's assertive diplomacy for an equal international position and its active participation in world politics in the period compelled their acquiescence in China's membership in international society.

Thirdly, with a presentation of Chinese diplomatic history of 1918–1920, this study also seeks to address the essential, yet controversial, questions central to the understanding of China's integration into the world, i.e. when and how the Middle Kingdom could be said to have entered the international society. It approaches the questions mostly from the historical perspective rather than from that of legal theory. It argues that, historically, China was accepted in 1918–1920 into the international society.

Chapter 1 addresses briefly questions of China's gradual integration into the expanding international system and the collapse of the Sinocentric world order. It argues that, by the beginning of World War I, China had been incorporated into the periphery of the European-dominated international system. Chapter 2 charts the Chinese preparations for and presentations at the Paris Peace Conference and studies the decision-making process of the Chinese Government in Beijing and of the Chinese Delegation in Paris in regard to China's signing of the Versailles Treaty. It contends that China was made a disappointed nation at Paris, and that its refusal to sign the Versailles Treaty was a national revolt against the continuing subjection of China in world politics. It also suggests that China's participation in the Paris Peace Conference, rather than in the Hague Conferences of 1899 and 1907, can be properly regarded as the beginning, when China was more 'conscious of certain common interest and common values', conceived itself 'bound by a common set of rules' in its relations with other nations, and shared in the working of common institutions in the emerging international society. Chapter 3 looks at the problem of the reconstruction of the East Asian international system after the Peace Conference from the perspective of the most interested Powers, Britain, America and Japan, and from that of China. The central theme of conflict is identified as China's place in the reconstructed international system. Chapter 4 is a study of China's overall assault on the Russian treaty rights and privileges in China to complete the picture of China's diplomatic efforts to win an equal international position in the post-war international order. The conclusion discusses the import of China's diplomacy in the period against the background of China's entry into the international society. It contends that the period is the point of entry of China into the emerging universal international society. But China's entry into that society is not marked by its meticulously fulfilling the European standard of 'civilization', but by a revolt against the treaty system imposed on China by the West and an assertion of its sovereign rights by invoking principles universally acknowledged among the European nations as governing their relations.

1 An Empire Contracted in a World Expanded

The idea that states and political communities on the globe today constitute a unified international system is only recent. Just as the image that our physical world is an indivisible whole was formulated slowly in history with discoveries and exploration of continents and gradually superseded the other images of the world, the idea of our political world as an interconnected and inseparable entity only emerged progressively as Europe expanded across the rest of the globe to incorporate other political communities into the states system originated in Europe. This chapter studies the meeting of two 'families of nations', the European and the Chinese, and traces the process through which the Chinese Empire was brought into the periphery of the global international system.

TWO 'FAMILIES OF NATIONS', EAST AND WEST[1]

Two developments in the 1640s, in Europe and in China respectively, viewed in retrospect today, have considerable significance in world history and in the evolution of the world-wide international system. In 1648, after years of changes as reflected in the Reformation and the Renaissance as a result of powerful intellectual, political and social forces at work,[2] the Peace of Westphalia, if it did not initiate a completely new situation in Europe,[3] at least did 'legalize a condition of things already in existence'.[4] This 'condition of things already in existence' turned out to be the emergence of a states-system among Christian states of Europe, later referred to figuratively as the European 'Family of Nations'. In China, 1644 marked the beginning of the Manchu or Great Qing Dynasty, the last of its kind, which was to last more than two hundred and sixty years. It inherited from its predecessor, the Ming Dynasty, the suzerainty over a number of states, including Korea, Siam, Liuqiu (Ryukyu), Vietnam, Burma, and Japan to some extent. The East Asian international system, isolated largely from the rest of the world and characterized by the tributary relations

6

between China and the other members of the system, can be said to have constituted its own world, a 'Family of Nations'[5] in the East, with China as the head of the family.

The significance of this of course lies not only in the emergence or the existence of the two Families of Nations, ignorant of each other at the time, but most importantly in their different perceptions of the world and in the different rules and principles governing the relations between members of the respective Family of Nations. In the evolution of the two systems of states and in the process of their getting to know each other, the differences, instead of being adjusted, became more outstanding. This foreboded conflict and confrontation between the two Families of Nations, representing two different civilizations, when they eventually met each other. This was what happened about two hundred years later in the Sino-British War in 1840.

The Family of Nations of the West consisting of the signatories of the Westphalia Treaty grew out of the medieval *Republica Christiana* where the Church and the Emperor were two superior authorities.[6] The *raison d'état*, which was embodied in Jean Bodin's celebrated words: '*majestas est summa in cives ac subditos legisbusque soluta potestas*',[7] was crystallized in international practices at Osnabruck and Munster. Thus Pufendorf was able to define in 1675 the system in Europe as 'several states that are so connected as to seem to constitute one body but whose members retain sovereignty'. When Rousseau wrote in 1756 that 'toutes les Puissances de l'Europe forment entre elles une sorte de système',[8] the concept of Europe being a Christian Commonwealth was no longer active in European international politics. The idea of a supreme authority and an organization above sovereign states was replaced by a notion that the states of Western Europe formed a single political system of equal sovereignty.

Voltaire qualified his description of Europe as 'a kind of great republic divided into several states'. He further elucidated the characteristics of this states-system. The states within the system, he observed, were

> all corresponding with one another. They all have the same religious foundation, even if divided into several confessions. They all have the same principles of public law and politics, unknown in the other parts of the world.[9]

Here, Voltaire makes two points: that common cultural background and universally accepted principles of law and politics are the basis of the European international system, and that, because of this, it is different from the other international systems, if any, in the world. What Voltaire failed to mention was underscored by Fauchille as 'la reconnaissance par les États européens de la solidarité de leurs intérêts politiques'.[10]

In the nineteenth century, Rivier, a celebrated international jurist, defined the legal concept of the Family of Nations. He wrote:

> C'est ... entre les nations qui ont avec nous une conscience juridique commune, que notre droit des gens règne et qu'il doit être appliqué, et ce sont ces mêmes nations que nous appelons préférence civilisées, parce que leur civilisation est la nôtre. Entre ces nations, qui toutes sont supérieures, règne une communauté et une réciprocité de droits ... Elles forment ce que l'on appelle la Société ou même la Famille des Nations: beau nom, destiné, on peut l'espérer, à devenir vrai de plus en plus.[11]

Emphasized here are again the common culture and common sense of justice in the European Family of Nations. The other features standing out in the definition are two fundamental principles of the European international society, namely, absolute sovereignty and juridical equality of states. It is these two fundamental principles that determined rules and institutions which functioned to regulate the relations between the European states and manage the order within the European Family of Nations. Operating in the framework of a common culture, '[T]his new system rests on international law and the balance of power, a law operating between rather than above states and a power operating between rather than above states'.[12] Complementary to the above two institutions were the congress and conference and diplomatic dialogue, mainly through resident embassies, to facilitate the communication between the states.

What characterized the Family of Nations in the West was completely missing in the Family of Nations in the East, which was based on the Chinese concept of 'Tian Xia Yi Jia' (All under Heaven are one family), as the Chinese always held to the family as the pattern for all forms of human association. The Chinese concept of 'Tian Xia' has two aspects. On the one hand, it presupposes the universal kingship which, Benjamin Schwartz maintains, is unique only when it is linked with the Confucian criteria of higher culture and moral order. The expression of this moral order is mostly found in *li*,[13] an all-inclusive term for ceremonies, rituals and rules of proper conduct. On the other hand, 'Tian Xia' refers to the Chinese Empire as well as China's known world. In the latter aspect, 'Tian Xia' is a dynamic concept as it changes with the expansion of the Chinese Empire and of the world to the knowledge of China. The Eastern Family of Nations, therefore, consisted of China, the 'Middle Kingdom', and states and political communities at the periphery of the Empire and sometimes in the areas of Chinese cultural influence. The latter were expected, at least in theory, to participate in the Family by recognizing the superiority of the Son of Heaven, the Chinese Emperor, and by observing appropriate procedures and ceremonies in their contact with the Centre. Specifically, the participation took the form of paying tribute to the Chinese Empire.

It follows that the Chinese world order was hierarchical and non-egalitarian, with the Chinese Son of Heaven at the apex. This is in sharp contrast with the European international order. This hierarchic order was, however, supported and eventually perpetuated by Confucian doctrines summed up in the Three Bonds and Five Relationships (*san gang wu chang*) governing the relations of benevolence and obedience, respectively, between father and son, husband and wife, sovereign and minister, the old and the young and between friends. As an ordering principle of the Chinese society, the Three Bonds and Five Relationships were repeatedly emphasized in the later dynasties by Confucianists and neo-Confucianists.[14] As the Chinese tended to think of the Empire and of the world in terms of an extension of the family, they often assumed that China's relations with the other countries and peoples were but an external expression of the internal political and social order of China and that China should act as an elder brother or a parent.

However we must guard against any oversimplification and generalization of the Chinese world order. A distinction has to be made between the subjective Chinese perception of what a Chinese world order should be and the objective realities of the history. It is by no means correct to claim that from the Han Dynasty (206 BC–AD 220) on, the Chinese rigidly applied a uniform system grounded upon the universal superiority of the Chinese in their relations with other countries.[15] Exploring the records of history, Professor Lien-sheng Yang of Harvard University wrote:

Politically and militarily, in several periods, China recognized neighbouring peoples as equal adversaries (ti-kuo). Note, for example, the relations between Han and Hsiungnu; T'ang and T'u-chueh or later T'u-fan; Sung and Liao, Chin and Yuan. In these relations kinship terms were often used.[16]

Historically, it is not the perception alone, but also the realities of the security and survival of the Chinese Empire that dictated the framework of the Chinese world order in different periods. The Chinese ways of dealing with outsiders were partly developed as a defence mechanism. As late as the Tang Dynasty (618 AD – 907 AD), 'efforts to seek peace through relations of equality or through relations of conquest were ... repeated'.[17] It is not until the Southern Song Dynasty in the twelfth century when the Chinese Empire was at its weakest and suffered humiliation as a result of invasion by the 'northern barbarians' that a dogma was worked out by the ascending neo-Confucian philosophy in regard to China's international relations. The dogma asserts that

> national security could only be found in isolation and stipulates that whoever wished to enter into relations with China must do so as China's vassal, acknowledging the supremacy of the Chinese emperor and obeying his commands, thus ruling out all possibility of international intercourse on terms of equality. It must not be construed to be a dogma of conquest or universal dominion, for it imposed nothing on foreign peoples who chose to remain outside the Chinese world. It sought peace and security, with both of which international relations were held incompatible. If relations there had to be, they must be of the suzerain–vassal type, acceptance of which meant to the Chinese acceptance of the Chinese ethic on the part of the barbarian.[18]

In the Ming Dynasty, however, this dogma generated a political system which is identified in contemporary studies of China and of international relations as the Chinese tribute system.

This is not to say that the tribute system came into existence only in East Asia in the Song (960–1279) and Ming Dynasties. The tribute system, in general, had existed in the old imperial order in the West and in the East alike. Vattel, in his *Law of Nations*, observed that

> The custom of paying tribute was formerly very common – the weaker by that means purchasing of their more powerful neighbour an exemption from oppression, or at that price securing his protection, without ceasing to be sovereigns.[19]

But the tribute system as such mentioned above is quite peculiar and is what concerns us here. The tribute system consolidated in the Ming Dynasty and inherited by the Qing Dynasty seems to have matched the Chinese conception of the world order, a cultural or psychological reality, with the existence of a Family of Nations with China as the superior a political reality.

This Family of Nations, which existed more in the minds of the Chinese than as an objective political fact, was ordered by China at the top of the hierarchy. The Chinese world order was accepted, sometimes reluctantly, by the other members of the Family. The Middle Kingdom, assuming its higher virtue and with its benevolence, ruled, as it were, the Family of Nations in the East by assigning to the other members their places in the Family. All the participants had to observe *li*, which Confucius regarded as 'the principle of a rationalized social order and through it everything becomes right in the family, the state and the world'[20] and as 'the foundation of the government'.[21] The *li* is actually inclusive of all prescribed appropriate formalities and ceremonies in their contact with the Empire.[22]

We may now sum up by comparing the two concepts of the Family of Nations. Both the European and the Chinese Families of Nations were built on the basis of a common culture and operated in the common cultural framework from which were derived institutions and principles governing relations between members of each Family. These institutions and principles rooted in two different civilizations were, however, incompatible with each other. First, while the legal principles of sovereignty and equality made all the European states theoretically equal and mutually independent, the Chinese world order was of a 'superordination and subordination'[23] pattern with its legitimacy coming from the mandate of Heaven. Secondly, in the Eastern Family of Nations, it was *li*, often vaguely defined, which took the place of international law in the Western Family of Nations in regulating the relations between China and the other members. It was the universal preeminence of the Chinese Emperor, the Son of Heaven, which superseded the balance of power as the managing institution to maintain order in East Asia. Thirdly, there were no such institutions as resident embassies and congress to facilitate the communication between members of the Family of Nations in East Asia. The diplomatic dialogue was virtually non-existent. The tributary missions were only expressions of tribute states' participation in the Chinese world order. Fourthly, whereas the European Family of Nations was a political order with the consent of all its members who shared common interest in maintaining that order, the Eastern Asian Family of Nations was, in contrast, more of a moral order, culturally based and politically oriented from the Chinese side. There was a conspicuous absence of common interest and consent among its members in maintaining the arrangement. Finally, it should be observed that the two Families of Nations firmly rooted in respective indigenous civilizations were at the time only vaguely aware of each other's existence.

PROBLEMS OF COMMUNICATION BETWEEN THE TWO CIVILIZATIONS, EAST AND WEST

The different values found in the two concepts of the Family of Nations in the East and in the West reflected two different civilizations which were separated by vast geographical barriers but which were destined to meet eventually. As each civilization at the time was a self-contented entity and conceived itself the centre of the world, there arose problems of communication between the two civilizations. These problems, which caused further estrangement of Eastern Asia and Western Europe, were three-fold: geographical, political and cultural.

Joseph Needham once observed that 'For three thousand years a dialogue has been going on between the two ends of the Old World.'[24] The dialogue, if any, was at best sporadic and casual. The communication between the two worlds was greatly hampered by the geographical barriers which were hardly surmountable before the dawn of the modern age. The immense physical distance in between simply separated the two societies in the East and in the West from each other. The Tibetan mountains and the Gobi desert, where the spread of Chinese civilization stopped, were as formidable to the Chinese as to the Europeans. Until May 20, 1498, when Vasco da Gama dropped anchor off Culcut in India, the Oceans were but 'the nameless perils in the world that be, Shipwrecks and sharks and the great deeps of the sea'.[25]

The difficulties were accentuated by the fact that interposed between the two worlds were first the Parthia and subsequently the Arabian and Islamized nations of the Middle East, who acted as intermediaries. Pratt described the function of these intermediaries as that of a 'curtain'. In his words,

the tribes and nations inhabiting Western Asia and the lands at the head of the Persian Gulf and on either side of the Red Sea were able to levy toll on the traffic through their territory. The curtain they let down between Europe and the East prevented direct contact between Rome and China. Each was a world civilization surrounded by a fringe of outer barbarians, each heard of another civilization at the other end of the world, but the two civilizations never met. They just touched with the tips of their antennae and that was all.[26]

The only exception which can be made here is the period during the Yuan Dynasty in China (1271–1378 AD). The Mongols established an empire which extended beyond the confines of Asia to the heart of Europe. The *Pax Tartarica* enabled the caravans, travellers and priests to pass with some freedom and security for the first time in history through the whole width of Europe and Asia. The story of Marco Polo was a case in point. It was owing to this situation and to the exploratory overtures of a few Venetians that Europe gradually became fully conscious of the 'spacious seat of ancient civilization which we call China'.[27] With the collapse of the Mongol power and the revival of Islam before the end of the fourteenth century, the 'curtain' was down again and direct land communication between Europe and China was cut off.[28]

The most acute and lasting problems of communication between the two civilizations are, however, cultural differences. When modern science and technology made it possible to overcome those physical barriers and to bypass the 'curtain', cultural differences loomed larger in the cross-cultural communication problems. Needham held that the two systems simply could not communicate with each other intellectually. China and Europe had developed entirely different modes of thought and their systems of thinking had been so fixed in the tenth century AD that observations, ideas and theories, whether pertaining to philosophy or to science, of either side could not adjust to those of the other and neither could accommodate the concepts emanating from the other.[29]

This incompatibility of Chinese civilization with that of Christian Europe, in a broad sense, can be accounted for by the origins of each civilization. The Western civilization may be thought of as being derived from three countries on the Mediterranean–from Rome, it inherited an idea of law; from Greece, philosophy, especially its notion of social and political order; and from Palestine came the belief of personal salvation for redemption of man's evil nature. The Chinese civilization, on the other hand, is based on the Confucian teachings which looked to the sages for inspiration and for principles. The essential values of the two civilizations were, therefore, different. For example, while Western Europe emphasized government by law, the Chinese believed in government by virtue and benevolence, just as Confucius remarked, if the people be led by laws and their conduct be regulated by punishments, they may try to avoid the penalties, but they have no sense of shame. Lead them by virtue and standardize them by rules of propriety, and they will not only have a sense of shame, but they will also become good.[30]

The Chinese in this way actually stressed one's obligations rather than one's rights as the Western civilization did. One historian, in reviewing the history of modern Sino-Western relations, observed that 'The troubles which have disturbed relations between China and the West since the end of the eighteenth century are mainly due to conflicting views regarding the rule of law and the rights of individuals'.[31] This is certainly true, though it is not the whole story of the conflict.

Cultural differences apart, the fundamental stumbling-block in the way of mutual understanding between the East and the West was cultural pride founded upon a series of unspoken assumptions manifested in the two civilizations. This self-conceived cultural superiority, which, it must be pointed out, was accompanied usually by ignorance, functioned to prevent the evolution of intercultural affinities between the East and the West. For the Chinese, the inheritors of an ancient civilization, and one geographically far removed from any other culture of comparable significance, their sense of being superior was deep-rooted in their way of thinking. It was difficult for them to conceive how any other people could be cultured yet live in a manner different from theirs. They were inclined to think that all alien cultures they came into contact with were inferior, hence barbarian. Likewise, in Western Europe, the Christian religion required its adherents to believe that their religion was perfect and to look upon Oriental religion as false, inferior or heathen. It was their holy duty to Christianize the world. Bozeman depicted the Western cultural pride at the end of the sixteenth century as follows:

> When Liz de Camoes reviewed the world before he died in A. D. 1580, he saw all history converging upon Christian Portugal. From here, he felt, had sallied forth a race of heroes, the Lusiads, destined by Providence to join the oceans and the continents in the service of all humanity and for the greater glory of Christianity and Western Europe.[32]

The pride and prejudice of the West were buttressed by the sudden outburst of scientific genius in the eighteenth century which led to the Industrial Revolution and an immense increase in wealth and power in

Western Europe, enabling it to overtake the other civilizations in many aspects. The Europeans were firmly convinced of the superiority of their culture and began to view everything from the standpoint of the morality, religion and culture of the West. In China, the sense of cultural superiority was stereotyped and seemed to have reached an extreme in the late seventeenth and early eighteenth centuries. The Chinese despised and showed contempt for everything and anything from the West. In receiving Lord Macartney's mission in 1793,[33] Emperor Qian Long wrote a poem which reads:

> Formerly Portugal presented tribute;
> Now England is paying homage.
> They have out-travelled Shu-hai and Heng-chang;
> My ancestor's merit and virtue must have reached their distant shores.
> Though their tribute is commonplace, my heart approves sincerely.
> Curios and the boasted ingenuity of their device I prize not.
> Though what they bring is meagre, yet,
> In my kindness to men from afar I make generous return,
> Wanting to preserve my good health and power.[34]

As late as 1839, the Viceroy in Canton ordered the Hong merchants to instruct the foreigners in the tenets of the Chinese civilization and to repress their pride and profligacy.[35]

The two civilizations as such could not hope to develop any significant cultural and political understandings between them, whereas, in their confrontation, each was inclined to deny the title of 'civilized' to the other. There was no meeting of minds whatsoever. Lord Macartney in his diary of January 15, 1794, wisely remarked that 'Nothing could be more fallacious than to judge of China by any European standard.'[36] It is, however, the fallacy of judging one by the standard of the other that both China and Western Europe committed when their two opposite conceptions of the world and of the social order came into conflict as a result of the West's expansion into Asia. Just as Mo Zi (Mo Ti) observed, 'Where standards differ, there will be opposition. But how can the standards in the world be unified?'.[37]

THE COLLAPSE OF SINOCENTRISM I

The historical development of the unification of the world in the form of the European expansion to incorporate all the other nations and states into a world-wide international system is partly attributable to the fact that modern science was generated in Europe. Modern science provided members of the European 'Family of Nations' not only with means with which to unify the world, but also with an encouraging sense of being superior, not only in their economic and military power, but also in their institutions and value systems. 'In their eyes modern civilization was synonymous with European ways and standards, which it was their duty and their interest to spread in order to make the world a better and safer place.'[38] The two Families of Nations finally met and clashed, as symbolized by the hostile confrontation between China and Great Britain in the beginning of the nineteenth century. Because 'the most fundamental incompatibility was each civilization's deeply ingrained self-assurance and self-righteousness',[39] the contact was a series of conflicts. The expanding West sought to impose its values and its world views upon China, and China tried to resist the imposition and held on to the conception of itself being the centre of the world.

The process through which China was forcibly drawn into the world-wide European-dominated international system is that of the demise of Sinocentrism. In the sixty years after 1840, China was, in reality, fully incorporated into the expanding European system of states, in the sense that it was in regular contact with other members and there was 'interaction between them sufficient to make the behaviour of each a necessary element in the calculations of the other'.[40] The Middle Kingdom became one of the many members of the global international system which linked all regional international systems into one. The collapse of Sinocentrism in the development of world politics was also a process of China's struggle to resist aggressive European expansion, to adjust itself to the changing international realities, to meet its problems without totally abandoning its imperial tradition, and finally to accept slowly and gradually, though sometimes reluctantly, some of the European standards, institutions, rules and values. If we telescope the changes of the Chinese views of the world and of their dealings with the outside nations and states in the years from 1840 to 1900, it is clear that the physical demise of Sinocentrism can be found in China's recognition of equality of other states with China; institutional changes including the establishment of Zongli Yamen[41] and of diplomatic relations with Western Powers; acceptance of the basic values and rules of international law; dispatch of diplomatic missions abroad; loss of all vassal states; and participation in international conferences and organization. In the reality of world politics, the world where the

Middle Kingdom assumed the central position was no longer in existence.

Notwithstanding its significance, the signing of the Treaty of Nanjing in 1842 after the first clash between the Oriental Empire – China – and an Occidental imperial Power – Great Britain – did not signal the opening of an era wherein China descended from the apex to accept equality with other states, not even with Great Britain. In fact, the Treaty was, in the eyes of Emperor Dao Guang, but a device to 'permanently prevent further troubles from happening'.[42] The five ports opened to the foreign merchants were, to the Chinese, like the factories at Canton previously, places where foreigners should be contained. As a *modus vivendi*, this amounted to a kind of 'extraterritoriality' imposed by China within its gates. The rights and privileges granted also aimed at the control or a loose rein of foreigners. In short, China responded to the Western challenge 'in terms of its own tradition'[43] The 'Board of Barbarian Affairs' continued to be responsible for the management of foreign affairs and its dealings were mainly conducted in Canton, far away from the capital, Beijing. Resident diplomacy at the capital was regarded as incompatible with the traditional institutions of Imperial China and, therefore, was not allowed, though consular relations were established in the treaty ports. In the first twenty years of the serious encountering of the two Families of Nations, China 'did not westernize its foreign relations because it saw no need to do so; it seemed to outsiders to be responding slowly precisely because its traditional institutions continued at first to function so well. In short, westernization was not the only response available to it'.[44]

China's official recognition of juridical equality with other states was later found in an imperial edict issued by Emperor Xian Feng after the joint Anglo-French Expedition in 1860 which invaded Beijing and forced the Emperor to flee. In an edict sanctioning the signing of the Treaty of Tianjin in 1861, the Emperor reluctantly decreed, 'England is an independent sovereign state, let it have equal status [with China].'[45] Before this date, the British feeling of not being treated equally could also be found in statements by British diplomats and politicians. Frederick Bruce, British Envoy Extraordinary and Minister Plenipotentiary to China, declared in Beijing in 1859 that he came to China to 'establish, on a proper footing, once and for all, our [the British] diplomatic relations with the Court of Pekin'. At about the same time, Viscount Palmerston contended in London that, if Britain continued to be treated on terms prescribed by the Chinese Government, and if it could not have either a resident minister in Beijing or a right to visit the capital, Britain was actually 'placed in a position of inferiority in regard to the Chinese Government'.[46]

China's recognition of the equal status of other states was followed and partially borne out by two institutional changes in the 1860s in the traditional Chinese system and statecraft – the compulsory acceptance of diplomatic representation of Western powers in Beijing and the initiation of Zongli Yamen, a government office to handle all aspects of relations with Western powers.[47] Both suggested the beginning of China's adoption of European ways of conducting foreign affairs, a significant change in the *Tizhi* (system and institutions) of Imperial China. Banno was certainly right to claim that the establishment of Zongli Yamen marked 'a turning point in China's foreign relations'.[48] That China had to change was not only because of the pressure from the West, but also because of the recognition among some Chinese officials of the 'changed situation unprecedented in the last thousand years'. In a memorial proposing the creation of Zongli Yamen, Prince Gong, who was later to become the principal minister of the Yamen, admitted that 'the present case is somewhat different from the [barbarian invasions] of former dynasties'.[49]

The significance of Zongli Yamen, the prototype of a foreign office, can be found in three aspects. Firstly, it signalled the beginning of the end of the traditional tributary system based on unequal relations and the acceptance of the existence of foreign relations defined by the European international society. 'Barbarian affairs' partly became foreign affairs. Secondly, as China's first formal centralized organ to manage its foreign affairs, the Yamen soon succeeded in establishing its working relations with the British, French, American, Russian and other treaty powers' envoys who were allowed, for the first time, to reside in the capital. Thirdly, it marked the beginning of a reform of institutions, in spite of the reluctance of Chinese officials,[50] which eventually brought China's diplomatic practice into line with that of the European international society.

Of other institutional changes, China's 'discovery' and adoption of international law and its dispatch of diplomatic missions abroad are also of great significance.[51] As observed previously, the concept of law was alien to Confucianism and incompatible with *li*, a traditional institution in the rule of the Middle Kingdom. However the Chinese officials were very much impressed that Western powers generally observed treaties faithfully. Prince Gong said in a memorial that 'After the exchange of treaties, the barbarians withdrew to Tientsin and sailed south in groups. Moreover, all their requests were based on the treaties.'[52] Shao Chaolin, President of the Board of War at the time, also observed that the British and French forces 'departed [from Beijing which they occupied] after exchanging the treaties, leaving our Capital unharmed'.[53] When, in 1864, Prince Gong and Zongli Yamen heard of the existence of international law, he reported that 'We have learned that there is a book called *Wan-Kuo Lu-Li* (Laws and Precedents of All Nations)'. He further recommended that 'there are points in it which may be adopted', although it was 'not entirely in conformity with Chinese institutions'.[54] In the same year, Henry Wheaton's *Elements of International Law*, translated into Chinese by W. A. P. Martin, was published and three hundred copies were distributed by Zongli Yamen to local officials for reference.

The extension of this exclusive European institution into the Oriental Empire and China's gradual adoption of it was an important step towards shattering the Sinocentric order. Soon, China had its first experience in the application of international law.[55] In 1878, it was invited to attend the sixth meeting of the Association for the Reform and Codification of the Law of Nations. Guo Songtao, Chinese Minister in London, who attended the meeting, spoke of improving the law of nations *'for the benefit of all governments and peoples'* (my emphasis). He explained that because of China's different cultural and political background, China had not completely subscribed to the rules of international law. He was, however, 'very desirous of attaining a knowledge of the science, in the hope that it will be beneficial to our country'.[56] By the end of the century, T. E. Holland, making a comment on both sides' observation of the conventions of war in the Sino-Japanese War, was able to say that China had adopted the 'rudimentary and inevitable conceptions of International Law'.[57]

The other change, which pushed China further into the interaction between states, was the establishment of resident diplomatic missions in foreign countries – after years of delay.[58] It was fifteen years after the minister of Britain took up his residence in Beijing that China had its first legation set up in London in 1877. This was followed by the establishment of legations in Germany in the same year, in the United States and France in 1878, in Russia and Spain in 1879, and in Peru in 1880. China finally accepted diplomatic representation abroad as a normal function of state diplomacy, a Western value. This facilitated the normal communication and regular contact between China and the outside world and involved China more in the international system. The interactions were such as to make it necessary for China to take into account the behaviour of other members of the international system, and at the same time to be taken into account by them.

These changes, significant as they are, do not amount to China's being accepted into the European Family of Nations. Even if, as Immanuel Hsu argued, China had by 1880 'realistically, if also painfully, assumed her place in the world community of nations',[59] it would still be difficult to sustain that this assumption was accepted by the European Family of Nations. Moreover, what China's place was remained a big question mark. From the European perspective, even at the turn of the century, the Middle Kingdom 'was only a candidate for admission to the Family of Nations'.[60] In the broader historical context, this 'diplomatic phase of China's entrance into the Family of Nations' was no more than China's being forcibly drawn into the expanding European international system and the beginning of its sustained contact with the West.

Finally, the death knell of the Sinocentric world order was sounded by the Empire's loss of its periphery, the so-called vassal-states, to Western imperialist powers. The expansion of Europe in the form of British, French and Russian imperialism, and later the Japanese imperial expansion, reached the peripheral areas of the Middle Kingdom from the 1870s onwards. Of all the tributaries listed in the 1818 edition of the *Collected Statutes of the Qing Dynasty* (Dai Qing Hui Dian),[61] Liuqiu went under the protection of (and later in the 1870s was annexed by) Japan; Britain took Burma after the third Anglo-Burmese War in 1885 and made it a province of British India in 1886; France colonized Annam twenty-five years after its first invasion in 1858; Laos became first a province of Siam and, in 1893, a French protectorate; and Korea was lost to Japan in 1895 after the Sino-Japanese War. Only Siam escaped from the European imperialist colonization in South East Asia, the price of its retaining the independence being to become a buffer zone between the British and French colonies in the area. Simultaneous with the imposition by the Western powers of 'unequal treaties' upon the Middle Kingdom, the disappearance of the traditional tributary system only made way for the 'treaty system' in which China was not at the centre as the arbiter but at the centre as a target of European imperialist power politics in East Asia.

Parallel to China's loss of its suzerainty could be seen its active participation in international conferences and activities, with China behaving more like a nation-state than a universal empire. As early as 1873, China was represented at international exhibitions at Paris and

Vienna. As already mentioned, China attended in 1878 the sixth meeting of the Association for the Reform and Codification of the Law of Nations, which was 'a novel feature in the history of the Association and, indeed, in the history of European Congresses'.[62] It joined the Universal Postal Union in 1862, the Red Cross in 1904, and the International Institute of Agriculture in 1905. Significantly, the two Hague Peace Conferences in 1899 and 1907 also witnessed Chinese participation.

By the end of the nineteenth century, the Middle Kingdom had undergone a drastic metamorphosis to assume a quasi-nation-state status by tacitly renouncing its claim to a Confucian universal empire. Its admission of the existence of other strong and independent nations beyond China and its actual dealings with them were more than a disavowal of the Chinese claim to universal overlordship. China was now incorporated into the world community of nations but was only brought to the 'outer courts of the charmed circle'.[63]

THE COLLAPSE OF SINOCENTRISM   II

It would be rash to assert that the factual collapse of the Sinocentric world order would naturally bring to an end Sinocentrism in the mental world of the Chinese, the conceptual Sinocentrism. In fact the collapse of the latter was long antedated by that of the former and to some extent can hardly be said to have been complete.

By 'conceptual Sinocentrism' is meant not only Chinese perception of China being the centre of the world, but more essentially the Chinese belief in the cultural and moral superiority of the Chinese civilization, deserving universal application. In the traditional Chinese thinking, there were three kinds of living beings on earth: the Chinese, the barbarians and the beasts. While the Chinese were the most cultured and the beast uncultured, barbarians, i.e., peoples outside the benevolence of the Chinese culture, came in between.

The Chinese were not fully aware of the existence of five continents beyond China, where peoples of different races and cultures lived until 1601 when Matteo Ricci, a Venetian Jesuit, presented to Emperor Wan Li of the Ming Dynasty a map of the world.[64] And in 1623 another Jesuit, Julio Aleni, wrote a book, *Zhi Fang Wai Ji* (Geography of the World), in an effort to tell the Chinese that there existed a world outside the Chinese tribute system. In the Preface it was stated that, 'since the Earth is a globe, any place can be the centre', bravely challenging the Chinese concept of China as the centre of the world. Jean Rodriguez commented later that

> The map of the world puts the Ming Dynasty at the centre so that it is convenient to look at. In terms of its place on the Globe, every country can be regarded as the centre. The Chinese, having seen the map and the Westerners, know now how big the world is and how many countries there are [in the world].[65]

What was said in the first part is right and in the second part an exaggeration. The knowledge was actually limited to the Court circle and to a few scholar officials. Most of the Chinese remained ignorant of the outside world. And, furthermore, this knowledge was almost lost when China was faced with the British challenge more than two centuries later.

It was after 1840 that the geographical concept of the Middle Kingdom as the centre of the world surrounded by barbarian states and tribes came under serious challenges again. Translation of passages from Murray's *Cyclopaedia of Geography*, sponsored by Commissioner Lin Zexu in Canton, was published in Chinese in 1841 under the title of *Si Zhou Zhi* (A Gazetteer of the Four Continents). In 1843, Wei Yuan published his *Hai Guo Tu Zhi* (Illustrated Treatise of the Maritime Countries), a work of fifty *Juan* (volumes). From 1840 to 1861, more than twenty-two books were written on the subject of world geography. Some of them, like Wei Yuan's *Hai Guo Tu Zhi*, were widely read among the scholar officials. These scholars and their efforts were thus 'instrumental in changing the Chinese geographical picture of the outside world. In so doing, they played a significant role, for they not only introduced new knowledge of the West, but also began to dissolve the Sinocentric view by showing that China was in reality not the Middle Kingdom'.[66]

The first sign of the disintegration of conceptual Sinocentrism was evidenced in the drop of Sinocentric terminology. For example, the use of *yi* (barbarians) to refer to foreigners, which was barred from official documents by the Treaty of Tianjin, was less frequently seen in official communications between Chinese officials. Instead, foreigners were called *Xi Yang Ren* (Western ocean people), or *Yang Ren* (foreigners). Even such a term as *Tian Xia* (all-under-heaven) was called into question. It was not an adequate term to describe China, some contended, because China was only one nation in the Family of Nations. If it could not face this reality, China would not be psychologically prepared to accept the idea of international law.[67]

Other scholars came to use the historical analogy of Warring States period (474–221 BC) to describe the world in which China found itself at the time. In 1873, *kotow* was officially abolished in Sino-foreign relations.

Another important sign of the disintegration of conceptual Sinocentrism was the emergence of what Paul Cohen called 'incipient Chinese nationalism' among a small number of Chinese officials, intellectuals and merchants.[68] Wang Tao's early call for the abolition of extraterritoriality in the 1870s[69] certainly found its parallel in Guo Songtao's submission in 1877 to the Emperor entreating the urgent need to abrogate this right and his talk with Lord Salisbury on the matter in London the next year.[70] Merchantile nationalism found its expression in the demands for the recovery of economic control *(shouhui liquan)* and the commercial rivalry *(shang zhan)*. These were certainly notions behind Li Hongzhang's initiative to set up the China Merchants' Steam Navigation Company and the Shanghai Textile Mill.[71]

These changes in the 1860s and the 1870s, significant in themselves, nevertheless did not touch the essence of conceptual Sinocentrism, the overwhelming sense of self-conceived Chinese cultural superiority. T. T. Meadows remarked in his *Desultory Notes on the Government and People of China*, in 1847, that the Chinese 'take the tone of superiors quite unaffectedly, simply because they really believe themselves superior'. He quoted a Chinese as saying:

> It is the great size and wealth and the numerous population of our country; still more in its excellent institutions, which may contain some imperfections, but which after all are immeasurably superior to the odd confused rules by which these barbarians are governed, but above all, in its glorious literature, which contains every noble, elegant, and in particular, every profound idea; everything, in short, from which true civilization can spring, that we found our claim to national superiority.[72]

This mentality persisted well into the 1870s and 1880s. The *Yangwu* (literally, Western affairs) or the Self-Strengthening Movement as it is commonly known in the West, was based on the notion of adopting western learning to preserve traditional Confucian way of life. For such 'liberal-minded' officials as Zeng Guofan and Li Hongzhang, who sponsored the *Yangwu*, western techniques were 'superior' and therefore, the Chinese should 'be humble-minded and bear humilia-tion, so that they can learn one or two secrets from the Westerners to benefit ourselves'.[73] The students sent abroad were also to 'improve in proper progression and peep into the subtle secrets [of western learning]'.[74] To Xue Fucheng, another reform advocate, the purpose of taking over the Westerners' knowledge of machinery and mathematics was 'to protect the way of our sage-kings Yao and Shun, Yu and Tang, Wen and Wu, and the Duke of Zhou and Confucius, and so make the Westerners not dare to despise China'.[75]

More conservative elements still refused to face the fact that there existed civilizations other than the Chinese, which might have some higher values. When Guo Songtao, the first minister from Imperial China to reside in a Western country, was preparing his trip to Britain in 1875, he received a letter from one of his friends, suggesting that he should spread Confucianism to England.[76] Moreover, when Guo's diary was sent to the Zongli Yamen as part of his official report and was later published by the Yamen in 1877, he was severely censured and impeached as a betrayer of the Dynasty as well as of the Chinese civilization because he noted in his diary that the Western people were different from previous barbarians and they also had two thousand years' civilization. The Court was influenced by the protest, so much so that the matter was closed only after the printed blocks of the book were ordered to be destroyed.[77]

Up to the 1890s, Western cultural impact remained singularly marginal on the Chinese scholarly world. Little had been done in the first forty years of Sino-Western contact to facilitate the intellectual communication between the two societies. The missionaries had no significant influence in the scholar–official circle. Chinese education remained oriented to the civil-service examination system. As late as the early 1890s, in the curricula of *Shuyuan*, or local school, there was almost no place for the so-called 'Western learning'. This amounted to an intellectual insulation of the Chinese literati. It is no exaggeration to observe that 'The majority of Chinese gentry–literati still lived in the mental universe of their own tradition'.[78]

It was the disastrous defeat of China in the Sino-Japanese War of 1894–1895 which crushed the pride and complacency of the Chinese scholar–officials. This event was historically significant in three aspects: it proved that thirty years' efforts by China in *Yangwu* were a total failure; it surprised Chinese scholar–officials that the Empire could be defeated by Japan, formerly a cultural borrower but now Westernized; and it turned the Chinese attention critically to defects of its own institutions and systems. National crisis was accompanied by a sense of cultural crisis. Not only the institutional legitimacy of the entire traditional political order but the tradition *per se* were called into question. Chinese culture was subject to some reinterpretation. 'Confucian confidence had gone and China was open to the penetration of foreign ideologies'.[79]

There is no question that the tempo of change in the cultural transition from traditional to modern China accelarated in the 1890s and the Western culture had more appreciable impact upon the Chinese scholarly world. The question is why. The secular role of so-called 'cultural brokers' – the missionaries – in spreading western knowledge and ideas, the mushrooming of newspapers and the publication of political writings of reform-minded Chinese scholars were not convincing explanations.[80] The change of tempo owed much more to the fact that survival of China as a nation was now taking priority over all other values and beliefs. It should also be observed that the Chinese mind was more receptive to the Western ideas and values after dozens of years' physical, commercial and intellectual contact with the West. Scholars' accumulated knowledge of the West gradually, though slowly, deepened their appreciation of the West – the Western culture, institutions and systems and cherished values – which were behind their steamships and cannons. The disappointment at the inertia and ineffectiveness of the traditional institutions and the political order hardened this appreciation. The Reform Movement in the 1890s saw Chinese intellectuals looking both beyond the horizon of the Chinese civilization and deeply into China's past for intellectual guidance and reorientation. Here we spot significant but reluctant disintegration of Sinocentrism.

Both Kang Youwei and Liang Qichao, the leading elements in the Reform Movement, sought the justifications of institutional change in China's tradition which, they believed and tried to prove, possessed the basic values and institutions they admired in the Western civilization. For Kang Yuwei, Confucianism was still universally applicable but only through reinterpretation to encompass the ideas of democracy and probably science. For Liang Qichao, 'Western histories say that the democratic conception arose in Greece and Rome. Liang Qichao considers that age to have been non-democratic. If that is called democracy, then our China, too, in ancient times could be said to have democracy.' And in China, 'although there was not the name of representative government, there was yet the fact of it'.[81] It is interesting to note that at this stage what the leading intellectuals tried to prove is not that Chinese culture had what the Western culture did not have but that it had, although this was probably long forgotten, what the Western culture did have. This is, if not an admission of cultural inferiority, at least an acknowledgement of cultural equality.

If we regard acculturation as the process of displacement or modification of the institutions, values and attitudes of one culture by those of another, the cultural transition of traditional China to modern China was such a process. The acculturation which Chinese intellectuals were undergoing represented the penetration of Western culture from the periphery into the centre of the Chinese tradition. Its immediate effect was to precipitate the crumbling of Sinocentrism in the mind of Chinese intellectuals. While the Western culture remained at the periphery of the Chinese intellectual world and Chinese culture held on at the centre of the Chinese scholarly world, the world was Sinocentric culturally, though not geographically. Now that the Western culture squeezed into the centre, Chinese intellectuals suddenly realized that culturally as well as geographically, China was by no means the centre, but rather a periphery in a world ordered by the West. The emergence of modern Chinese nationalism in this period was another expression of this realization.

THE 'CORE' AND 'PERIPHERY' IN THE INTERNATIONAL SYSTEM

By the time China was brought to the realization of the superiority of the West, Europe, which had a 'highly inventive and dynamic civilization' but 'did not have room enough for the power of all its active thrusting communities',[82] had, through its expansion in all directions from the fifteenth century onwards, unified the world for the first time in history into one single international system. It linked together the regional international systems, such as the Islamic and the Chinese, through their contact with Europe and involved the states and empires outside Europe in constant and regular political, economic and military interactions with the European states.[83] This all-inclusive 'Family of Nations' had three salient features: geographically it encompassed the entire globe; culturally it included all civilizations on the earth; but economically, politically and militarily it was dominated by Europe. Keylor calls it 'a genuine interlinked and interdependent world with Europe as its focal point'.[84]

With the benefit of hindsight, the growth of the conventionally called 'European-dominated international system' can be regarded as having undergone three stages by the end of the nineteenth century.[85] These three stages were marked by European colonization and expansion into different geographical areas of the world and by the chronological differences in the admission by the European states of those outside states into the European international system. It should not be neglected that cultural homogeneity and geographical propinquity played an essential role in deciding the chronology of the incorporation of other states in this emerging universal international system.

The first stage was characterized by the recognition of the European settler states of the Americas as sovereign and juridically equal members of European international society, a process which was completed in 1823 when the British Foreign Secretary George Canning announced the British recognition of the rebellious Latin American states. Little difficulty arose here. The United States and other American states were 'easily admitted'[86] because the Americans, as inheritors of European political ideals and Christian culture, had similar political institutions, economic practices, religious beliefs and cultural traditions.

The acceptance of the Ottoman Empire into the club of European powers could be taken as the second stage. The signatory powers of the Treaty of Paris in 1856 declared 'the Sublime Porte admitted to participate in the advantages of the Public Law and System [Concert] of Europe'. Three important facts must be remembered however. First, the Ottoman Empire was geographically present in Europe but culturally distinct. Second, long before its admission, it had participated in European politics and interacted with European powers and was a factor to be reckoned with. Third, after the formal admission, the Ottoman Empire was still to be subject to the capitulations system for more than sixty years.

At the third stage, Europe expanded overall into areas of Asia and Africa which were far away from Europe and where civilizations were incompatible with that of Europe. States in these areas, China and Japan for example, entered the international system 'at the price of Westernization' and were first admitted under the capitulations system.

An overview and a general analysis of these three stages of the evolution of a universal international system point to the fact that, in its expansion, Europe took into its system first the culturally homogeneous states, then culturally heterogeneous but geographically contiguous ones, and finally those culturally heterogeneous and geographically distant states. While the culturally homogeneous states were included readily, the culturally heterogeneous states were accepted reluctantly and conditionally. The international system in the second half of the nineteenth century, therefore, was composed of two distinguishable groups of states and political communities: the European society of states (including the American states) which was characterized by their consent to common rules, institutions and recognition of common interests; and the non-Western states which had established contact with the European society of states under the conditions and rules laid down by the Europeans.

In this 'European-dominated international system', it is possible to identify a 'core' and a 'periphery'. Martin Wight, in his *De Systematibus Civitatum*, divided the expansion of the Western states system into four phases and contended that

> In each phase, there has been a highly organized geographical core, with a periphery of powers or regions more loosely connected with the system.
> To 1500   core, Italy; periphery, Transalpine Europe
> 1500–1763   core, Western Europe; periphery, Eastern Europe
> 1763–1914   core, Europe; periphery, the Americas and the traditional states of Asia
> Since 1914   core, roughly the states which helped to found or were members of the League of Nations; periphery, the ex-colonial states, especially in Africa.[87]

It is not enough just to point out the existence of a core and a periphery in the expanding European states-system. Such an existence nevertheless could be proved not unique in the then existing international systems, if we define periphery as 'a surrounding region, space or area' (*Oxford English Dictionary*) or as 'a surrounding power' (Wight). The significance lies rather in identifying the special features of the core and the periphery in each specific period as well as the special relationships between them. Wight made two general observations towards this direction in his argument above: the location of the core and the loose connection between the core and the periphery. As regards the period of concern to this study,[88] two questions arise: What is the implication of this geographical location of the core? And what does 'loose connection' mean?

As it expanded to include non-Christian communities in its states system in the nineteenth century, Europe, originally the geographical centre of the European international system, assumed more and more cultural implications. This was reflected in the Eurocentric views of world politics which seem to have taken shape only in the nineteenth century. Hedley Bull lent his support to this point when he wrote, by taking Euro-Asian relations as an example, that

> Indeed, in the three centuries from 1500 to 1800, as European involvement in Asian politics persisted and grew, and with it the armed rivalry of the European powers in Asia, a loose Eurasian system or quasi-system grew up in which European states sought to deal with Asian states on the basis of moral and legal equality, until in the nineteenth century this gave place to notions of European superiority.[89]

This superiority was factual and material as well as conceptual and cultural. It was factual and material in the sense that, as a result of Industrial Revolution in the eighteenth century, Europe had experienced a transformation from an agricultural to an industrial society and had seen an enormous increase in wealth and in economic and military power, which put Europe in the dominating position in the world and substantially increased the disparity, in terms of military potentialities, between Europe and the non-European world. This, in turn, reinforced a sense of the cultural unity of Europe which tended to increase its sense of distinctness from the non-European world and consequently generated in the minds of Europeans a sense of cultural and moral superiority over the rest of the world invariably seen as either barbarian or savage. Further, the ancient Asian civilizations were regarded as decadent. The solemn responsibility of such leading imperial powers as Britain was 'to provide the uncivilized, backward peoples of the colonial world with the fruits of Britain's superior culture, in particular the spiritual inspiration of Christianity and political benefits of enlightened administration'. The role of Europe was 'rescuing the indigenous populations of the non-European world from the superstitions of their primitive religions and the barbarity of their native customs'.[90] In a word, a civilizing mission was born to force the other peoples 'to bow before the moral power of the civilized West'.[91] The European expansion, which was originally concerned with trade, settlement and occasionally the balance of power, became now a morally justifiable mission to impose European rules, institutions and administration on states and political communities in Asia and Africa, to induce or to force them to conform to the standard of European international society. In the nineteenth century, therefore, Cassese argues, European countries developed two distinct classes of relations with the non-European world: capitulations and appropriation.[92] 'Thus the rules and institutions which the Europeans spread out to

Persia and China in the nineteenth century were those which they had evolved with the Ottomans (e.g. capitulations, consulates with jurisdictions over their nationals) rather than those in use within Europe itself (e.g. free movement and residence virtually without passports).'[93] Essentially, therefore, the 'core' and 'periphery' theme in the nineteenth century international system was culturally European versus non-European.

In such a situation, the 'loose connection' between the centre and the periphery took on special meaning and was culturally determined. The connections between the European and the non-European states were loose, not only in the sense that communications and contacts between them were much less regular, less constant, and less frequent than among the European states themselves, but more in the sense that they perceived no common interest between them to facilitate their contact and there were no common institutions to regulate their relations. It is the Europeans who set the conditions and terms for the non-European political communities in their relations with Europe. The 'loose connection' then in the way of capitulations and appropriation took the form of European imposition of its value system on the 'outside' world. The basis of the contact was therefore an unequal relationship between the centre and the periphery, which was another characteristic of the 'loose connection'. The 'most idiosyncratic trait' of the international system in that period was 'the existence of deep factual inequalities and widespread relations of domination'.[94] Europe assumed a dominating position politically, economically, militarily and culturally in the universal international system it had, probably unintentionally, brought into being.

It is important to note that some publicists at the turn of the century tried, deliberately or not, to foster in the domain of international law a notion of centre and periphery by accentuating the exclusiveness of the European 'Family of Nations'. As mentioned previously, Holland, in his *Lectures on International Law*, had spoken of the 'outer court of the charmed circle' wherein China, Persia and Siam had been brought after their participation in the Hague Conferences.[95] He suggested explicitly here that, in the domain of international law, there was a exclusive centre (the charmed circle) and a surrounding region or area (outer court) to which non-Western states might be admitted. Similarly, W. Hall called on the states outside European civilization to 'formally enter into the circle of law-governed countries'.[96] J. Lorimer expounded the principles of the natural law school in the matter of political recognition by classifying it into three categories: plenary political recognition, partial political recognition, and natural or mere human recognition. To quote him,

> The sphere of plenary political recognition extends to all the existing States of Europe, with their colonial dependencies, in so far as these are peopled by persons of European birth or descent; and to the States of North and South America which have vindicated their independence of the European States of which they were colonies. The sphere of partial political recognition extends to Turkey in Europe and in Asia, and to the old historical States of Asia which have not become European dependencies – viz. to Persia and the other separate States of Central Asia, to China, Siam, and Japan. The sphere of natural or mere human recognition, extends to the residue of mankind.[97]

Lorimer further explained that civilized communities which enjoyed plenary recognition were surrounded by partially civilized communities. Similarly when Oppenheim specified three conditions for an outside country to be recognized legally as a member of the expanding European Family of Nations,[98] he must have been aware of an outer area where states could stay as 'probationary' member and could learn to be 'civilized'.

Of the contemporary scholars of international studies, Bull spoke of 'an immense periphery looking to a European centre' in the nineteenth century;[99] Cassese used 'the margin of the international community'[100] to describe the place wherein non-Christian states for long found themselves; and Gong mentioned a non-European periphery in the process of the emergence of a universal international society.[101] Not only the Europeans saw the 'outside' world as a periphery in the world politics of the nineteenth century. The non-Western countries also acknowledged or had to acknowledge the central role and dominating position of Europe in the universal international system. Their acceptance of unequal terms dictated by the Europeans in their mutual relations, as manifested in the capitulations system, their efforts at Westernization or modernization of their foreign relations institutions, economic activities and legal systems, their looking to Europe for intellectual inspiration, their changes, adaptations and adjustments to the modern world shaped by the Europeans, their attempts to meet the standard of 'civilization' so as to enter the 'Family of Nations' formerly exclusive to the Europeans – all this demonstrates that, from a non-Western perspective, the role of Europe as political and probably also cultural centre of the global international system was also accepted and acceptable. Bozeman sums up the situation concisely:

> Most of the peoples outside the Atlantic community of nations accepted the standards of intellectual and material achievement that Occidental thought and enterprise represented, subscribed to the vocabulary of political symbols that had been composed in the West, adopted the forms of government that Europeans and Americans had devised, and acknowledged the validity of the tenets of international intercourse long associated with the European system of states. They thus came to see both their present and future in terms of Western aspirations and achievements.[102]

Now the notion of periphery can be subjected to an analysis from two different perspectives. From the European (or centre's) perspective, the 'peripheral' states and political communities were legally not full subjects of international law, or at least were not granted full international legal personality. In Lorimer's words, they were either protected states or belonged 'partly to the category of recognized states and partly to the category of protected states'.[103] They were at most marginal or partial members in the European Family of Nations because they were still regarded as 'lesser breeds without the law'[104] and not yet able to meet the standard of 'civilization' set out by the Europeans.[105] Politically, 'it was an established custom for tensions and conflicts at the core of the system to be resolved by suitable adjustments of resources and territory at the periphery'.[106] Bismarck's open suggestion after the Franco-Prussian War in 1870–1871 that France annex Tunisia, and the British and French compromise after the Fashoda crisis in 1898 are two classical examples. The non-European states, consequently, were sometimes the 'playground', so to speak, of European power politics and remained mostly passive objects to be acted upon by European politics.

From the non-Western (or periphery's) perspective, the 'peripheral' states accepted, sometimes reluctantly and forcibly, the domination of the Europeans and at the same time aspired to membership in the European Family of Nations. For this purpose, the Ottoman Empire had to modify its theory that the relations between the faithful and the infidel were only constant unrelenting wars and the Chinese had to abandon their ethnocentric view of the world, both under the capitulations system. On the other hand, there was strong resistance from each state or political community against being drawn forcibly into the universal international system at the expense of its own culture and civilization. This was in the form of an assertion of local culture and a rejection of total Westernization. Finally there was, from the very beginning, resentment from those non-European states and political communities regarding their treatment in European-dominated world politics. Paradoxically, the resentment was transferred to loud protest only when the non-European world at the periphery gradually acquired the knowledge of the existence of international law and absorbed Western values such as the principles of national sovereignty and juridical equality between states.

To sum up, the core–periphery divide in the nineteenth-century international system was, in cultural terms, found in the confrontation between European culture and other indigenous cultures. While the European culture claimed its superiority and asserted its leading role in the nineteenth-century world, the other cultures, trying to preserve their own identity, nevertheless acquiesced in its superiority, made necessary adjustments to fit in with the world modified by the Europeans and adopted some of the European institutions. This was a process wherein interactions between the European and other cultures took place. It was a transitional phase from a universal international system to a global international society.

In actual world politics, the idea of the core and the periphery in the nineteenth century international system was embodied in the relations of the dominating and the dominated between the Europeans and the non-European world. While the Europeans regarded the non-European communities and states as only objects in European power politics, the non-European world came to assert itself in world politics by registering in action its protest and resentment against its treatment at the hands of the dominating European powers. It was a theme of conflict which was characterized increasingly by the periphery's revolt against the centre's domination. The legacies of the 'core' and 'periphery' theme in world politics of the nineteenth century can still be felt today.

A NATION AMONG THE NATIONS

The first decade of the twentieth century was the last phase of China's metamorphosis to become a nation-state under the impact of the West. By the end of 1911, Imperial China was gone and the Republic of China was proclaimed. Nominally, the process of China's transformation, sometimes painful, from a universal empire to a member of the multi-state world was completed. China no longer constituted a world itself, but a part of the world and a unit in world politics. After a long and sustained resistance of Sinocentrism, the Chinese world order collapsed, only to give way to an international order defined by the Europeans. In the confrontation of the two civilizations and two political traditions, the Middle Kingdom compromised here with its adaptations so as to fit into the framework of the expanding European international system. As Sun Yat-sen proclaimed in the capacity of Provisional President in January 1912, the Republic of China would try its best 'to carry out the duties of a civilized nation so as to obtain the rights of a civilized nation'.[107]

The final phase of the Middle Kingdom's metamorphosis was acknowledged as a period of reform and revolution. Most scholars see both the Imperial reforms and the Republican revolution as a means to resist the relentless imperialist encroachment on China and to save China from national extinction. Some scholars also argue that the Imperial reforms carried out in this period had, directly and indirectly, precipitated the revolution and speeded up the collapse of the Qing Dynasty.[108] There is certainly more to say about all this. What has up to now failed to be recognized is that these are some of those 'domestic processes of political and social reform which narrowed the differences between them [Asian and African political communities] and the political communities of the West, and contributed to a process of convergence'.[109] In other words, China's adopting Western political institutions which even the Empress Dowager in 1901 believed were 'the fundamental source of Western government',[110] actually prepared China for its entry into the universal international society. This can hardly be overemphasized.

Take for example the four series of major Imperial reforms listed in Mary Wright's illuminating introduction to *China in Revolution, The First Phase 1900–1913*. The educational reform as found in the abolition of the civil examination system and creation of a Ministry of Education in 1905, in Wright's words, 'altered with one stroke the basis of gentry power and of the recruitment of the bureaucracy. It also removed much of the premium on Chinese classical learning and cleared the way for the new educational system'.[111] The military reform and the creation of a 'New Army' modelled on the Japanese and German armies initiated a modernization process of the Chinese military, the structure of which was gradually put in general accord with that of the Western military organizations. The military now aimed more at the national defence than at dealing with internal disturbances. The organizational reform of the entire administrative apparatus of the Empire certainly brought China's government organization very much more in line with that of the Western states. The most illustrative instances are the authorization of elected assemblies at the provincial and national levels and of other organs of local government and the establishment of Wai Wu Bu (Ministry of Foreign Affairs) in 1901 to replace Zongli Yamen and that of Fa Bu (Ministry of Justice) in the place of Xing Bu (Board of Punishments) in 1906 and the creation of a Ministry of Education (1905) and a Ministry of Commerce (1903).[112] Last but not least, reform measures to encourage commerce and industry were a 'reversal of an imperial policy that had been taken for granted for two millennia', as was admitted in an Imperial edict ordering the creation of a Ministry of Commerce in 1903, that

> Commerce and the encouragement of industries have ever been from ancient times to the present matters of real importance to governments, but according to an old tradition we have looked upon matters of industries and commerce as matters of the last importance.[113]

Another instructive example is the judicial reforms, which are not included in Wright's list. Originated as a technique to abolish foreign extraterritoriality, the proposed judicial reforms were to alter China's traditional legal structure so as to satisfy foreigners. This meant an adoption of and adaptation to Western styles of judicial codes and procedures. A law school was established in Beijing in 1905 and a new courts system independent of administrative offices was decreed in 1907. A commercial law was proposed and an entirely new criminal code was drafted, revised and imperially approved before the 1911 revolution. Such radical institutional change invariably touched upon 'formal ethics, more subtle moral feelings, and inherited social relations'.[114]

Indeed, what characterized these reforms were their assaults on the traditional political and social orders of the Middle Kingdom, just as Levenson argued that

> the means of survival are the ultimate national values; if adherence to tradition is incompatible with the adoption of these means, tradition must go.[115]

That is probably why, even with limited achievements in some cases, the Imperial reforms in the first decade of the century had instituted fundamental changes in nearly every sphere of Chinese life. The changes in the Chinese values system and traditional institutions they had brought about and were to bring about called into being a New China similar to the rest of the world in its political attitudes and values and in its legal institutions. Whether intentionally or not, this was not just a transformation of an empire, but that of a civilization.

The Imperial reforms, it has been well argued, were precipitated by a sense of national crisis, particularly after the Allied pillage of Beijing in the wake of the Boxer Rebellion. Morse pointedly characterized the final phase of Imperial China in its foreign relations as the 'period of subjection'.[116] The 'scramble for concessions' from 1897 to 1900 had further entrenched imperialist powers in different parts of the Middle Kingdom which they did not hesitate to claim as their exclusive 'spheres of influence'. The imperialist powers seemed to have shifted from a policy of checking one another to 'outgrabbing' one another. 'Talk of partition of China was still common among Western diplomats in Peking. Even if few favoured it, many anticipated it'.[117] The foreign omnipresence was further evidenced by sixty-two treaty ports and extensive treaty rights and privileges which Willoughby tried in 1920 to describe in his 600-page book, *Foreign Rights and Interests in China*.[118] It was found in the handling of China's maritime customs funds, in the ownership of the major iron and steel plants, in the control of the salt monopoly, and in the administration of justice, particularly in Shanghai. The total foreign debt amounted to 800 to 1000 million taels in 1911 and it was estimated that for China to buy back its railways alone would need 1,617,000,000 francs.[119] China had mortgaged almost everything for loans and Jordan, the British Minister in China, claimed in 1913 that 'China no longer has any tangible security to offer'.[120] It must be also remembered that China had long lost its autonomy of tariff and its foreign relations were invariably based on 'unequal treaties'.

No one could deny this picture of China suffering the stigma of the capitulations system in its extreme form at the beginning of this century. Another aspect of China in international life, though not so conspicuous at first, should not, however, be overshadowed by this picture. It was not so much that China had been invited to attend the two Hague international peace conferences in 1899 and in 1907, which, some international jurists maintained, was 'from courtesy',[121] but that the Middle Kingdom reciprocated this 'courtesy' by participating in both conferences. More important, China went on to sign and ratify or adhere to international conventions and acts concluded at the two

Hague conferences. According to MacMurray, China had by 1911 become a signatory of seventeen Hague conventions and declarations out of the twenty-two he listed in his book, including Convention I of 1899, and that of 1907 for the Pacific Settlement of International Disputes, and the Final Acts of the First and the Second International Peace Conferences at the Hague.[122] This was the beginning of China's perception of common interests and common values with other political communities in the world and of its share by consent in the working of common international institutions.

It would be difficult, however, to sustain with only this evidence the argument that China entered the emerging international society at the turn of the century. For one thing, China's participation in world politics was still minimal. Its consciousness of common interests and share of common institutions with other states were still so limited as not to have developed to a point where both China and other states 'conceive[d] themselves to be bound by a common set of rules in their relations with one another'.[123] Moreover members of the European Family of Nations were far from ready to admit China into the circle. From their point of view, China had not yet graduated to membership of the emerging international society and was therefore still denied full international statehood. Its relations with foreign nations were, without exception, based on 'unequal treaties'. In other words, all changes considered, China still possessed more attributes of membership of an international system than of an international society. It stayed at the margin of the expanding international system.

However differences should not be overlooked between China as a member of the international system in the late nineteenth century and China at the beginning of the twentieth century. If the Middle Kingdom had initially been forcibly and involuntarily drawn into the expanding European states system, the first decade of this century certainly saw the first signs of China's active and voluntary participation in international affairs. If China's initial resistance to the Western assault on its world order was Sinocentric and xenophobic, its resistance to further imperialist encroachment on Chinese sovereignty after the Boxer Rebellion in 1900 was certainly nationalistic. Indeed, the final phase of China's metamorphosis into a nation was accompanied by rising Chinese nationalism. This was another driving force which changed the Middle Kingdom, probably inexorably, into a modern nation. The Chinese nation-building efforts in the early years of the present century were, as argued by Mary Wright, 'directed towards action and change in three different, though related spheres'. They were, first, resistance to imperialism as reflected in China's assertion of its sovereignty along the frontier areas and in the watchword 'recovery of sovereign rights'; secondly, organization of a modern centralized nation-state, capable of both forcing back the imperialists and forwarding China's aspirations in political, social, economic and cultural life; and last and less important, the overthrow of the Manchu Dynasty.[124] These were in fact the responses China developed to the imperialist danger it was faced with. It is interesting to note that the Nationalist Revolution in 1911 only accomplished the least important task of Chinese nationalism. The change of body politic further prepared China for its role in the global international system. Yet China as a nation was still groaning under crippled sovereignty and impaired territorial integrity. Chinese nationalism was yet to accomplish its other two tasks. As the first Foreign Minister of the Republic of China, Liang Ruhao, wrote privately in November 1912,

> I consider that it is about time that our China should make a diplomatic stand against the present aggression, for our easy yielding in their most immoral international conduct would in my opinion lead to other equally uncalled for claims on the part of other land grabbing nations of which we had too sad experience during the recent period of the late reign ... The game has to be stopped, otherwise this paring process must inevitably end in our extinction as a nation.[125]

China as such was still struggling for its survival and groping for its rightful place in the world community.

2   A Disappointed Nation at Paris, 1919

The metmorphosis of China in the last few decades of its imperial history was both momentous and sweeping. Seventy years after the impact of European expansion was first seriously felt, the Middle Kingdom – a universal empire – was replaced by a nation-state, the first republic in Asia. This signified the total collapse of the traditional Chinese world order which had to give way to the European-defined international order of modern times. In the confrontation of the two civilizations, the Chinese civilization, of which China had been so proud, had to adapt itself and adopt some Western institutions such as, for example, those elaborated in international law for the conduct of relations between modern states. It was a gradual and sometimes painful process to transform the old Confucian Empire so as to be accepted by the European international system. In this way, China, half reluctantly and half willingly, was put into the framework of the European international system.

China was now a republic. But the Republic was in a state of nominal independence but was to all intents and purposes a colony. Unfortunately, the change of the body politic–the establishment of the Republic of China – did not succeed, as was hoped by many Chinese, in recovering lost rights by the voluntary surrender of the Powers. Indeed

> The enthusiasm of the republicans for Western forms of government was partly due to the belief that by establishing these institutions China would automatically become a real member of the Club, and would be treated as equal. The special rights might be justified by the archaic character of the Manchu Government; but a republic was surely a modern state by definition; to retain extraterritorial rights and concessions, leased territories and legation guards in the territory of a sovereign republic was unseemly.[1]

Prior to World War I, China remained a pawn in the game of the balance of power in East Asia played by the rival Great Powers – Russia, Germany, Britain, France and Japan, and less so the United States.[2] The total subjection of China by an imperialist Power or imperialist Powers was still a possible prospect lingering on the horizon. By the end of 1913, China was still 'teetering between precarious national existence and a slide into complete foreign domination, with the present changes in favour of the slide'.[3]

The outbreak of World War I in August 1914 was both a blessing and a curse for China. It was a blessing because, as almost all European Powers were deeply involved in the War, they had to loosen their grip on China, and the war gave China a breathing space to develop its own infant industries. It was a blessing also because, probably unseen at the time, it meant the breakdown of the European system of balance of power and it carried a prospect of reorganization of the international system after the war, an opportunity for China to readjust its relations with the Powers and to find its own legitimate standing in the new international order. It was a curse because the war immediately spread to East Asia and because, as was soon proved, Japan was out to entrench itself and to bid for its supremacy in China at the expense of the interests of other Powers.

China was little concerned with the complicated issues which in August 1914 plunged Europe into war. It was, nevertheless, involved in the war from the very beginning, with Japan's declaration of war against Germany in August 1914 and its eventual occupation of the German leased territory of Jiaozhou in Shandong Province in October. There were two drastic developments in the war years which were to have decisive importance in the reconstruction of the post-war East Asian international order. The war-time Japanese expansion in China in the form of its Twenty-One Demands in 1915 and of its tightened economic control foreshadowed the Sino-Japanese confrontation in the future peace settlement. On the other hand, China's participation in the war on the Allied side in August 1917 changed its position *vis-à-vis* Japan and eventually secured it a seat at the future peace conference.[4] The war henceforth involved the former empire inextricably in the evolving international system.

In a broader perspective, the democratization of the post-war international system held out an encouraging prospect for China to be fully incorporated into the emerging international society. It was a process started, during the war, with the democratization of foreign policy, which was thereafter transferred from private Cabinet meetings to the public gatherings, and was complemented by a diplomacy of mass persuasion. It reached a point of no return when Woodrow Wilson decided to throw American might behind the Allies and to turn the War into an ideological crusade to make the world safe for democracy. The dynamic principle of national self-determination, promoted by Wilson, and also in some way by Lenin, was a fundamental challenge to the legitimacy of the pre-war international order and was to change both the face and the structure of the international system forever. The proposed League of Nations – a democratic-type international institution – represented an ideal projected by Wilson to prevent war and to maintain peace. It was not only a denunciation of the legitimacy of the balance of power regime, but also presupposed political and economic cooperation of states and political communities in reconstructing and maintaining peace and order. China, as we will see, readily cashed in on this transformation of the international system. It began both to demand and to assert readjustments of its foreign relations in the wake of the war. However, whether the prospect of China's full incorporation could be materialized was to be decided first and foremost by the development of world politics at the peace conference at Paris during the first half of 1919 which professed to aim at ushering in a new international order based on international justice, equality between states and national independence.

GETTING PREPARED

At the eleventh hour on the eleventh day of the eleventh month in 1918, guns and cannons in Europe were finally silenced with the signing of the Armistice with Germany by the Allied and Associated Powers. The convening of a peace conference was now on the immediate agenda of all the Allied leaders.

In China, the people learned 'with great joy that the terms of the Armistice have been accepted by Germany, thus the cause of justice and freedom has been vindicated and its final triumph has been won by the Allied arms'.[5] The news of the Armistice was accordingly greeted with 'joy and cheerfulness' and a 'continuous round of festivities and celebrations' in which 'the foreign and Chinese communities joined wholeheartedly'.[6] The culmination of the celebrations of the Allied victory was the great Government-organized national celebration held in the Imperial Palace on November 28, 1918. Reinsch later recalled,

We gathered in the pavilion of the Ta Ho-men, the gate which leads into the court immediately before the main Coronation Hall of the Imperial City. Here in the very inner sanctuary of the thousand-year-old imperialism of China, the victory of freedom was celebrated. On the ascending terraces stood thousands of guests, the military and officials in uniform; over the balustrades waved forests of flags of the Associated Nations, as well as long floating banners with Chinese inscription in gold.[7]

The Chinese excitement and joyfulness was more over the prospect which the Allied victory would probably hold out for China as a weak nation than over the Allied victory itself. The Chinese were 'greatly excited over President Wilson's speech on the fourteen principles on which peace is to be based'.[8] They believed,

> The war is now ended, and Right has emerged triumphant from the conflict. China is now free to tell the world her grievances without fear of further outrages being committed against her, and moreover the Great Powers which have been fighting on the side of Righteousness are now more determined than ever to maintain the cause of Justice throughout the world . . . In view of President Wilson's declarations regarding the freedom and independence of small and weak states, and the entry of England into the war to uphold the sanctity of treaties, we can safely trust these two Great Powers to see to it that justice is rendered to us.[9]

In the official circle, Xu Shichang, the President, in a mandate issued on October 29, when negotiations for the Armistice were going on, had also hinted at Chinese aspirations inspired by the Allied war aims. He stated that

> the objects of the Entente countries in declaring this war have been repeatedly declared to be to uphold the principle of humanity, international law, the equality of nations and liberty of the people. Our government and our people have heard these declarations with the highest admirations.[10]

Earlier, on his assuming the presidency, Xu stated in a reply to a telegram by President Wilson offering his congratulations that he would put forth his best effort to 'meet the wishes of the people of the whole country that in coming councils of family of nations our country may assume its rightful place'.[11] On November 2, in a speech at a banquet in honour of members of the Chinese Congress and Senate at Huairentang, the President made the point publicly and explicitly when he said that in view of the approaching conclusion of the war in Europe, he would hope that China could gain an equal position in the Family of Nations in the post-war peace.[12] For the coming peace conference, he also expressed the confidence and hope that China would 'continue to work hand in hand [with the Allies] for the cause of freedom, justice and fair dealing'.[13]

When China entered the war in 1917, it did not formulate any specific war aims, though it had asked for certain benefits to be granted as *quid pro quo*.[14] However it did show great concern over its prospects at the peace conference and its international position after the war. Both President Li Yuanhong and Vice-President Feng Guozhang wished first to be assured that, in making common cause with the Allies, China would be treated with due respect in the Family of Nations and entitled to all the privileges accorded by international law to the smallest member state in the European Family of Nations.[15] Clearly, the Chinese were greatly encouraged by such war messages addressed directly to the Chinese as that the British Empire was fighting bravely for victory so that 'the nations great and small are secured in their right to pursue their development free and unmolested'[16] and that the American crusade was 'to maintain in the world the right of peoples to decide their own destinies unhampered by the wrongful exercise of power'.[17] The Four Principles expounded by Wilson 'represent the aspirations of the Chinese people'.[18] Consequently the Chinese were led optimistically to look to the peace conference for the redressing of wrongs done to China and for a readjustment of China's existing relations with the Powers according to the new principles conducive to the new international order.

A careful examination of the Chinese and foreign diplomatic archives has revealed that, contrary to what has been commonly believed and alleged, the Chinese preparations, both before and after the Armistice, for the coming peace conference were early and extensive.[19] As early as April 1918, a Preparatory Committee for the Coming Peace Conference was set up in the Foreign Ministry and began to hold regular meetings with the attendance of Foreign Minister Lu, Vice-Foreign Minister Gao and Foreign Ministry counselors.[20] There was a common realization that

> our country is no longer in an era when it was closed to international intercourse. If [our nation] is to compete and survive in the world, it is important that [we] must study all problems of international significance and prepare ourselves in advance so as to be ready to take the good opportunity of the peace conference to raise them. This is a matter concerning our international standing. We must do our best.[21]

According to the minutes of the Ninth Meeting, Premier Duan had called the attention of the Committee to the questions of the League of Nations, tariff autonomy and national self-determination. 'What the Premier means is that the Committee should concern itself with all the matters related to the preparations for the peace conference'.[22] A wide range of topics had been discussed. Among them were the revision of the 1901 Protocol, restoration of Jiaozhou, abrogation of extraterritoriality, and tariff autonomy. From the minutes preserved it seems, however, that nothing definite had been decided by August 1918, as regards the Chinese demands at the peace conference.

Meanwhile the Chinese Government had asked its foreign advisers to present their opinions on the subject: China and the Peace Conference. At least five of them duly submitted their memoranda:[23] *China and the Coming Peace Conference* by Dennis, dated March 1918; *La Participation de la Chine au Congrès de la Paix* by Georges Padoux was received in September; *China and the Peace Conference* by Konovalriff, in October;[24] *Observations with Regard to China's Position at the Peace Conference* by Willoughby, in November; and Dr. Nagao Ariga's *Observations on China's Preparations for the Peace Conference*, probably also in November.[25] Their views, however, do not seem to have had much weight in the decisions of the Chinese Government.[26]

A number of other memoranda were also submitted, at the request of the Foreign Ministry, by the Chinese officials on the questions connected with the post-bellum peace-making, each touching a specific subject. These subjects included the development of a positive diplomacy after the war,[27] customs and tariff autonomy, revision of the 1901 Protocol, the abrogation of extraterritoriality and the disposition of former German colonies and occupied territories.[28] In mid-August, the Foreign Ministry produced its first draft of questions which were to be raised by China at the peace conference. They included (1) revision of the 1901 Protocol; (2) recovery of former German and Austro-Hungarian concessions; (3) abrogation of extraterritoriality; and (4) restoration of Jiaozhou.[29]

Before the end of the war, China seemed to have gone a long way in preparing itself for the peace conference. On October 17, the Chinese Minister in Washington, Dr. Wellington Koo, received instructions from the Foreign Ministry about the proposals China intended to present to the future peace conference, and was asked to make them known to the State Department. He was informed at the same time that the Chinese Cabinet had decided to appoint him as one of the Chinese delegates to the future peace conference in Europe.[30] Immediately after the Armistice, on November 15, Koo had an interview with Robert Lansing, the American Secretary of State, and orally informed him of the Chinese Government's proposals. Ten days later, Koo sent Lansing an informal memorandum outlining those proposals. They were elaborated under three headings: (1) Territorial Integrity, under which were proposed abrogation of foreign concessions and settlements, and relinquishment of leased territories; (2) Preservation of Sovereign Rights, under which were listed abrogation of Articles VII and IX of the Protocol of December 7, 1900 and the 1901 Protocol, and abolition of extraterritoriality in China; and (3) Economic and Fiscal Independence, under which were demanded freedom of tariff and administration and renunciation of spheres of influence.[31] On November 27, Koo called on Breckinridge Long, the Third Assistant Secretary of State, and discussed with him the Chinese proposals.[32]

The proposals the Chinese communicated to the Americans, and probably to them only,[33] were more the desires and aspirations of China than its practical programme at the peace conference. They could be regarded as a broad outline of a comprehensive plan to readjust China's foreign relations. They did show, however, as Koo said to Long, 'the extent of encroachments effected by the foreign powers upon the independence and freedom of China as a sovereign nation'.[34] With regard to China's desiderata at the peace conference, opinions differed. At a Cabinet November meeting discussing the Chinese demands at the peace conference, General Duan Qirui the former Premier who had sponsored China's entry into the War,[35] advised that China

> should not make excessive demands [at the Peace Conference] because our declaration of war [against Germany] was too late and our participation in the war was nominal. In addition to the demands for rehabilitation of the German and Austrian concessions and abrogation of their consular jurisdiction and other privileges, we could demand revision of the customs tariff and repeal of the articles in the 1901 Protocol on the stationing of foreign troops in China. As to Qingdao, Japan has declared again and again its intention to restore it to China. I believe that Japan won't break its promise. We'd better, therefore, see how Japan proposes and act accordingly.[36]

Clearly, the fact that China had not made a great contribution to the Allied victory and that the proposed desiderata, in some aspects, would affect not only the future position of the enemy states but also existing rights of the friendly Powers was in practice a serious consideration in the minds of the Chinese decision-makers. This consideration seemed to have modified considerably China's conditions for peace to be proposed to the peace conference. On November 24, about one week before his departure for Paris to attend the Peace Conference, Foreign Minister Lu Zhengxiang informed the British and American ministers in Beijing in personal conversations of the proposals that the Chinese Delegation was to make. They were extremely modest and concerned only with the enemy states, mainly Germany and Austria. The proposals as summarized in Reinsch's report to Lansing were:

> First. The settlement of proposals relative to the annulment through declaration of war of the treaties between Germany, Austria-Hungary and China, particularly with respect to permanent abrogation of the protocol of 1901 and treaty ports concessions as far as concerns Germany and Austria-Hungary.

> Second. That in the matter of damages for injury suffered the Chinese delegation would be guided by the general principles adopted by the Allies.

> Third. That in eventual making of new treaties with Germany or Austro-Hungarian states the principle of equal international rights implying complete reciprocity should be taken as a basis.[37]

Lu, however, expressed his Government's hopes and trust that the friendly Powers at the Peace Conference, 'in accord with the new spirit which now animates international relations', would 'make such arrangement as would effectively protect the integrity and independence of China particularly by discontinuing localization [sic] foreign interests and influences in different parts of China'.[38]

This then, is, the picture of China's preparations for the Peace Conference. On the one hand, China did formulate some policies and came up with some proposals to be presented at the Peace Conference; on the other hand, there was a lack of coordination of its policies and an air of inconsistency and indecisiveness in its proposals. There was a clear contradiction between China's aspirations and its practical policies at the Peace Conference. This fact did later on have some impact on the actions of the Chinese Delegation at Paris. It can be accounted for, however, by both domestic and international constraints. Internally, the Beijing Government was not entirely the master of its own house because of the political division of the North and the South and factional struggles of the warlords. Externally, any positive foreign policy had to be accepted by the Allied Powers. Furthermore this was almost the first time China participated in the work of an international conference. Its delegates had 'little or no experience of international conferences, and would be quite at a loss how to put their cause properly'.[39]

None of this seemed to hamper the organization of the Chinese Delegation to the Peace Conference. In mid-November, Foreign Minister Lu was already preparing himself for his departure for Paris as the head of the Chinese Delegation. On November 30, the Chinese Ministers to America, Britain and Belgium, Wellington Koo, Alfred Sze and Wei Chentsu, were each 'nominé Délégué Plénipotentiaire au Congrès de la Paix' by a Presidential mandate.[40] Aware of the danger to China of divided counsels at such a crucial moment and of the advantages of presenting a united front at the Peace Conference, a reconciliation between the North and the South[41] was effected with the appointment of Dr. Chengting Thomas Wang from the South as one of the Chinese Delegates on December 27, 1918.[42]

Meanwhile, well before the Peace Conference, the Chinese diplomats went out of their way to enlist the sympathy and support of the Powers for their cause at the Peace Conference. But the responses were not altogether encouraging. On November 26, 1918, Koo was granted an interview with Wilson in the White House which lasted 15 minutes. The President, while assuring the Chinese Minister that 'he would gladly do his best to support China at the peace conference', told Koo that 'there was one difficulty in the case of China, i.e. there were many secret agreements between the subjects of China and other powers', and that his Fourteen Principles were 'probably more difficult to apply to the Far East'.[43] Hu Weide, Chinese Minister to France, also saw the French President and reported that the latter only said that France would support China 'so far as it can'.[44] On December 18, at Paris, Hu Weide, Alfred Sze and Wellington Koo talked with Robert Lansing about the Chinese questions at the Peace Conference. Lansing's answer was quite non-committal. He told the Chinese that

The position of the United States in the Conference was peculiar. It had no interests of its own to serve, but it had interest in the questions of all countries. Other countries, however, had very substantial interests and were naturally desirous of promoting them. The role of the United States would therefore be to readjust the conflicting interests of the different powers by concession and compromise as was done in the case of the federal constitution of the United States. It was probable that the result would be satisfactory to none. Consequently the United States might find it necessary to modify its views relating to Chinese questions after consultation with the other Governments.[45]

The British reply to China's proposed desiderata at the Peace Conference, as furnished by Macleay,[46] was almost all negative.[47] Only Colonel House, when approached, talked in general terms about a satisfactory solution of China's questions and its relations to the world peace. He told Koo that he

had studied the questions of China and considered that, just as the Balkans were the storm centre of the peace in Europe, so China was the storm centre of the peace in the Far East. To have a permanent peace in the Far East, there must be a durable settlement of the status of China and no settlement could be durable unless it was satisfactory.[48]

If the status of China in the post-war international system was China's long-term concern, its immediate and more urgent concern was surely its independent position at the Peace Conference. It feared being represented by Japan. As early as November 1915, the Japanese Foreign Minister Kato denied that China, a neutral, had any right to attend the future peace conference, as the disposition of Jiaozhou was a matter between Japan and Germany.[49] In 1917, 'the fact that Japan had already made efforts to assure for herself the right to speak for China was worrying the Chinese. With the Premier, as with the President, the idea that through breaking with Germany, China could assure herself of an independent position at the peace table had much weight'.[50] In mid-November 1918, while the Chinese Minister in France reported that Pichon, the French Foreign Minister, had told him positively that China would have a seat at the Peace Conference,[51] the 'Japanese Legation [in Beijing] has intimated in several quarters that the Japanese Government may be found ready to settle Shantung question by returning Kiaochou leased territory to China in accordance with the original declaration of that Government in 1915 and that under such circumstances there would be no occasion for China to be represented at the Peace Conference'.[52] In January, Foreign Minister Lu was told by the Japanese that they were not pleased with the presence of Wang and Koo in the Chinese Delegation.[53] As late as January 23, 1919, after the arrival of the

Chinese Delegation at Paris and the opening of the first Plenary Session of the Peace Conference, 'the Chinese are still perturbed over the report, emanating from Paris, that Japan is to represent China at the Peace Conference. No explanation – no confirmation or denial – has been received and naturally the Chinese are uneasy, fearing that Japan may be attempting another ballon d'essai'.[54]

Japan did not get its own way and China was represented at the Peace Conference. There brewed, however, an air of suspicion and confrontation. Japan, as one of the principal Allied Powers, had prepared itself systematically and pragmatically for the Peace Conference. It would be difficult to show that Japan had any definite and consistent war aims. Its ambition was, nevertheless, clear: the expansion of Japan, to say the least, on the Asian Continent and in the Pacific, which was clearly revealed by its actions during the war years and also in its conditions for peace. In contrast to China's enthusiasm for the Allied victory,

> the news of the armistice is viewed by the Japanese press and people with a detached attitude. Satisfaction is professed but without enthusiasm. Newspaper comments reveal a keen interest in Japan's aims at the Peace Commissioners [Conference?], chief emphasis being laid on the necessity of securing recognition of Japan's paramount position in Eastern Asia.[55]

As to the Fourteen Points put forward by President Wilson as the basis of peace, the Japanese Foreign Minister Uchida told the Chinese Minister to Tokyo on October 11, 1918, one month before the Armistice, that there were three points which were of vital importance to Japan: disarmament, the principle of self-determination and the League of Nations, and that Japan would reserve its approval until after its more careful study of them.[56]

On December 9, 1918, Uchida handed to Baron Makino, one of the Japanese envoys to the Peace Conference, instructions setting forth Japan's demands at the Peace Conference as conditions of peace. Of all the conditions, the first and primary one 'in which Japan alone has an interest independently from the Allied and Associated Powers' was 'to demand the cession without compensation of Germany's territorial rights to Tsingtao and to the Pacific Islands north of the equator' and 'of rights and titles which Germany possesses as a State and the properties owned by Germany or by German public corporations with respect to Shantung Province and the Pacific Islands north of the equator'.[57] In the supplementary papers attached to the instructions, the Japanese demands and the tactics to achieve them were further elaborated. One paragraph reads:

> No. 1. Of our demands concerning Tsingtao, the cession of the Shantung Railway and mines is the most important element apart from the demand for the cession of the lease of territory and territorial waters itself. Therefore, in presenting our demands, you will do your best in the negotiations to secure success, arguing on the firmest grounds and displaying a fair attitude.[58]

The tactics were 'to stress the indivisibility between the lease and the rights to construct or run the said railway and to exploit mines' and to 'set forth plain and straightforward political arguments founded on the rights of victor'.[59] On January 18, 1919 when the Paris Peace Conference had its first Plenary Session, the Japanese Cabinet at home finally formulated conditions of peace in which Japan alone was interested and which were to be incorporated into the draft treaty. Article 2 and Article 4 read respectively as follows:

> Article 2. Germany shall transfer and cede to Japan the lease of territory and territorial waters, all the rights, titles, privileges, concessions which she has in Shantung Province by virtue of treaties, arrangements or custom, as well as all the other rights, titles, privileges and concessions concerning the railway and mines, etc., and all rights, privileges and concessions which constitute a part of the above rights, titles, privileges and concessions, or which exist outside Shantung Province in connection with them.

> Article 4. Germany shall cede to Japan the Tsingtao–Tsinanfu Railway, and its branch lines, as well as all the mines which belong to that railway or which are managed for its benefit in the said region, as well as all the rights, titles, privileges and properties belonging to the said railway and mines in the same region.[60]

It is clear that, while China would claim back the German-leased territory and the German privileges in Shandong, on the principle of national sovereignty and integrity, Japan simply regarded the disposal of Jiaozhou and the German interests in Shandong Province as a matter between Japan and Germany, without considering the sovereign right of China over the area. The Japanese Government were determined to have their claims established at the Peace Conference on the basis of their contribution to the Allied cause during the war, their actual occupation of the claimed area, and the secret agreements reached between Japan and other Allied Powers for further extension of Japan's imperial power in Asia. The Japanese attitude cast a shadow over the prospect of China's fulfilling its national aspirations, even that of recovering Jiaozhou, and foreboded a serious confrontation between Japan and China at the Peace Conference. As it turned out later, the Shandong question became, so to speak, a bone of contention and a touchstone for the Wilsonian principles. A Chinese delegate to the Paris Peace Conference later remarked that 'it was for the satisfactory solution of this problem that our delegates fought to the bitter end. It was this question which caused the Chinese people to alternate between great hope and profound disappointment.'[61]

A BONE OF CONTENTION

The Chinese Foreign Minister Lu, as head of the Chinese Delegation, arrived at Paris on January 11, 1919. By then, most of the fifty-two members of the Delegation were in Paris and were allocated Hotel Lutetia as their principal residence and headquarters. In addition to five plenipotentiaries, the Chinese Delegation was composed of seventeen technical advisers on political, legal, diplomatic, economic and military questions, five technical experts who were all foreign,[62] and twenty-five secretaries.[63] It seemed that China, a 'probationary' member of the emerging international society, was recognized as equal, at least nominally, to other members of the expanding European Family of Nations. Most Chinese believed that, with such a grand delegation at the Peace Conference, it would be possible, for the first time since its contact with the West, to take an active stand in world politics.

Yet China was in no position to bargain, for it was weak, not fully sovereign, and had not acted to the satisfaction of the Allies Powers in its war efforts in such matters as the deportation of enemy subjects in China. What gave the Chinese inspiration and what they could possibly rely upon at the Peace Conference were the principles Wilson proclaimed during the war years. As observed earlier, many of the Chinese desiderata therefore consisted of China's aspirations and expectations inspired by Wilson's Fourteen Points, which the Chinese believed would be the basis of the peace. These principles and points were soon to be put to a crude test in the power politics at Paris. China's lot at the Peace Conference fluctuated with that of those principles.

In Paris, before the formal opening of the Peace Conference, the Chinese felt 'slighted' when China, classified as a 'power with special interests', was allocated only two seats.[64] Lu had written to Pichon on January 14 in the hope of getting 'another allotment'. He reminded the French of the assurances 'given by the diplomatic representatives of the Allied and Associated Powers at Peking, on August 14, 1917, that they ' "will do all that rests with them to insure that China shall enjoy in her international relations the position and regard due to a great country" '.[65] But the response from the British and the French was 'far less encouraging'.[66] They told the Chinese that in this case the country's war efforts counted most.[67] The Chinese delegates were especially depressed when they learned that Brazil, Belgium and Serbia, after their protesting, had succeeded in increasing their seats to three. The Chinese obviously took it as a matter of equality and of the Powers' recognition of China's position in the world community.[68] The result was taken as a bad omen. Much to the disappointment of the Chinese, as subsequent events would show, China was still among the suitors and supplicants at the Peace Conference.

The chance for China to make an official presentation of the Shandong case, although expected by the Chinese Delegation, came unexpectedly quickly and at short notice. At lunch on January 27, a telephone call came through to the Chinese Delegation from E. T. Williams, Chief of the Far Eastern Affairs Division of the State Department and adviser in the American Delegation, who told the Chinese informally that they would be invited to attend the afternoon session of the Council of Ten to present China's case. He expressed the hope that the Chinese could prepare themselves for it. He also told the Chinese that a formal invitation would be sent to them by the Secretary-General of the Conference.[69] The Chinese delegates were having lunch together except for Lu, who was indisposed. The message obviously caught them unprepared and they 'wondered what the nature of the proposition discussed would be'.[70] It was about one hour before the afternoon session was due that the formal invitation came into the hands of the Chinese.[71] They hastily decided that Wang and Koo would go and participate in the session, with Wang representing the South.[72] At 2.30 pm, Wang and Koo went in a hurry to see Lansing, explaining that they would need some time to look over the problem of Jiaozhou to prepare the presentation, and asking whether it was proper for them to ask for an interval. They also inquired about the American support for China on the restoration of Jiaozhou. To both questions, the American Secretary of State gave Wang and Koo affirmative answers. As to the validity of the secret agreements between China and Japan, Lansing seemed to have demurred and as to the attitude of Great Britain, France and Italy, he was 'somewhat apprehensive'.[73]

On January 24, the disposal of former German colonies had been brought up in a discussion at the Council of Ten at which the British Dominions presented their claims with respect to German East Africa and the Pacific Islands south of the equator. On Monday morning, January 27, the problem came up again, when 'President Wilson, referring to the discussion of the previous Friday, asked whether it was wise to deal with the Pacific piecemeal. He asked whether the Japanese should not be heard before any final decision was taken'. Baron Makino, the Japanese delegate, sought, in his argument for the Japanese presentation, to include Jiaozhou and the former German Pacific islands in a one-package deal, arguing that 'the capture of both had been the result of one campaign'. While contending that 'he had no objection to the presence of any interested Power', he tried to exclude China from the discussion of the Jiaozhou problem, stating,

> The presentation of the Japanese case concerning Kiaochow would be made with reference to Germany only. Japanese relations with China on these questions were on a different footing. The claim he would put forward was addressed to Germany alone, not to China. He did not wish to discuss in the presence of the Chinese delegates Japanese relations with Germany.[74]

Wilson expressed the view that he did not understand the Japanese contention that the disposition of Jiaozhou did not affect China, and insisted on China's presence.[75] It was the decision of the Council of Ten on the same line that led to the summons of the Chinese Delegation to the afternoon meeting.

At three o'clock, at the Quai d'Orsay, the Japanese delegate, Baron Makino, advanced at the tenth meeting of the Council of Ten the Japanese claims against the German Government for the unconditional cession of the leased territories of Jiaozhou, together with the railways, and other rights possessed by Germany in Shandong Province, on the following grounds. First, Japan had eliminated the German bases and influence in East Asia 'at no small sacrifice', and Germany could not be allowed to revive its interests and to reoccupy its leased territories. Secondly, Japan was in actual occupation of Jiaozhou and had since its seizure 'continued in possession of the rights then enjoyed by Germany'. Thirdly, Japan had made a great contribution to the victory of the Allies, which rendered it only 'just and fair' that Japan should retain the German interests there.[76] The Baron, however, 'said nothing about Japan's intention to restore Kiaochow to China'.[77] After the Japanese statement, Clemenceau, as the Chairman of the Council, asked the Chinese delegates whether they would like to make a reply now or to take time to prepare one. Wang, after consultation with Koo, rose to say that 'the question was of such vital interest to China that he hoped the Great Powers would reserve decision until the views of China had been heard' and asked the Council of Ten to allow the Chinese delegates some time to prepare themselves. Clemenceau said that the Council of Ten would like to hear the Chinese view the next day.[78]

Immediately after the session, at 5.45 pm, Foreign Minister Lu and Koo went to see President Wilson, asking for advice on China's presentation of its case. The Chinese seemed to be quite encouraged when the President remarked that he 'had listened not only with surprise but with distress to the claims made by Baron Makino in such plain terms to the Pacific Islands north of the Equator and to the leased territory of Kiaochow in Shantung Province'. The President suggested that Koo might 'speak just as plainly about her [China's] desires as Baron Makino did in behalf of Japan'. He said he would do his best to help China and also promised that he would try to secure British support for the American stand, 'although Great Britain's hands were tied by her alliance with Japan'.[79]

On the following day, January 28, Wang and Koo again attended the meeting of the Council of Ten. Koo, as the 'spokesman of 400 millions', made the official Chinese presentation, asking the Conference for the direct restitution of the German leased territory of Jiaozhou and other related rights and interests. He supported his argument by invoking the principles of nationality and territorial integrity which had been universally accepted as the basis of the forthcoming peace. He contended that 'the territories in question were an integral part of China. They were part of a province containing 3 million inhabitants, Chinese in race, language and religion.' He called the Council's attention to the fact that the said lease of the territory was 'extorted' from China by force. He further defended China's claim on economic, cultural and strategic grounds. Economically, 'the introduction of a foreign Power could only lead to the exploitation of the inhabitants', as the Province was already densely populated, thus not suitable for colonization; culturally, Shandong was 'the cradle of Chinese civilization . . . and a Holy Land for the Chinese'; and strategically, China could not allow any foreign power to have 'claims to so vital a point, which commanded one of the main gateways of North China and controlled one of the shortest approaches from the sea to Peking'. In his further contentions for China, in answer to Baron Makino's argument about the Sino-Japanese agreements, he reminded those present that the Sino-Japanese Agreement of 1915 was reached under duress and observed that China had always considered all the Conventions with Japan as provisional and subject to revision by the Peace Conference. China's entry into the war, he argued, had so vitally changed the situation contemplated in the Treaty that on the principle of *rebus sic stantibus*, it ceased to be applicable. China's declaration of war also brought to an end the lease obtained by Germany in Shandong.[80] Koo's speech seemed to have appealed to the Allied leaders (except the Japanese, of course!) and quite impressed them.[81] When the meeting adjourned after Koo's speech, President Wilson went over to congratulate him on his excellent presentation of China's case. So did Lloyd George, Clemenceau, Balfour and Lansing.[82]

The report of China's argument at the Council of Ten on January 28 in the Paris press soon reached China and aroused great hopes in China that the case of Jiaozhou would be decided in China's favour. The President, the Premier and the Foreign Ministry as well as the Parliament all sent telegrams to Paris, expressing their congratulations and their raised expectations that China could win at the Council table. The Chinese Delegation also received telegrams from various provincial authorities and from government officials and student associations in the Shandong Province, fully supporting the stand the Chinese Delegation took at the Conference. Nation-wide, there prevailed a general belief that a triumph of China over Japan was almost achieved. The Chinese Delegation at Paris was also quite optimistic about the prospect of China's case.[83]

Coincidentally, it was on the eve of the Chinese New Year that the news of Koo's presentation at the Peace Conference was spread throughout China. The excitement of the Chinese people was all the more apparent, it was reported, and

Not since the Imperial regime has China's New Year been so enthusiastically celebrated as it is now. Everybody seemed to have been spending money, buying food and luxuries, and generally preparing for a good time, which was emphasized by continuous cracker firing which marked Friday night and Saturday morning.[84]

The apparent excitement of the Chinese seemed to be not merely over the success, if any, of their delegates in raising China's demands but over the recognition of China as an equal in the Family of Nations accorded by the Powers through the recognition of its delegates. The *North China Herald* reported:

> When [the] telegram reported that Dr. Wellington Koo and Mr. C.T. Wang had successfully crossed swords with the Japanese representatives, that in fact, China had got a hearing, there was a distinct feeling of jubilation. Not only China received a hearing, but her delegates had been recognized.[85]

China's feelings of elation at the strong position its delegates won for China at the Peace Conference were soon to be dampened, as the Japanese Minister to China, Obata, moved to dash them to the ground. On January 31, having received a telegram dated January 28 from Matsui,[86] Obata communicated to the Chinese Foreign Ministry his desire to see the Acting Foreign Minister Chen Lu on some urgent business.[87] The request was declined because it was the Chinese New Year's Eve. On February 2, however, Obata paid an unexpected visit to the Foreign Ministry and insisted on seeing the Acting Foreign Minister, to whom he expressed Japan's dissatisfaction with what he called the unfriendly attitude of the Chinese delegates towards Japan at the Peace Conference. He insisted that China must undertake not to publish or disclose to the Peace Conference secret agreements concluded between Japan and China without first obtaining Japanese approval.[88] He also threatened that if China disregarded Japanese advice, Japan would take necessary steps to maintain its international position.[89] It was widely reported that Obata intimated to Foreign Ministry officials that Japan might resort to economic pressure and even military force to stop China from publishing Sino-Japanese secret treaties.[90]

The move Obata made 'brought forth a storm of protest' within China.[91] The World's Chinese Students Federation dispatched a telegram to President Xu, declaring that, 'If we yield it will be tantamount to acknowledging Japan as our master. We cannot remain still, to see our nation humiliated.' They asked the Chinese Delegation 'to stand firm for China's cause' and assured them that 'the whole nation is united to support you'.[92] The President and the Government, under the pressure of public opinion, accordingly sent telegrams to the Chinese Delegation in Paris, assuring their support.[93] The so-called 'Obata Incident' helped to inflame the anti-Japanese sentiment among the Chinese and to intensify the Chinese nationalism already awakened. Contrary to the wish of Obata, the position of the Chinese delegates was reinforced by the nationalistic feelings further aroused partly by him.

In Paris, the Japanese move aroused considerable attention. Macleay of the British Delegation minuted a Foreign Office document as follows:

> there seemed to be no doubt that the Japanese Minister in Peking did use threats in his endeavour to induce the Chinese Government to send a telegram to their delegation here to modify their attitude over the Kiaochow question.[94]

Wilson, upon hearing the news, instructed that a telegram be sent to the American Ambassador to Tokyo to inquire into the matter and at the same time advised the Chinese Delegation not to submit to the Peace Conference the Sino-Japanese secret agreements before Japan did.[95]

It must be remembered that the controversy over the publication of the Sino-Japanese secret agreements was started during the January 28 session of the Council of Ten. Shortly before Koo presented China's case, Clemenceau, in his capacity as Chairman of the Council, requested on behalf of the Conference full information as to the Sino-Japanese engagements in regard to Shandong, because 'as notes had been exchanged, he thought that a statement of these engagements might be worth the consideration of the members of the Council'. President Wilson then asked Makino whether he proposed to lay these notes before the Council. In reply, Makino said that he did not think the Japanese Government would raise any objection, but, as the request was an unexpected one he would be compelled to ask its permission. In answer to the same question raised by President Wilson to the Chinese delegates, Koo said that the Chinese Government had no objection.[96]

Of all the war-time secret engagements between Japan and China, two were of vital importance to the disposal of Jiaozhou: the Sino-Japanese Treaty of 1915, and the exchange of notes between the two Governments on September 24, 1918. A Chinese note to the Japanese Foreign Minister stated that the Chinese Government were 'pleased to agree' to put into the hands of Japan and Germany the disposal of Jiaozhou in the post-war peace settlement in exchange for the withdrawal of Japanese troops and of the Japanese civil administration bureaux from areas outside Jiaozhou.[97] The exchange of notes had legally put Japan in an almost impregnable position in regard to its demand to inherit the German rights in Shandong. Later on, in April, it was this agreement between China and Japan which would doom China's claim for the direct restitution of Jiaozhou.

The shadow of secret agreements between the Allied Powers also overcast the Shandong case in Paris. On January 30, Foreign Minister Lu went to see Clemenceau and was told that on the previous day the Japanese envoy had produced in front of him the agreement between Japan and France in February 1917 on the disposal of Jiaozhou and asked him for an explanation. Clemenceau said that he told the Japanese that, if there had been no such agreement, he would have supported the Chinese claim.[98] On February 7, Lu had an interview with Lloyd George who told the Chinese Foreign Minister that there were Anglo-Japanese secret agreements and it would be difficult for Britain to support China in matters related to them. He suggested, however, that China should submit to the Conference all Sino-Japanese secret agreements before Wilson left for the United States on February 14, as the Americans were not bound by any secret agreement.[99]

The secret agreements referred to above between Japan and the other Allied Powers, Britain, France, Italy and Russia, had been concluded in February and March of 1917, when 'the submarine campaign had become very formidable' and 'Japanese help was urgently needed'.[100] These secret agreements guaranteed the Allied Powers' support for Japan at the future peace table in the matter of its claim to German rights in Shandong, as well as the German colonies in the Pacific north of the Equator.[101] As a *quid pro quo*, Japan agreed to dispatch two cruisers to patrol the Mediterranean and to cooperate with other Allied Powers to sponsor China's entering into the war, so as to liquidate the German influence in China. It should be noted that all this happened after the United States severed its diplomatic relations with Germany consequent to the latter's universal submarine warfare. In fact, as revealed later by the publication of secret treaties by the Bolsheviks and by the other sources, the Japanese move was taken as a preventative measure in anticipation of China's participation in the war on the Allied side, which would completely change China's position *vis-à-vis* Japan and would obtain for China a say at the future peace conference. Krupensky, the Russian Ambassador to Japan, reported to the Russian Foreign Minister on February 8, 1917 about the Japanese approach to him for a secret guarantee, stating that

... the minister [Motono, the Japanese Foreign Minister] pointed out the necessity for him, in view of the attitude of Japanese public opinion on the subject [Japan's right to claim former German rights in the Far East and in the Pacific], as well as with a view to safeguard Japan's position at the future peace conference, if China should be admitted to it, of securing the support of the Allied Powers to the desires of Japan in respect of Shantung and the Pacific Islands.[102]

Japan, by virtue of these secret agreements which came to be known only at the Peace Conference, had practically preempted Allied interference in the matter. Shandong became not only a matter of territorial sovereignty and national integrity but also a problem over which battles had to be fought against the spectre of secret agreements. Both China's demands and Japan's claims hung on the Powers' attitude towards these 'ugly old entanglements'.[103]

While the 'Obata Incident' was still arousing vehement protests in China, the Japanese Delegation in Paris informed the Chinese Delegation on February 7 of the secret agreements it intended to submit to the Peace Conference.[104] Likewise, the Chinese Delegation, before its submission, also informed the Japanese Delegation of the secret agreements they proposed to submit, which included the full text of the Sino-Japanese Agreement of 1915.[105] On February 15, the Chinese Delegation duly submitted, together with the Sino-Japanese war-time secret agreements, China's claim for direct restitution of the leased territory of Jiaozhou to the Conference.[106]

However, the Sino-Japanese controversy over Shandong was shelved for quite some time because the attention of the Council of Ten was engaged on more urgent matters such as the drafting of the Covenant of the League of Nations, and because of the absence from the Conference of Wilson and Clemenceau from mid-February to March.[107]

AN UNREWARDING SUPPLICATION

At the same time that China made its submission to the Peace Conference of its claim for direct restoration of Jiaozhou, it was also actively preparing the presentation of its other demands in readjusting its foreign relations. Lu reported to the Cabinet that

[We] have submitted only this claim because the Shandong problem is the most urgent one [for us] now. [We] are afraid that if [we] submit at once all the other proposals and demands, we might be isolated, for it might turn the European Powers and America to support Japan because of their common interests [in China].[108]

The other proposals and demands mentioned above were embodied in the January 8, 1919 instruction from President Xu to the Chinese Delegation. The instruction pronounced that 'In accordance with the principles enunciated in numerous speeches by the American President and the British Premier, our nation should try to obtain international equality [at the Peace Conference]'. Five proposals, he instructed, should be made to the Peace Conference for this purpose: (1) revision of all unequal treaties between the Chinese Government and the foreign governments and individuals, including restoration of leased territories and withdrawal of foreign post offices in China; (2) abrogation of consular jurisdiction on the condition that China reform its legal system and the civil, criminal, commercial and procedural laws be promulgated and enforced; (3) tariff reciprocity and autonomy; (4) withdrawal from China of foreign troops sanctioned by the 1901 Protocol; and (5) relinquishing of the remaining part of the Boxer Indemnity and using it for educational purposes in China.[109] This was the final instruction the Chinese Delegation received before the opening of the Conference as to China's policy at the Peace Conference. It was a more detailed outline for the realization in China of the three principles in Koo's memorandum presented to the Americans in Washington in November 1918, namely political sovereignty, territorial integrity and fiscal independence. It was a more clearly elaborated version of China's hopes and aspirations expressed by Lu in the same month to the American and British Ministers in Beijing.

At Paris, from the very opening of the Peace Conference, the Chinese Delegation involved itself deeply in preparing the proposals. A suggestion was adopted at the second meeting of the Chinese Delegation on January 22 that, in presenting to the Conference China's conditions on matters concerning Germany and Austria–Hungary arising directly out of the War, China should also express its hopes for a total readjustment of its external relations to see how the Allied Powers reacted to them.[110] On the afternoon of January 28, apparently encouraged by Koo's impressive speech at the Council of Ten in the morning, the Chinese Delegation meeting decided the 'division of labour' among its members in preparing the details of those proposals for submission.[111] About one month later, at the twenty-sixth meeting of the Chinese Delegation on February 26, the draft proposal on the abrogation of consular jurisdiction was presented.[112] At the following two meetings, the draft proposals for the withdrawal of foreign post offices and for fiscal independence were handed in by Sze.[113] On March 3, Koo submitted the draft proposal asking for the relinquishing of leased territories.[114] All these drafts were presented to the Delegation meeting, subject to the discussion and comments of other members of the Chinese Delegation. At the beginning of April, final versions were agreed upon and were put to print.[115] Acting on the decision of the sixty-seventh meeting, on April 10, the document *Questions for Readjustment* was submitted to the Conference on April 15.[116]

The Chinese supplication attracted little attention at the Peace Conference because, it was alleged, the problems did not arise directly out of the war. The document has similarly been neglected in academic studies of China's presentation at the Paris Peace Conference.[117] This document, however, was actually a manifesto of China's nationalistic aspirations and desires and an overall plan to readjust China's international relations with foreign Powers to put China on an equal footing with other nations in the expanding international system. The fact that the Chinese justified their demand for such an overall readjustment by invoking principles of equality, justice and respect for sovereignty showed how much China had advanced towards accepting the common values of the European international society to qualify itself for the membership of that community. It also showed how extensive the foreign encroachments were on the Chinese sovereignty. It is more important to note, as will be studied later, that China went on with its own line after the Peace Conference to implement the readjustment in spite of oppositions from the Powers. This document gave a sense of direction to Chinese diplomacy in the forthcoming years. Part of those nationalistic aspirations expressed in the document would before long be realized at the Washington Conference in 1921–1922 when the Powers' were compelled to consider the matter.[118]

The actual Memorandum consisted of nine parts. In the first part, the short introductory remarks, the Memorandum stated that China had made remarkable progress since the founding of the Republic in political, administrative and economic fields. There were, however, hindrances of an international nature in the way of China's progress. 'Of these hindrances, some are the legacies of the past due to circumstances which do not exist now, while others arise from recent abuses which are not justifiable in equity nor in law.' The Chinese Delegation decided to submit the Memorandum to ask for readjustment 'so that all hindrances to China's free development be removed in conformity with the principles of territorial integrity, political independence and economic autonomy which appertain to every sovereign state'. They believed 'the Peace Conference seeks to base the structure of a new world upon the principle of justice, equality and respect for the sovereignty of nations'.[119]

In demanding the renunciation of the spheres of influence in China, the Memorandum argued that the claim for spheres of influence was initiated by Germany over the Province of Shandong in 1898, and later, in what was known to be the 'scramble for concessions', other Powers, 'apparently out of a desire to maintain the balance of power in the Far East, advanced similar claims in regard to other parts of the territory of China'. China asked the Powers to renounce their respective spheres of influence because the very existence of them was 'impairing the sovereign rights of China' and 'threatening her [China's] territorial integrity and political independence as well as giving rise to international jealousy and thereby jeopardizing the peace of the Far East'.[120]

On the matter of foreign troops and police in China, the Memorandum elaborated the extent of their presence. They were divided into two kinds: those under the sanction of the 1901 Protocol, and those introduced against the repeated protests of the Chinese Government. Under the former heading were listed Legation guards stationed in Beijing and along the railways between the capital and the sea, which numbered around 9,000 immediately before the war. Under the second heading were listed, among other things, 1,500 Japanese troops outside the treaty port limits in Hankou, 2,200 Japanese troops outside the former German-leased territory of Jiaozhou and 150 Russian troops and 30 British-dispatched Indian soldiers in Kashgar in the Province of Xinjiang. Japan also had set up 27 police agencies in Manchuria, arguing such a privilege was 'but a corollary of the right of extraterritoriality'. The Memorandum contended that the principal reasons for demanding their withdrawal were that 'the respect of the Chinese for foreign lives and property in recent years has been striking and beyond criticism, even in time of internal disturbance' and that it 'does violence to the sense of pride of the Chinese people, in that they are a standing derogation of China's sovereignty'. Such a practice had 'no parallel' in other countries. It also denied that any grant of extraterritoriality included the right of establishing police agencies.[121]

As to the foreign post offices, the Memorandum pointed out that the 'opening of these offices was not based on any treaty provision or concession. Their existence and gradual increase since has merely been tolerated by the Chinese Government'. It went on to spell out that the institutions of the Chinese postal service had rapidly developed, so much so that it had 'already for over five years taken its place as a fully equipped member of the Universal Postal Union'. Therefore, 'the Chinese Government are of the opinion that the time has now come when their own postal service should become the sole establishment of the kind carring [*sic*] on postal work within the limits of the Chinese territory, as is the rule in every other independent country'.[122]

The Memorandum asked the Powers to promise to relinquish their consular jurisdiction upon China's promulgation of its civil, criminal and commercial laws and laws of civil and criminal procedure, and upon its establishment of new courts in the districts of prefectural divisions. It dwelt upon the incompatibility of consular jurisdiction with the exercise of the right of territorial sovereignty. The consular jurisdiction in China 'is not and was not based upon any principles of International Law, but was merely created by the Treaties' when there were 'fundamental differences between the Chinese and foreign laws and the imperfection of the Chinese judicial system'.

In asking for the relinquishment of the leased territories, the Memorandum asserted that the existence of leased territories 'jeopardizes the territorial integrity of China' and 'greatly prejudiced China's interests'. They were 'demanded by the Powers in the main avowedly to create a balance of power, not between China and another country, but as between foreign aspirants to power and advantage at a time when the territorial integrity of China under the misrule of the Manchu Dynasty appeared to be in imminent danger'. They constituted a 'virtual *imperium in imperio*' in China and very often became *points d'appui* for developing spheres of influence. The Memorandum justified the Chinese demand on the ground that it was detrimental to the integrity of Chinese territory and that the new international order after the war with the League of Nations would totally change the pre-war situation in East Asia, thus dispensing with any necessity for maintaining balance of power therein.[123]

The Memorandum made the request that the Governments of the Powers holding concessions and settlements in China agree to restore them to China in five years time. Although the 'settlements' or 'concessions' were granted by the Treaties, it argued, practices and claims had for years been introduced on the part of foreign authorities in the concessions to exercise power and jurisdiction out of the reach of treaty provisions. 'This assertion of exclusive authority and power has made each concession virtually "un petit état dans l'état" to the impairment of China's rights as a territorial sovereign'. It also hampered China's work of administration. As municipal administration in China had seen great progress in recent years as exemplified in the case of Beijing, the Chinese Government believed itself 'prepared to assume the responsibilities for effective administration' of those areas. Besides, China had taken over the German and Austro-Hungarian concessions in both Tianjin and Hankou since 1917 and administered them without hearing 'serious criticism'.[124]

On tariff autonomy, the Memorandum denounced the conventional tariff imposed upon China as 'unfair and unscientific' because there was no reciprocity, and no differentiation, for example, between necessities and luxuries, and the tariff had undergone no real revision since 1858. Consequently, it provided only insufficient revenue for China. 'It is clear therefore that in the matter of tariff, China does not enjoy the same right as is granted practically to all nations.' The Memorandum urged that, 'To conform to the aim and object of the League of Nations, it is urgently desired that the right of China to revise the existing tariff conventions should be recognized and agreed to by the friendly Powers.' It also expressed the hope that 'friendly Powers will restore to China the same fiscal right as is enjoyed by all independent nations so that the Chinese people may develop their natural resources, become better consumers of the world's commodities, and contribute their share to the progress and civilization of mankind'.[125]

Finally, that the Chinese were appealing to the theme of common interests shared by members in the expanding international society was clearly reflected in the concluding remarks of the Memorandum. They stated that, although the Chinese Delegation 'are not unaware that the questions herein dealt with did not primarily arise out of this World War', yet they believed that 'these questions demand readjustment by the Peace Conference because, if left unattended to, they contain germs of future conflicts capable of disturbing the world's peace again'.[126]

It should be noted that, in pleading to the sense of justice of the Powers, China also promised more reforms of its institutions so as to come into line with practices of the civilized nations. Among other things, China promised further legislative and judicial reforms, including promulgation of five Codes[127] and establishment of new courts in all the localities where foreigners resided, so that the Chinese state of laws and their administration would gradually reach the stage 'as has been obtained by the most advanced nations'.[128] In tax reform, *likin*[129] would be abolished if concessions could be made by the Powers before China achieved its full tariff autonomy.[130] The Chinese Government would also undertake, as an obligation, to protect and safeguard the rights of property-owners in the leased territories and settlements upon their eventual restoration to China.[131]

It would not be difficult to see that the Chinese pleading was mostly based on commonly accepted principles of international justice, equality among nations, respect for national sovereignty, and unmolested and free national development in the post-war international order. Significantly, China, in striving to conforming to the standard of 'civilization' so as to gain the full membership of the Family of Nations, now also asked to be treated in accordance with the standard and values professed by the Western nations as the common basis of the expanding international society. This demand to revise regulatory rules and institutions, which the West had introduced to regulate relations between European and non-European nations, could probably be regarded as the beginning of China's active participation in the shaping of the international system.

By the time the Chinese Delegation submitted this Memorandum in the middle of April, the Peace Conference was engaged in settling more pressing European matters, with the prospect of the Germans coming to Paris in two weeks' time. Some of the Chinese proposals, when known to the French and the Americans, commanded their sympathies. But it was almost out of the question that the proposals would ever be dealt with during the Peace Conference, not merely because of pressures of time, but also because they entailed an overhaul of the Powers' interests in and policies towards China. It was natural that the Chinese entreaties attracted little attention, other than an acknowledgement that they had been received by the General Secretariat of the Peace Conference.[132]

AN 'EVEN BREAK'?

From February to mid-April, the Sino-Japanese controversy over Shandong was not on the agenda of the Peace Conference. But it certainly lurked in the background. Paris was full of intrigues and plots.[133] Baron Makino, aware of the land grabbing of other European Powers at the Conference,[134] once implied to Colonel House that the Japanese demands for German transfer of Jiaozhou and the Pacific Islands north of the Equator were probably too modest.[135] In early

March, the correspondent of the *Kokumin*, a Japanese newspaper, complained in Paris that

> Japan is losing all points at the Peace Conference; that control of the Pacific islands will probably go to Australia, that the Tsingtau and Shantung railway will probably be returned to China, that the question of racial discrimination has been tabled and this is Japan's supreme moment when she must decide which alternative to adopt, to join the League of Nations without securing any rights in the world or secede from the League on the grounds that Japan's rights to equal treatment is not acknowledged by the Powers.[136]

Clearly, what the Japanese were after at Paris was not merely a Great Power status as symbolized by its presence at the Council of Ten, but 'equality' with other Great Powers measured by its gains out of the Peace Conference.

Meanwhile, the Chinese Delegation was continuing its solicitation of help from the Powers, especially from the Americans, for a settlement of the Shandong question in favour of China. On the afternoon of March 24, Koo secured an interview with President Wilson and inquired about the prospect of an early solution of the Shandong question. The President, instead of answering directly, informed Koo that the Japanese delegates had asked him for an interview to discuss privately the Shandong question before the Conference took it up again. He asked Koo whether the Japanese, in doing so, would propose to keep the railway while returning to China the leased territory– Jiaozhou. Koo told Wilson that that was probably the Japanese intention. It was one of the reasons why Japan had asked for German surrender of Jiaozhou directly to Japan together with the Shandong Railway. Most likely, Japan would also want to attach conditions for the restoration of Jiaozhou to China. Koo further contended that

> If Japan was to have the railway and exclusive settlement in the best part of the leased territory, it would mean the returning of the shadow to China, while leaving the substance to Japan. China would be getting nothing back.[137]

Wilson showed his understanding by saying that he was now clear in his mind on principles involved in the question.

Apparently encouraged by the formation of the Council of Four from which Japan was excluded, the Chinese approached Colonel House and Lansing on April 2 and on April 4 respectively to press for an early solution of the Shandong dispute, preferably in the Council of

Four.[138] Chinese courage seemed to have been boosted by Lansing who told them that

> Although there were secret agreements between Japan and other great powers, the Shandong question could be settled only by applying the principle of self-determination. He was opposed to settling it on any other principle and he knew that President Wilson would be opposed to it also ... He felt ... that China's position *vis-à-vis* this question at present was very favourable.[139]

On April 8, Koo, in sending Lansing an aide-mémoire of their conversation on April 4, intimated his hope that Lansing would see his way 'to lay the matter before President Wilson at an early date'.[140] On the same day, Lu sent a letter to Balfour, expressing the Chinese desire that the matter be solved in the Council of Four.[141] Before then, on April 5, Lu also talked with Pichon about the Chinese contention for direct return to China of the leased territory.[142]

April was indeed the month for decisions in Paris, with the prospect of the Germans coming for the reading of the draft treaty. Unfortunately, it was also 'the Dark Period of the Peace Conference'.[143] In March, House had already 'realized that the only possible peace would not be the ideal settlement he had hoped for'.[144] Lansing now privately remarked that 'Gloom is everywhere. Paris is steeped in it. Distrust and depression have succeeded the high hopes with which the Council of Four was greeted'.[145] Colonel Bonsal's observation on April 12 was sharp: 'As the Conference stalls', he observed,

> the programme is torn to bits, and the men who came as peace talkers put on their war paint and fight like tigers, not for the common good but to safeguard what they hold are their vital national interests.[146]

At the Council of Four, at the mercy of which the fate of small and weak nations was to be decided, President Wilson confronted the same 'wiliest politicians in Europe'[147] and the same problems as two months before. Yet his position at both Paris and Washington had been seriously weakened. His word now was 'no longer supreme in the world Council of the Allies as it most certainly was a few short weeks ago– before the Armistice'[148] and at home support for him was 'dropping sheepishly away behind him'.[149] He had to make uneasy and unstable compromises of his principles,[150] so as to wind up this unpleasant business, if the Peace Conference was to get anywhere.

In mid-April, the Sino-Japanese controversy over Shandong slipped back to the Conference table. On April 15 and 17, Lansing twice suggested at the Council of Five that 'all questions relating to the renunciation of territorial rights and privileges and to the abandonment of claims by Germany should be decided *en bloc*' and that, along this line, Germany would renounce its rights and privileges in China 'in favour of the Five Great Powers acting as trustees'.[151] On both occasions, 'the Foreign Ministers of Britain, France and Italy remained silent',[152] while Makino argued that Jiaozhou was an exceptional case because it was not a German colony and because of the treaties entered into between China and Japan.[153]

Lansing was not alone in making this proposal. On April 18, at the Council of Four when the Jiaozhou question was brought up for discussion, Lloyd George claimed:

> I do not know why Kiaochow should not be treated in the same way as all the other overseas German possessions, whose surrender by the Germans to the Great Powers has been decided, with the right to deal with them as they see fit.

Wilson echoed his suggestion in saying that 'this is Mr. Lansing's opinion and I consider it the best solution'. The Four reached a decision:

> It was agreed ... that the Japanese Plenipotentiaries should be asked to accept the same formula for Kiaochow as was adopted in the case of the German colonial decisions. That is to say, renunciation in favour of the Allied and Associated Powers.[154]

The situation at Paris at this moment became extremely trying. Colonel House began to advise Wilson to

> accept the line of the pact of London, as far as it touches the boundaries of the old Austro-Hungarian Empire ... because if Italy refused to sign the Treaty with Germany and if Japan also refused, and there is some danger of this too, then conditions would be serious.[155]

Another American Commissioner, General Bliss, predicted on April 19, after a conference with Wilson, that 'in a few days we shall have settled a peace of a "blow-up" '.[156]

Wilson, however, personally made a proposal along the line suggested at the meeting of the Council of Four on April 18 to Makino and Chinda on the morning of April 21 in his house in the

Place des États-Unis, only to find that the Japanese were 'very stiff' and that they stood absolutely upon their original demands regarding Shandong.[157] The Japanese actually rejected the proposal for the reasons (1) that there had already existed an agreement between China and Japan concerning the disposition of Jiaozhou; (2) that the mandate system should not be applied to the territory of such a culturally advanced nation as China; and (3) that the Japanese people would never accept it because it meant that the Powers were suspicious of Japan's goodwill and sincerity in fulfilling its treaty obligations towards China.[158] The Japanese also intimated to the President that, if the solution of the Shandong question was not to Japan's satisfaction, Japan would not sign the treaty.[159] At the afternoon session of the Council of Four, having heard President Wilson's account of the Japanese attitude, the Council decided to summon Japan to its morning session the next day.

The sessions on April 22 of the Council of Four were most crucial to the settlement of the Shandong problem. The Japanese attended the morning session, at which Baron Makino presented the Japanese claims again. Lloyd George promptly expressed his readiness to stand by the pledge of his predecessors to support Japan on the issue. But he also suggested that the general principle governing the disposal of other German colonies be applied to Jiaozhou and that Japan make no specific provision in the treaty for its disposition so that Australia and New Zealand would not make similar demands on German colonies in the Pacific.[160] To this, Chinda argued that Jiaozhou was not part of a former German colony and that he could not see why the solution should be 'put in abeyance'. He stated that the Japanese Delegation was under express instruction from the Japanese Government that, unless they were placed in a position to carry out their obligations to China, they were not allowed to sign the treaty.[161]

The Japanese 'bluff' seemed to have worked well. Clemenceau had remained silent before and said nothing during the discussion afterwards. Lloyd George mumbled a few words not quite relevant to the subject. Wilson spoke a lot but only lectured on broad principles and his hopes without even challenging the validity of the secret agreements Japan made with China or with the Allied Powers.[162] The Japanese obviously observed this, probably with relief. They reported to Tokyo that Wilson 'was more friendly and conciliatory in both attitude and speech than on the previous day'. They left the session with the impression that 'the discussion was fruitful not only in softening the opposition from the United States President but also in making him understand Japan's firm attitude on this question'. They also interpreted the attitude of Clemenceau and Lloyd George at the session as an acquiescence in Japan's demands.[163]

The Japanese were not far wrong. At the afternoon session to which the Chinese were summoned, the changing attitude of Wilson was more apparent. From the very beginning, the Chinese were lectured not on principles of the peace but on the secret treaties concluded during the war. Wilson reminded the Chinese of their agreements with Japan in 1915 and 1918 and even read aloud the exchange of notes between the Chinese Minister in Tokyo and the Japanese Government in September 1918. He went on to emphasize the 'embarrassing position which had been reached' because of China's secret agreements with Japan. China's declaration of war against Germany might have invalidated the Sino-Japanese Treaty of 1915, but not the Agreement of September 1918. Great Britain and France were bound by their war engagements to support Japan to get whatever rights Germany had in Shandong. 'Because', he said to the Chinese, 'the War had largely been fought for the purpose of showing that Treaties could not be violated.' Wilson even defended the secret agreements between Japan and the Allied Powers. 'The engagements were unfortunate', he maintained, 'nevertheless, they had been entered into for the salvation of China, because they had been entered into for the salvation of the world, of which China was a part. In fact, it would be said that the very engagements were instruments for the salvation of China.' The Chinese delegates were then asked by Lloyd George and Wilson whether they would prefer the observation of their treaty with Japan to observing those between Japan and Britain and France. In spite of Koo's protest that both were unacceptable choices, Lloyd George proposed to put this question to be examined by American, British and French experts to 'learn their views as to which course would be best for China'.[164] His proposal was agreed.[165]

This practically sealed the efforts on the part of China to have the Shandong question settled in its favour. It was the last time the Chinese were ever consulted on the matter before the final decision at the end of April.[166] Anyway, was there such a need for further consultation? The lot had been cast and the basic line drawn. There was little doubt after April 22 that the matter of Jiaozhou was to be settled, if there was any settlement at all, along the lines predetermined in the secret engagements during the war.

The Chinese seemed to have only a belated recognition of changes of Wilson's attitude and still cherished a hope against hope that Wilson would not abandon totally his principles of self-determination and just peace. Koo went to see Lansing on the evening of April 22, asking him to tell Wilson that either to carry China's treaties with Japan or to observe treaties between Japan and the Allied Powers on the disposition of Jiaozhou would deeply disappoint the Chinese and that they hoped that Wilson would insist in the Council of Four on a more favourable settlement for China.[167] On April 24, the Chinese Delegation submitted to the Council of Four a memorandum, proposing:

1. Germany renounces to the five Allied and Associated Powers her holdings, rights and privileges in Shantung for restoration to China.

2. Japan, being in possession of the said holdings, rights and privileges, engages to effect the said restoration to China within one year after the signature of the Treaty of Peace with Germany.

3. China agrees to make a pecuniary compensation to Japan for the military expenses incurred in the capture of Tsingtao, the amount of the said compensation to be determined by the Council of Four.

4. China agrees to open the whole of Kiaochow Bay as a commercial port, and to provide a special quarter, if desired, for the residence of the citizens and subjects of the Treaty Powers.[168]

This last Chinese supplication, with considerable concessions, for a just settlement of the Shandong question fell on deaf ears.

For the last few days of April 1919, the Shandong question was entirely in the hands of the Great Powers. The Japanese were invited to talk with Balfour on the afternoon of April 26 to 'dispel the suspicion' on the part of the British as to the motives of Japan's insistence on holding the railway and its concentration of troops at Jiaozhou.[169] On the evening of the same day, they went to see Lansing and Williams to 'soften' their attitude, only to find Lansing still insistent on the invalidity of the secret treaties and suspicious of Japan's purposes in Shandong.[170] For Wilson, American public opinion was a serious concern, as he frankly admitted to the Japanese that

It was extremely difficult for him in the face of public opinion in the United States of America to assent to any part of the arrangement. He was seeking a way to make it possible for him to agree, and it was not a simple matter. Public opinion in the United States did not agree to the transfer of the concession.[171]

He was trying to wring concessions from the Japanese to reconcile American public opinion and, probably, to ease his conscience as well.

The British played the role of mediator. Balfour had hinted to the Japanese on April 16 that Britain and France were both concerned with conditions upon which Japan would return Jiaozhou to China and that Japan had to make concessions to a certain extent so as to reach a compromise.[172] After his meeting with the Japanese on April 26, he drafted and submitted a proposal which was made known to the Japanese at the meeting of the Council of Four on April 29. To satisfy Wilson and to allay the Chinese resentment, Balfour proposed that Japan make a public statement of its policy toward China, as follows:

1. The declared policy of Japan is to hand back to China at the earliest date the sovereignty of Shantung Peninsula and to retain only the economic privileges possessed by Germany.

2. The intention of the clauses relating to the police on the railway is merely to give the owner of the railway security for traffic and will be used for no other purposes.

3. Such Japanese instructors as may be required to assist in policing the railway may be selected by the company.[173]

With much consultation, but not much amendment, the Balfour proposal was adopted by the Japanese as a semi-official oral statement issued at the Council of Four on April 30.[174] This seemed to have satisfied Wilson, who took this statement as a Japanese commitment to return the sovereignty of Jiaozhou to China. The Big Three finally committed themselves to incorporating into the Peace Treaty the draft clauses proposed by the Japanese with regard to the Shandong question, which eventually became Articles 156, 157 and 158 of the Versailles Treaty.[175]

The fortune of China, ranged as one of those 'suppliants and suitors' at the Peace Conference, was thus decided by the Supreme Authority of the Peace Conference. Wilson told Grayson that it was 'an even break'[176] and thought that it was the best he could get 'out of the dirty past'.[177] House thought it was 'bad enough, but it is no worse than the doubtful transactions that have gone on among the Allies themselves and indeed, that are going on now'.[178] Lansing condemned it as 'an immoral bargaining away of principles and of the rights of China'.[179] Whatever it was, the break was certainly not 'even'. Wilson himself admitted later that he had to give and had given Japan 'what they should not have'.[180]

Still more of a myth exists as to why Wilson yielded to Japan and abandoned his principles in the case of Shandong. Wilson himself explained to the press at the end of June that he was firm on Fiume because Italy wanted to annex it for good, while in the case of Shandong, Japan had promised to return to China its political sovereignty and there were also Sino-Japanese agreements to consider. On top of that, Japan must be kept in the Conference to make the League of Nations work.[181] This was probably the explanation. Wilson's faith in the League of Nations revealed his belief that the post-war international order should be managed, not by political rivalry among Great Powers of the pre-war kind, but by co-operation of five Great Powers acting as trustees for the world peace. Whatever price had to be paid, Japan must be incorporated into the framework of the League of Nations to cooperate with the other Powers. As for China, he had told the Chinese that it was difficult to apply his Fourteen Points to the Far East and there were China's secret agreements with Japan to blame. China had to depend on the League of Nations to redress wrongs done to it. In the final analysis, what could China do to effectively challenge the international system to be ushered in by the Powers?

Wilson seemed to have genuinely believed that Japan, if refused Jiaozhou, would withdraw from the Conference and that the Japanese were not bluffing him. Other historians who specialized in the study of the Peace Conference, notably Fifield, have supported the thesis, with their studies of the Japanese documents, that Japan would definitely have refused to sign the Treaty if their demands were rejected.[182] There is, however, some substantial counter-evidence which does not seem to have come to the attention of historians. In general, it is arguable that Japan, with the memory of Three Powers' intervention in 1895, and fearing isolation would have given up its privileged international position, recognized by the other Powers, so readily. More specifically, two other pieces of evidence may be suggested here. First, in Paris, Marquis Saionji, the head of the Japanese Delegation, practically told the other Japanese delegates at the end of April that nothing could be more stupid than to lose their heads over a petty imbroglio about Shandong, abandon the League of Nations, and withdraw from the Conference. He shouted at them 'However, if you want to withdraw, do so! All of you! I'll stay here on my own, so you can go straight away.'[183] Secondly, the Japanese Prime Minister, Hara, in his diary entry of April 30, 1919 explicitly stated that he had instructed the Japanese delegates in Paris to wait for further instructions if Japan's claims should be rejected.[184]

While it is still a matter of speculation as to whether Japan would have refused to sign the Treaty if its demands had been turned down, it became before long a fact that China decided to stay away from the ceremony of signing the Peace Treaty on June 28, 1919 at Versailles.

NATIONALISM AND THE MAY FOURTH MOVEMENT

The news of the Big Three's decision in Paris to transfer Jiaozhou and former German interests in Shandong to Japan, when reaching Beijing, immediately threw the Chinese from pious hope to deep despair. 'Young's China's faith in Wilsonian idealism was shattered to dust. "The New World Order" was no more!'[185] This frustration and exasperation was soon transferred into a national protest against the Paris decision on Shandong. An 'unpremeditated nationalist movement'[186] was started by students in Beijing on May 4, 1919. Whether or not China would sign the forthcoming German Peace Treaty with the Shandong provisions, i.e. whether China would accept the verdict of the Peace Conference, became a national issue in the eventful days of May and June.

The existing studies of the period are heavily concentrated on the so-called 'May Fourth Movement', either as a populist movement against the alleged intention of the Government in Beijing to sign the Treaty without reservations, or as an intellectual revolution in modern China.[187] Neither the process of the Government decision-making in Beijing on the issue of China's signature nor the absence of the Chinese Delegation from the signing of the Versailles Treaty has received more than a fleeting mention in those studies. More regrettably, there has been little serious attempt to investigate the subject. Consequently, there has been oversimplification and sometimes an erroneous assumption that, because of the government's repressive measures against the students' radical actions during the May Fourth period, there was a direct confrontation between the students' nationalistic demands to save the country by not signing the Treaty and the Government's 'traitorous' policy to 'sell out' China by signing the Treaty with the Shandong clauses. Little appreciation has been shown of the assertion of Chinese official nationalism in the matter of China's signning of the Versailles Treaty. The question why China finally refused to sign remains unsatisfactorily explained.

If very few people at Paris had envisaged any prospect of China's refusal to sign the Peace Treaty with the Shandong provisions,[188] even fewer could foresee that the Chinese were capable of putting, with such determination, their disappointment and discontent with regard to the Peace Treaty into concrete expression of political nationalism in the form of nation-wide demonstrations, petitions, strikes, press campaigns and anti-Japanese trade boycott. Beginning on May 4, 1919 in Beijing, when some three thousand students from thirteen institutions of higher learning staged a demonstration in front of Tiananmen at the centre of the city, the nationalist agitation lasted about two months, until after June 28, when the Chinese Delegation in Paris withheld their signature from the Treaty. This was soon dubbed by the Chinese students as the 'May Fourth Patriotic Movement', or the 'May Fourth Movement' for short.[189]

There has since been confusion about the use and definition of the expression the 'May Fourth Movement'.[190] It has been used interchangeably with the 'New Culture Movement'. By the same token, it has been interpreted as an 'intellectual revolution', the 'Chinese Renaissance',[191] a 'democratic revolution',[192] an 'anti-imperialist and anti-feudalist bourgeois democratic revolution' and 'part of the world revolution of the proletarian class',[193] or an 'iconoclastic cultural revolution'.[194] All these interpretations seem to have committed the fallacy of incorporating the May Fourth Movement *per se*[195] into the New Culture Movement and used the former to designate the latter and consequently cost the former its own identity.

The May Fourth Movement *per se* is probably no more than a 'patriotic movement against the Pan-Asianism and aggression'[196] and an 'anti-power-politics movement'[197], aimed at the rejection of the Great Powers' disposal of Jiaozhou in favour of Japan in disregard of China's nationalist aspirations and demands. More broadly, the May Fourth Movement was a continuation of China's search for an answer or a resistance to the expansion of the West (now including Japan) into China after 1840. It was a reflection of the continuing agonizing concern of the Chinese, especially the Chinese intelligentsia, with the debilitation and dislocation of China in the international system after the complete change of their perception of the world. It was also a reflection of a continuing conflict between China and the West as regards China's position and status *vis-à-vis* the Western Powers and other states in the international system still dominated by the Powers of European culture. The difference now was that, whereas the earlier conflict between China and the West up to the turn of the century was the result of China's obstinate and persistent refusal to allow the

Western states an equal position in China's own world, the conflict at the Paris Peace Conference in re-establishing a new international order arose from the Powers' denial of China's equality and full sovereignty in international society and its continual refusal to grant China 'qualifications' for full membership of the post-war international system.

Further, what makes the May Fourth Movement *per se* unique and unprecedented is probably not only its popular basis and nation-wide scope, as has been indicated.[198] More significantly, especially in the context of China's entrance into the Family of Nations, the uniqueness of the May Fourth Movement is that it was the first time since Sino-Western contact was made in 1840 that the Chinese people successfully transferred their discontent into a national rejection of an international order imposed upon China by the Powers. In view of China's role in the development of a global international system, it can be regarded as the first impact of assertive Chinese nationalism[199] on the modern international system.

Nationalism as 'a state of mind and an act of consciousness'[200] certainly has no place in the Sino-centric world order of a universal moral community. Traditional Chinese society was simply 'devoid of national feeling'.[201] The rise of Chinese nationalism, as mentioned in Chapter 1, resulted from the demise of Sinocentrism and the ancient Middle Kingdom's gradual acceptance of the ideal of nation-states and from a complicated process of Chinese intellectual adaptation and transformation which involved a reinterpretation of China's history and culture. Moreover the emergence of national consciousness in China was prompted by a sense of national crisis precipitated by constant Western encroachment upon China. The birth of Chinese nationalism was not, therefore, the inauguration of an ideological movement. Its very emergence did not imply any existence of a formulated political concept built upon precepts of European philosophers. Rather, it was a form of group consciousness primarily concerned with the survival of China as a nation. It was characterized by what Nehru later called 'an anti-foreign feeling'.[202] Mary Wright defined the massive Chinese nationalism as 'an intense, widespread fear that China would be partitioned and the Chinese disappear as a people'.[203] From the beginning of the century, nationalism had been transformed into massive actions to resist imperialist oppression and domination of China.[204]

The immediate forces of circumstance which provided the main stimulus for the nationalist movement in May 1919, if summarized briefly, were, first, the extensive Japanese wartime political and economic encroachments upon China; second, the disappointment with the Powers' betrayal of Wilsonian principles which had once inspired Chinese nationalist aspirations; and third, the disillusionment with the political disintegration of warlord China. However the nationalist movement in the May Fourth period felt the same concern as Chinese nationalism of the earlier periods. The popular fear at the May Fourth period was that power politics at Paris had again put into peril China's existence as a nation. The popular demand was that the Government should refuse to sign China's 'death warrant', (i.e., the German peace treaty with Shandong clauses) so as to protect China's sovereignty and territorial integrity. In this sense, the May Fourth Movement could be more properly regarded not as the beginning of modern Chinese nationalism but as its climax.

It is not to be questioned that the May Fourth Movement contributed heavily to China's final refusal to sign the Versailles Treaty and that nationalism in the May Fourth period was 'a movement that was directed against the world which "opened" China and impinged upon her'.[205] The question is rather whether the May Fourth nationalist movement alone can fully account for China's final decision not to sign the Versailles Treaty. Nationalism as a nation-wide phenomenon during the May Fourth period must have other manifestations. The May Fourth Movement heavily influenced the government decision-making. But it did not make the decision. What should be further observed is that the nationalist feelings during the May Fourth period, just as at the turn of the century, were shared by people of all social strata in Chinese society. The so-called 'official' nationalism and the populist nationalism shared the same concern and the same aspirations. The difference between them was probably that the populist nationalism tended to demand radical actions,[206] while the official nationalism tended to be more accommodating. In other words, the populist nationalists were impatient to revolutionize the existing order overnight by a mighty effort of human will. The official nationalists, on the other hand, had no alternative but to work within the existing framework of power politics in international relations from a position of China's weakness. As will be argued in the following study of the decision-making process of the Government in Beijing and of the Chinese Delegation in Paris, the conflict between the Government and the students during the May Fourth period was probably not that between the former's willingness to 'sell out China' and the latter's resolution to 'protect China's sovereignty', as is commonly alleged. It was a more complicated picture. Both for the Government in Beijing and for the Chinese Delegation in Paris, the primary consideration in their decision of whether to sign or not to sign was also how to protect China's sovereignty and territorial integrity and how to enhance its position in the post-war international system. China's final decision not to sign the Versailles Treaty was a national decision and must be seen as the work of combined efforts of Chinese populist and official nationalisms.

THE ISSUE OF SIGNATURE

The issue of China's signature was quite an unexpected problem for the Chinese Government. Prior to and during the Peace Conference, both the President and the Government had entertained high hopes for China's improved position *vis-à-vis* other Powers in the post-war international system. They had never prepared themselves for any decision by the Powers such as that on the Shandong transfer. Accordingly, they did not formulate any policy to meet the situation. On May 4, the Cabinet told Lu Zhengxiang in Paris:

> Now people pay very much attention to the Shandong question. Recently, Shandong people of all walks of life and Shandong members of the Parliament in Beijing have been aroused and indignant. They have been going around campaigning and appealing. The original position of the Government was to ask the Germans to return [Jiaozhou] directly. The concessions which can be made now [on the part of China] is that Jiaozhou should be handed over to the five Great Powers and returned to China at a set date.[207]

On May 5, another cable was sent to Paris by the Cabinet:

> We have received your telegram about the Japanese demand for incorporating a provision in the Peace Treaty to the effect that Germany handed Qingdao[208] to Japan for the free disposal of the latter. Our nation should insist to the last minute on not recognizing [it]. If the provision is incorporated into the Treaty, our nation should certainly not sign. Do as instructed.[209]

The official reaction was to be found somewhere else. On May 6, at Shanghai, the Internal Peace Conference between the North and the South held a special session to discuss the Shandong issue. On the same day, a telegram was dispatched to the Chinese delegates in the name of the chief negotiators of both the North and the South, Zhu Qiyin and Tang Shaoyi. They claimed:

> Qingdao is part of Chinese territory on lease to Germany. It is not a dependent territory ... If the Peace Conference should recognize the demand of another country and refuse to uphold China's position [on the Shandong question], we 400 million Chinese people, to uphold right and justice, will never recognize it. We ask you not to sign the Peace Treaty in order to promote international justice and preserve our international standing.[210]

On May 12, the Beijing Government invited members of the Parliament to a tea party to discuss the matter of signature. On May 13, members of the Senate, urged by the Government, also held a meeting to look at China's case in Paris. There seemed to have been a consensus among members of the Parliament that China should not sign the Peace Treaty as it was then presented. In the words of the President of the Parliament, he would 'rather forfeit Qingdao by withholding than affixing the signature, so as to leave some room to manoeuvre in the future [to rescue Qingdao]'.[211] The result of the meetings of the Government with members of the Parliament was the dispatch of a circular telegram to provinces on May 13, asking the Dujuns[212] and principal civilian officials to submit their views on the issue of signature. The telegram read in part:

> We have sent numerous telegrams to our special envoys [in Paris], instructing them to insist on direct return of Qingdao [to China] ... People of our nation now attach special importance to the matter. Since we could not attain the original goal – i.e. there is no provision about the direct return [of Qingdao] to China, our nation cannot recognize [the Treaty]. Nevertheless, if we refuse to sign just because of this, it would have an unhealthy impact upon our relations with the Allies and upon our position in the League of Nations. It is therefore very difficult [for the Government] to decide whether to sign or not.[213]

The Government, meanwhile, instructed Chinese delegates 'to withhold the signature for the time being'.[214]

In the latter half of May 1919, Dujuns in various provinces, in response to the May 13 circular telegram of the Government, cabled Beijing to express their views on the matter of signature. What was significant in their replies was that there seemed to be also a consensus among Dujuns and provincial officials on the rejection of the Treaty.

To give only two examples. In the words of the Dujun of Hunan Province,

> Whatever changes we may encounter in our relations with the Great Powers, if we cannot achieve the goal of restoration [of Qingdao], we should never yield and sign [the Treaty] to give away [Qingdao] willingly. It is a matter of sovereignty related to our territory. [We] should argue strongly on just grounds and not make the slightest concession.[215]

The Dujun of Jiangxi Province said in his telegram:

> Qingdao is part of our territory. The matter is related to that of our sovereignty ... Success or failure [in matters of restoration of Qingdao] has direct bearing on the national survival. [We] should contend vigorously and make not even the slightest concession. If our protest is to no avail, [we] have to refuse to sign.[216]

It can be seen that, in the initial period of the May Fourth Movement, the nationalist sentiment was as strong in the official circle as among the students and that few warlords were found publicly supporting the proposition that China should sign the Treaty. The consensus in China's initial reaction to the Powers' decision on Shandong at Paris was national, not only reflected in the students' demonstrations but also found in official pronouncements of the Central as well as local governments. China should contend for a revision of the Shandong provisions in the Treaty. Failing that, it should withhold its signature.

However such a refusal would involve many complications. It was clear from the very start that the Chinese dissatisfaction with the Treaty was only directed at the three clauses (Articles 157–159) regarding Shandong, not at the Treaty *in toto*. In fact, the other provisions of the Treaty concerning China were favourable to the Chinese. If China refused to sign the Treaty, it would not be able to benefit from those favourable provisions, including abrogation of German consular jurisdiction in China and return to China of the astronomical equipment plundered by the German soldiers from China in 1900 and 1901. Moreover, should China fail to sign the Treaty, would it still be able to join the League of Nations as an original member?[217] The Government was also worried that the action of abstaining from the signing would displease the Powers and that China would be accused of destroying the united front of the Allies *vis-à-vis* Germany in the peace-making, thus being isolated. There was even a fear that the state of war between China and Germany would not be easily brought to an end and in negotiation with Germany on its own, China would be in an unfavourable position to bargain with Germany.[218]

All these complications were systematically elaborated in a telegram sent by Foreign Minister Lu at Paris to the Cabinet on May 14. Unlike the normal official telegram, the May 14 telegram was exceedingly long and was divided into two parts: a normal text and an appendix. In the latter part of the telegram, Lu stated clearly that he was 'making bold to cable home [my] humble opinion' in his private capacity.

In the main body of the text, Lu informed the Government of his formal protest to the Conference on May 6 and China's statement of its reservation as to the Shandong clauses on the same day, suggesting that China 'forebear and submit to signing the Peace Treaty with reservations to Shandong clauses'. He further stated that

Although our statement as to the reservations has been recorded in the procedures of the Conference [on May 6], whether it can actually be made at the signing it is still very hard for every one we have asked to say definitely. This is what makes us hesitate as to whether the Treaty should be signed.

He asked explicitly whether, 'in the event that the reservations cannot be made as we wish, has it been decided not to sign?'.

The so-called appendix of the telegram in which Lu submitted his 'humble opinion' was actually a detailed analysis of possible alternative approaches China could adopt in the present situation, and their advantages and disadvantages. In his view, after the formal protest to the Conference, China could express its discontent in the following three ways: (1) to follow the example of Italy and leave the Conference to return to China; (2) to refuse to sign; (3) to sign with reservations to the provisions which China could not recognize. He dismissed the advisability of the first alternative and further contended:

For the second alternative, although we are discontented with the provisions about Shandong, there are other clauses related to Sino-German relations [which we are satisfied with]. For instance, abrogation of German consular jurisdiction in China, cancelling of the German portion of the Boxer Indemnity, tariff freedom in regard to Germany and as well as reparations. Besides, as long as we do not sign the Peace Treaty [with Germany], [we] will always be in a state of war with it. It is still a big question whether in the future [China] can assure itself as many advantages in a direct negotiation with Germany. For the third alternative, i.e. to sign with reservations to clauses on Shandong, as the Peace Treaty deals mostly with the German questions, it would not be out of expectation that the Powers would not allow China to make reservations on the ground that the enemy states would follow China's example [in making reservations].

Lu further contended that in the decision of the 'Big Three' was included a Japanese statement that Japan would return Jiaozhou to China with full sovereignty and its troops would withdraw. This would substantially modify the Japanese position in China obtained through the Sino-Japanese treaties of 1915 and 1918. He asked:

If we made a statement in the Peace Treaty not to recognize [the decision of the 'Big Three'], can our two treaties with Japan [in 1915 and 1918] be regarded as null and void? Otherwise, is it to our advantage to discard the decision [of the 'Big Three] and to retain the treaties [with Japan]? Moreover, the three leaders have mediated and discussed the matter for a few days and showed their good intentions. We have to consider carefully whether it will embitter international feeling if we continue to refuse to recognize [the Shandong clauses].

It should be noted that to sign the Treaty without reservations was not even considered at Paris as an alternative approach, though, by the arguments above, Lu was urging a measure of caution in the government decision not to sign the Treaty. This was further illustrated in his deliberations in the same telegram. He suggested that, 'in order to show our discontent, we should of course refuse to sign. Yet the matter seems still open to question if only we weigh carefully the disadvantages [of not signing] against the advantages [of signing]'. Lu was worried that China would 'not be capable of recovering Jiaozhou on its own' and believed that 'the situation in the Far East still depends on the Great Powers checking each other'. If China would not sign the Treaty or even sign with reservations on the Shandong clauses, Lu thought, 'it is expected that three Powers [Britain, America and France] will look on indifferently [when China negotiates with Japan in the future] because we [China] have not appreciated their mediation [at the Paris Peace Conference]'.[219]

On receiving Lu's telegram, Acting Foreign Minister Chen Lu sent a reply to tell Lu that 'the disadvantages of not signing the Treaty elaborated in your telegram are exactly what the Government is worried about'.[220] The Government's dilemma with regard to signing of the Treaty was two-fold. On the one hand, the Government was standing between the people and the Powers. It had to face both the people who had been nationalistically excited in opposition to the signing, and the Powers who had made the Treaty. Most expressive of this dilemma were the words of the Government itself that, 'if the Government signs the Treaty, it will not live up to the wishes of the people. Yet if it refuses to sign, it may lead to more international disputes and the Government has no proper policy to deal with the consequent situation'.[221]

On the other hand, either to sign or to refuse to sign would do harm to China's international position. According to a report by the Foreign Ministry in May 1919, there would be two disadvantages in signing the Treaty: that Japan would expand in Shandong, and that the expansion of Japan in Shandong would become the root of future trouble in East Asia. But there would be five disadvantages in refusing to sign. First, Qingdao was already under Japanese control, the status quo of which could not be changed by refusing to sign the Treaty. Second, the problem of Qingdao, thereafter, would not be solved through the mediation of the Powers, but through direct negotiation between China and Japan. China, weak and helpless, would be in a disadvantageous position. Third, China would alienate itself from the Powers and would not be able to get international support even if Japan acted against international law. Fourth, China could not join the League of Nations. Fifth, China would fail to benefit from other favourable clauses of the Peace Treaty.[222]

The report suggested that 'Disadvantages are different in degrees ... The Government has weighed carefully the advantages and disadvantages and believes that it is less dangerous to sign'. It went on to state, however, that 'whether to sign or not is to be decided by the public'.[223] The arguments in the report did, nevertheless, constitute the basis of the so-called policy of 'choosing the lesser evil' to be adopted later by the Government.[224]

In the second half of May, a few developments at home and at Paris both encouraged and discouraged the Chinese Government towards making up its mind to sign the Treaty even without reservations. On May 16, the Chinese Minister to France, Hu Weide, explicitly expressed his support for signing in a telegram to the Government, using arguments similar to Lu's.[225] Before that the Government had already received a telegram sent on May 8 by the Chinese Minister to

Italy, Wang Guangxi, in support of signing.[226] On May 18, the Chinese chargé d'affaires in Tokyo informed his Government of the semi-official statement made publicly by the Japanese Foreign Minister, Uchida, that Japan would return Qingdao to China with full sovereignty.[227] This message was communicated by the Cabinet and the Foreign Ministry to the Chinese Delegation in Paris on May 21 with the instructions:

> Since Japan has formally made this statement, it is in the interest of our nation and of our friendly relations with other Powers that our nation should first strive to make reservations. Should that fail, we should sign the Treaty *in toto* so as to consolidate the position of our nation. Do as instructed.[228]

As the Chinese diplomatic documents reveal, this was probably the first time that the Chinese Government instructed the Chinese Delegation to sign the Treaty even without reservations. What should be noted is that the instruction had emphasized that efforts should first be made to obtain reservations and that, failing that, it was for the sake of strengthening China's international position that the Treaty should be signed.

In Beijing, advice from the foreign Legations also backed China's signing the Treaty. The Chinese delegates in Paris were told:

> The Legations here [in Beijing] have also stated their views on gains and losses with regard to our signature ... The British and French Ministers maintained that we should sign anyway. The American Minister holds that, if reservations cannot be made, we have to sign so that in the future League of Nations, America can do its best to help [China]. Otherwise, it will be very difficult [to do that].[229]

At Paris, the prospects for making reservations were gloomy. On May 19, Lu reported that he met Pichon that day at the Association of International Law and raised the question of reservation at the signing. The latter replied that 'it will never be allowed'.[230] On May 22, the Chinese delegates were also told by the British in Paris that 'The Peace Treaty is a treaty between the Allied and Associated Powers and the enemy states. There cannot be any reason not to sign or any reason to make reservations.'[231]

On May 24, the Cabinet sent out a circular telegram to inform the provinces that the Government now decided after careful consideration that we should first try to make reservations so as to leave the [Shandong] question open for future settlement. But if the reservations are too difficult to make, we have to sign. The Government have consulted with the Speakers of both the Congress and the Senate[232] and with former Premier Duan [Qirui]. They are of the same opinion.[233]

On the same day, Duan also sent out in his name a circular telegram to provincial Dujuns and civilian governors to entreat their support for the signing of the Treaty. The replies from the provinces this time seemed to be in favour of the signning.[234]

On May 27, the Government's explicit instructions were sent to Paris: 'First, try to make reservations. If that is not possible, [we] have to sign'.[235] Three days later, on May 30, again, the Government reiterated:

The Government attached great importance to the Peace Treaty of the European Conference. To avoid damaging our international standing and other rights, it is advisable not to refuse to sign the Treaty.[236]

It is of special importance to note that, first, all instructions stressed the need to try to make reservations initially. In fact, the Government could be regarded as being as nationalistic as the students were in its consideration of China's signning. Second, both those opposed to signing and those advocating signing showed great concern with China's position in the post-war world. In the arguments of both sides, China's international standing was invoked to justify their demand or decision. Not to sign was to resist the aggression of China by Japanese imperialism. To sign was 'for the sake of China's international standing, i.e., not to alienate the goodwill of the Western Powers and not to isolate itself from the international community, thus putting itself in a more vulnerable position'.[237]

The changing position of the Government, coupled with its repressive measures against the students' actions in late May and early June, further entrenched its confrontation with masses of the people and provoked strikes by merchants and urban workers.[238] The result was the resignation of the Premier and the collapse of the Cabinet on June 10. On June 11, President Xu, in his own resignation submission to the Parliament, observed that now that it was impossible to make reservations, he was faced with two crude choices: either to sign or not to sign. He repeated the Government position of 'choosing the lesser evil'. In his words,

> The public opinion of the whole nation is unanimous in resolutely refusing to sign. [I] intend to live up to the wishes of the people. Yet, after careful considerations of the advantages and the disadvantages, [I] cannot bear to be indifferent to possible crushing misfortune of the nation.[239]

Elsewhere, President Xu had indicated what he thought was China's dilemma, i.e., 'for the future of the nation, the Peace Treaty must be signed; yet for the present stability of the nation, the Peace Treaty should not be signed'.[240]

Xu's resignation was declined by the Parliament and he remained the President. The consequence of this government crisis, however, was a still more weakened caretaker cabinet[241] faced with ever increasing pressure from the public, and with the great urgency of dealing with the unsettled matter of China's signning of the Peace Treaty. In mid-June, the Parliament in Beijing held a special plenary session to discuss the government policy with regard to the issue of signature. It passed a resolution to send a circular telegram, in the name of all members of the Beijing Parliament, to make it clear to the whole nation that the Parliament's position on the matter of signature remained the same as it had declared in May 14.[242] That is: China should sign only with reservations to the Shandong provisions. On June 20, the Southern Military Government urged that the President should 'take into consideration the public opinion, preserve the sovereignty of the nation and never sign unconditionally'.[243]

The pressure upon the Government relating to the signature came also from the warlords. On June 15, General Wu Peifu, together with some 60 other generals and high-ranking army officers, sent a telegram to the President, repudiating the idea of signing away Qingdao. They said:

> [We are] surprised to hear the sad news that the Government would sign the Treaty ... We will never recognize [the signature] because whether we get Qingdao or not is a matter of national survival. Some people say that to refuse to sign would embitter the feelings of Britain, France and America. [We] have never heard that a nation should sacrifice its own rights and interests to curry the favour of other nations. We soldiers will never shirk from our duty of defending our country and will fight as vanguards for our Republic

... We entreat the Government to respect the public opinion, to have confidence in the morale of the army and to insist to the last minute on not signing [the Treaty].[244]

Under all these pressures, the Government wavered again. There was some confusion and contradiction in the government's instructions to Paris on China's signature. From what we can see in the archives, of a number of telegrams sent to Paris in the second half of June, only two clearly instructed the Chinese Delegation to sign. On June 16, President Xu asked the Acting Foreign Minister, Chen Lu, to send a private telegram to Lu in Paris, instructing him to 'sign [the Treaty] and do not consider overcautiously the internal and external situations'.[245] On June 19, the Cabinet reaffirmed to Lu that 'as to the Government's approval of the signature, it seems there should not be any further change'.[246] All other government telegrams insisted on making reservations first. In Beijing, the Acting Premier, in reply to General Wu Peifu's telegram, claimed, on June 20, that 'the Central Government has been insisting on the restoration of Qingdao and has cabled our envoys to protest and sign only with reservations'.[247]

In fact, the Government instructions to the Chinese Delegation were often also a sort of consultation. In early June, the Government had sent instructions to the effect that the delegates should consider carefully and exercise their own discretion on the issue.[248] This and the confusion in the government instructions in late June left the Chinese Delegation in Paris considerable room to manoeuvre.

As the date of signing the Treaty was approaching, the Government seemed to have decided to shift the responsibility to the Chinese Delegation at Paris, instead of making a decision itself. From June 24, the Cabinet repeatedly sent to Lu telegrams to the effect that the situation at home was extremely tense and the Government was under heavy pressure from the people, and that Lu should decide himself whether the Treaty should be signed or not.[249] In Beijing, the Acting Premier, Gong, told the mass media on June 24:

The Government has recently sent instructions to the [Chinese] delegates that as regards the matter of signature, they should size up the situation carefully on the spot and act at their own discretion.[250]

It seems, however, that the Government again changed its mind at the last minute, faced with mounting pressure from the nationalist movement. The final explicit government instruction sent to the Chinese Delegation on June 27 was that they should not sign the treaty without reservations on the Shandong provisions.[251] It was at about 5 pm on June 28, two hours after the signing ceremony began at Versailles, that the Chinese delegates received this instruction from the Chinese Government. By then, the Chinese Delegation had already assumed the initiative and 'made a collective decision not to go and sign the Treaty'.[252]

ABSENCE FROM THE HALL OF MIRRORS

While in May and most of June, the Government vacillated and hesitated in its final decision not to sign the Versailles Treaty, the Chinese Delegation in Paris were trying, by sustained efforts, to make reservations on the Shandong provisions in the Treaty. Failing that, they decided to stay away from the signing ceremony on June 28. Here 'official nationalism' was more manifestly at work.

China's case at the Peace Conference as regards Shandong was at once weak and strong. It was weak because China was a weak nation in a state bordering on internal political chaos and because it was confronted by one of the five principal Allied Powers which was bent on expansion in Asia as a reward for its contribution to winning the war. Legally, its arguments for the invalidity of Sino-Japanese agreements in 1915 and 1918 were open to attack. Even if, in consequence of China's declaration of war against Germany, the Sino-Japanese Treaty of 1915 could have been nullified, the declaration could not, in any case, have any effect upon the validity of the Agreement of September 24, 1918, subsequent to that declaration.[253] It was strong because its demands were based on accepted principles of political sovereignty and territorial integrity of a nation-state and were compatible with the new spirit promoted by the Allied leaders, especially President Wilson, and enthusiastically applauded by people all over the world. China was, therefore, able to appeal to the sense of justice of the supreme authority at Paris and to world public opinion, just as the Chinese Delegation admitted in its protest on May 4:

China, in coming to the Peace Conference, has relied on the Fourteen Points set forth by President Wilson ... and the principles laid down in his subsequent addresses, and formerly [*sic*] accepted by the Powers associated against Germany. She has relied on the spirit of honourable relationship between states which is to open a new era in the world and inaugurate the League of Nations. She has relied, above all, on the justice and equity of her case.[254]

Consequently, when the Powers retreated from their insistence on international justice and reconciled themselves with struggling for national interests, and especially when Wilson was ready to compromise his declared principles, China's case immediately became exceptionally vulnerable and the result could not but be 'a grievous disappointment' to the Chinese.[255]

On the evening of April 30, after the Big Three had disposed of the Shandong question, Baker of the American Delegation was sent unofficially by Wilson to 'explain it [the decision] in all its aspects' to the Chinese.[256] Baker handed to the Chinese Delegation an informal memorandum, imparting the gist of the decision by the Big Three. He stated that 'the President desired him to say that the President was very sorry that he had been unable to do more for China, but that he had been compelled to accede to Japan's demands "in order to save the League of Nations" '.[257]

Baker found the Chinese 'bitterly disappointed'.[258] One of the Chinese delegates, on hearing Wilson's message, replied:

First, that the League of Nations as yet has no existence; secondly, that if it is born its powers and authority will be problematical; thirdly, that in any event its real ruling force will be the same governments that made the decisions in Paris in the Shantung question and wrote the terms of the Treaty and Covenant; fourthly, it cannot be presumed either in law or logic that a League of Nations whose constitution is created in association with the Treaty is designed to reverse or to amend the terms of the Treaty; fifthly, that it is only the weak nations that are forced to depend on the League of Nations for justice, security and protection, while the Powers positively refuse to depend themselves on those guarantees, and state openly that they are inadequate.[259]

The Chinese resentment was also partly expressed in a protest sent to Clemenceau on May 4. The Chinese Delegation asserted that

If there was reason for the Council to stand firm on the question of Fiume, there would seem all the more reason to uphold China's claim relating to Shantung ... If the Council has granted the claims of Japan in full for the purpose of saving the League of Nations, as has been intimated, China of course would have less to complain of, believing as she does that it is a duty to make sacrifices for such a noble cause as the establishment of a League of Nations. The Chinese Delegation cannot, however, refrain from wishing that the Council had seen fit, as it would be far more consonant with the spirit of the League now on the eve of formation, to call upon strong Japan to forego her claims animated only by a desire for aggrandizement, instead of upon weak China to surrender what was hers by right.[260]

On May 3, the strongly-worded Chinese manifesto in French was published in Paris newspapers, stating, as Colonel Bonsal rendered it, that 'China has been stabbed to the heart in the house of its friends'. The Chinese delegates were 'furious' with Wilson, as Dr. Morrison, a technical adviser to the Chinese Delegation, informed the Americans, because the Chinese were united in regarding the decision as a 'base betrayal'.[261]

The Chinese were most dejected as there was no formal communication from the Council of Four to the Chinese Delegation about the nature and the extent of the Big Three's decision and the guarantees the Japanese promised to them. House wrote in his diary on May 1 that Wang went to him that day and that

He was distressed over the decision concerning Shantung. I made him admit that he did not know what had been decided, or how well China had been protected. I requested that he get a text, read it carefully, and then if he had any complaint, do let me know.[262]

It was, however, only after two weeks' strenuous efforts on the part of the Chinese that they were in the end acquainted with the full text of the Big Three's decision and Japan's verbal promise 'under a pledge of complete secrecy'. 'The full text, however, did not give us any less disappointment', Koo recalled.[263]

Immediately after they were informed of Wilson's message, the Chinese Delegation held a formal meeting on May 1[264] with the attendance of all its plenipotentiaries and also of the Chinese Ministers to France and Italy. It was decided to issue a protest to the Peace Conference on the Shandong settlement, which was duly presented to Clemenceau on May 4. It was proposed that the Chinese Delegation, by way of protest, might also (1) withdraw from the Conference, following the example of Italy; (2) refuse to sign the Treaty; or (3) sign the Treaty with reservations to the Shandong articles. The feasibility of the first two proposals seems to have been dismissed instantly. As for the third option, they believed that it would depend upon the Powers' attitude toward it and they had to 'consider carefully whether to do this will impair international friendship and sympathy [toward China] since the three leaders have showed their goodwill by serving as mediators [between China and Japan] and spent days [trying to resolve the Sino-Japanese dispute]'.[265] They decided to submit their opinions to the Beijing Government for instructions. Pending the instructions, they decided to adopt the third option in their action.

On May 6, Lu, the head of the Chinese Delegation, appeared at the plenary session of the Peace Conference and made a brief and formal protest against the Shandong clauses after a summary of the draft treaty was presented. He stated that China was deeply disappointed at the Shandong settlement, and in the event that no revision were to be effected, the Chinese Delegation regarded it as its duty to make there and then reservations as to the clauses with respect to Shandong.[266]

Revision of those clauses was out of the question by then. The draft treaty was to be presented to the German delegates the next day, May 7. Meanwhile, a storm of protest had broken out in China against the Shandong decision, which exerted heavy pressure on the Government at home as well as on the delegates at Paris.[267] It seemed that the only option open to the Chinese Delegation at Paris now was to try to secure reservations before affixing its signature to the Peace Treaty. The government's instructions in May and June, as we have seen, were generally in line with this.

In the second half of May, the Chinese delegates approached the French and the American Foreign Ministers and Macleay of the British Delegation separately for consultation on the question of China's reservations. Pichon told the Chinese that it was impossible to make reservations, whereas Lansing maintained that making reservations was permitted in international practice.[268] Macleay, when consulted, simply said that China could neither refuse to sign nor make reservations, because the Peace Treaty must be signed by the Allied and Associated States in a spirit of unity with the enemy state, Germany.[269] On May 26, during an informal meeting with Pichon, Lu told the French Foreign Minister that he had received the government's instruction that the Chinese Delegation should not sign the Treaty without making reservations on the Shandong articles and that the Chinese delegates were to submit a letter to this effect to the President of the Conference. Pichon warned the Chinese that, if China created a precedent by making reservations on Shandong, Italy might make reservations on Fiume. And if all other nations which were not fully satisfied with the Treaty followed the precedent and made their reservations, the Treaty would become a broken one.[270]

The Chinese did not seem to have been discouraged by the disheartening result of their consultations. On May 26, a formal letter was addressed by Lu to Clemenceau. Lu pointed out that, having examined the three articles regarding Shandong, the Chinese disappointment was made 'more poignant', for there was no provision in the Treaty to safeguard China's rights as a territorial sovereign over Shandong and the three articles were couched in such language as to convey unmistakably to the Chinese the painful impression that the transfer of German rights in Shandong to Japan was made at the expense of China, one of the loyal partners of the Allies. He stated that, faced with a popular demand from the Parliament, the Chambers of Commerce and the Educational Associations, and many other bodies, urging the Chinese Delegation not to sign the Peace Treaty, the Chinese Government had little choice as to the course open to them and had decided to sign the Treaty with the reservations he had made on May 6.[271]

The Chinese Delegation was not optimistic, however, about the prospect of their being allowed to make reservations.[272] On the morning of May 28, they held a secret meeting to discuss the disadvantages and advantages of signing the Treaty in the event that reservations were not allowed to be made by the Peace Conference. Wang argued forcefully against signing the Treaty if reservations could not be effected. He contended that, first, the three articles about Shandong amounting to conceding China's full sovereignty were worse than the Sino-Japanese Treaty of 1915; second, to refuse to sign could rally the public opinion of the whole country and help to bring about the reunification of the South and the North; and third, it would not be difficult for China to conclude a separate peace treaty with Germany.[273] He also observed that China in its previous diplomacy had invariably yielded to the Powers and lost various rights. It had to change its policy now. Koo echoed Wang's argument by saying that Japan was bent on expansion in China and that refusing to sign the Treaty could boost people's morale to oppose the Japanese aggression, whereas to sign would cause further internal dissensions. Sze suggested that China could refuse to sign, because the Treaty could not stand for long for the reason that many small states were not satisfied with it. The counter-arguments at the meeting warned that refusing to sign the Treaty would cost China some advantages it might gain from the Treaty, such as redemption of the German settlements and concessions and relinquishment of the German portion of the Boxer Indemnity. Moreover China might be shut out of the League of Nations by not signing the German Treaty. China, as a weak nation, could not afford that.[274]

The possibility of China's being excluded from the membership of the League of Nations in the event of its refusing to sign the Treaty was a serious concern for the Chinese Delegation. For the Chinese, the membership of the League of Nations had practical as well as symbolic value. The Chinese still hoped and believed that membership would make it possible for the new international organization to hear the Chinese grievances and have them redressed. Membership of the League of Nations would also signify the acceptance of China by the Family of Nations originated in Europe and the recognition of China as a member of the emerging post-war international system. Koo offered to look into the problem, and found 'a beam of light in the darkness': China could become a member of the League of Nations by signing the Austrian Treaty, which also had the Covenant of the League of Nations as its first part.[275] 'With this discovery', Koo recalled, 'I was more firmly convinced that if a reservation was out of the question, impossible to secure, China should refuse definitely to attach her signature to the Peace Treaty'.[276]

By the beginning of June, in China, the popular concern with China's signning of the Peace Treaty had developed into a turbulent nation-wide movement to force the Chinese Government not to sign the Treaty without reserving the Shandong provisions. The Premier and the Cabinet resigned on June 10. With a weakened caretaker cabinet and mounting pressure of an increasingly vehement nationalism in action, and with the approaching date for the signing ceremony, the situation became more delicate. As has been argued previously, in the second half of June, with the Government vacillating, the issue of signature was more in the hands of the Chinese Delegation.

On June 24, Koo talked with Dutasta, Secretary-General of the Peace Conference, on China's reservations.[277] On the afternoon of June 25, the issue was discussed briefly at the Council of Four, now with Baron Makino of the Japanese Delegation also present. Clemenceau refused to consider the Chinese demand because 'Nous ne l'avons accordé ni à la Roumanie ni à la Serbie'.[278] Lloyd George was worried that Italy would follow China's example. Baron Makino simply threatened that, if China's reservations were to be accepted, Japan would also reserve accordingly.[279] The demand of the Chinese Delegation to sign the Treaty with reservations was again frustrated by the 'wiliest politicians' of Britain and France and by the Japanese bluff.

The same evening, Koo went to see Wilson, petitioning the latter to support China on the reservation issue. Wilson made it clear to him that he would not agree to any formal reservations.[280] The only suggestion he offered was that China might send in a letter, declaring that it had the right, when deemed opportune, to reopen the question of Shandong in the future.[281] The Chinese Delegation seemed to have decided to adopt this suggestion. Koo saw Pichon on the morning of June 26 and told him that the Chinese had to make reservations on the Shandong issue, if not within the Treaty itself, at least in a document attached to the Treaty.[282] On the afternoon of June 27, Koo saw Pichon again, only to be informed that the Council of Four had decided to allow China to present their declaration concerning the reservations on the Shandong question *after*[283] signing the Peace Treaty.[284] Koo was furious and told Pichon that, in view of the Powers' uncompromising and unsympathetic attitude toward China's intention to sign with reservations, in the event that the Chinese Delegates were not able to append China's signature to the Peace Treaty, the Peace Conference, not the Chinese Government, would be blamed for that.[285]

The ceremony for signing the Peace Treaty had long before been set to be held on the next day, June 28. The moment for final decision had now come. Koo went to St. Claude Sanitarium in the suburbs of Paris to report the whole situation to Foreign Minister Lu, who had been laid up there for more than ten days. He told Lu that it was impossible then to make reservations and the Chinese political leaders, students organizations and Chinese community representatives in Paris were daily bombarding the headquarters of the Chinese Delegation with the request for a definite assurance that China would not sign the Treaty without reservations.[286] Lu and Koo decided then that they should make their last efforts on the morning of June 28, by sending in a separate declaration on the Shandong provisions, to be registered before the signing, but not to be attached to the Treaty itself. Failing that, China should refuse to sign the Peace Treaty.[287]

Koo saw Dutasta early the next morning and handed to him a draft declaration of reservations by the Chinese Delegation.[288] The meeting lasted only five minutes, as the latter refused adamantly to admit any declaration contemplated by the Chinese.[289] The final efforts made by the Chinese Delegation were doomed.[290] At 2.30 pm, just half an hour before the signing ceremony, the Chinese Delegation informed the Conference that 'they do not feel warranted to sign the Treaty at Versailles today'.[291] In the afternoon, the two seats reserved for the Chinese Plenipotentiaries in the Hall of Mirrors remained empty throughout the ceremony of signature. China became the only nation represented at the Paris Peace Conference which did not affix its signature to the Peace Treaty.

On the same day, the Chinese Delegation issued a public statement to the press in Paris, explaining the reasons for China's absence from the Hall of Mirrors. It stated that

> the Peace Conference having denied China justice in the settlement of the Shantung question and having today in effect prevented them from signing the treaty without sacrificing their sense of right, justice, and patriotic duty, the Chinese delegates submit their case to the impartial judgment of the world.[292]

Later the same day, after receiving the Government's final instruction to sign only if allowed to make reservations,[293] Lu reported to the Chinese President that

> It is to our surprise and indignation that the Peace Conference should have acted in such an autocratic way, without showing even an infinitesimal degree of consideration toward the honour and dignity of our country. In diplomatic negotiations, weak nations resisting at the beginning and giving way in the end has become almost an axiom. If we forebore and signed the treaty this time, then farewell forever to any possibility of exercising diplomacy in our country. Both dictated by our own conscience and guided by foreign public opinion, there is no reason why China should recklessly sign the treaty.[294]

China was made a disappointed nation by the Peace Conference. It had hoped that the Peace Conference would review its treaties with Japan during the war and would redress the wrongs done to China in the spirit of equality and justice. Yet the Conference honoured the war-time secret treaties, and China could only blame itself. China's disappointment was more acute because, unlike Germany, it was in the Allied camp; but it regarded itself as being treated like the vanquished, to be sacrificed, when necessary, to keep peace among the Powers. It was also because, unlike Italy and Japan, China's demands were not to expand, but only to restore its lost territory and lost rights, fully in line with the principles and the spirit of the new international order. Yet its demands were denied, simply for the reason that the confrontation it met was from a principal Allied Power and that, in practice, the professed principles had to be compromised with power politics.

It should be noted that, at that time, the Chinese people 'were being whirled in the vortex of old and new. The old organization was beginning to crumble, the new had not yet taken shape'.[295] They had rejected the old traditional order prevailing in China for thousands of years, and were in a process of state-building and naturally eager to find China's place in the new order they were to accept. Consequently, when its delegates were accorded a hearing, they took it as a recognition of China's rightful place in the Family of Nations and were accordingly elated; whereas when Shandong was finally handed to Japan without the Chinese delegates being consulted, they were dejected. The disappointment and disillusionment of the Chinese at the failure of Wilsonian idealism and at the prospect of China's place in the emerging international society were as bitter as their hopes had been high before and during the early period of the Conference.

China was made a disappointed nation at Versailles by the Peace Conference on which, paradoxically, China had placed such high hopes at the end of the war for restoring its lost sovereign rights and for regulating its relations with foreign powers on the basis of new principles. Its demands for the restoration of Shandong were reduced to sheer discontentment with the benevolent professions by the Western Powers of lofty principles such asnational self-determination and freedom, equality and independence of small and weak nations. Its fortune at the Peace Conference proved that, contrary to what it had hoped, power politics was still very much alive in post-war international relations and so was the concept of 'spheres of influence' in the Great Powers' policy toward China. China's place in the future international order was not determined by its acceptance of principles of international law or those of the new international order but by the Powers at the top of the hierarchy of the international society. China's aspirations to stand on equal footing with other nations and to play a positive role in the future international system were still to be fulfilled

But China's refusal to sign the Peace Treaty was a bold step towards its rejection of the unjustified, and in the eyes of the Chinese unjustifiable, international order to be imposed upon it in spite of its protest. It was a clear expression of its assertion against any further subjection of China in world politics. Moreover, with hindsight, it signified the beginning of China's taking initiatives to exert influence upon the development of the international system, especially that in East Asia.

China's presence at Paris marked the beginning of China's active participation in managing world affairs which, China realized, had become part of its national concern. China's participation in the Paris Peace Conference, and thus in the process of shaping a new international order, was itself significant. It was an indication that China was coming out of subordination and capitulations to be accepted by the West as a member, though not yet with full sovereignty, of the emerging international society. China's desire to become part of the world received recognition. It was the first time that China concerned itself as a member of the global international society with international affairs, some of which were only remotely or not at all related to China's national interests.[296] This was particularly indicative of China's perception of common interest with other members of the international society. China's enthusiastic acceptance of democratic ideals and of the Wilsonian principles as the basis for constructing the post-war peace was a reflection of common-value consciousness on the part of China. Surely, by its presence and active diplomacy at the Paris Peace Conference and later in the League of Nations, China now began to share with other members of the international society the working of common institutions.

China failed to recover Jiaozhou directly from Germany at the Peace Conference, yet China's diplomacy at Paris during this period can hardly be regarded as a failure. In fact, the overall picture should be seen as more of a success. Although China did not sign the Treaty of Versailles with Germany, groundwork was laid for the future Sino-German Peace Treaty by which China was to abolish the German extraterritorial rights in China, to recover the German concessions in China and to put Sino-German relations on the basis of equality. At the Peace Conference, by signing the Treaty of St. Germain with Austria, China recovered from Austria part of its lost sovereignty, such as tariff autonomy, and revoked the extraterritoriality once granted to the Austro-Hungarian Empire. In so doing, China actually initiated a break in the 'united front' of the privileged West in China. More significantly, the Chinese delegates had effectively used the Peace Conference as a forum to tell the world its sorrows and its aspirations and to call attention to China's problems. This helped to raise the so-called 'Far Eastern question' in international relations which 'had scarcely risen above the horizon' in 1914.[297] By participating in the Peace Conference and eventually by signing the St. Germain Treaty with Austria, China won a seat at the first world organization with globe-wide representation, the League of Nations.

Furthermore the rise of Chinese nationalism and China's rejection of the Versailles Treaty were also of great historic importance. First, we must remember that the action was unprecedented in the history of China's diplomatic relations with the West since 1840. In the past, China had refused to come to the negotiation table and was several times compelled or coerced by *force majeure* to conclude what were later termed 'unequal treaties'. Now China came to the international conference of its own accord, but refused to sign the Treaty only because of the unfair treatment it felt it had received at the Peace Conference. China's rejection of the Treaty was not of the Treaty *per se*, but was clearly an attempt to reject an international order which the Powers intended to establish in post-war East Asia. China's action promptly put the West on the defensive as to the legitimacy of their visions of the post-war East-Asian international system, in the light of their proclaimed principles and democratic ideals. China's response now, if any, to the West, was no longer on the terms set out by the West but more in the terms of the proclaimed principles of the European international society.

Second, the fact that China did not sign the Treaty left unsettled the Shandong question and consequently Sino-Japanese relations. Coupled with the uncertain fate of the third Anglo–Japanese Alliance and the American-Japanese rivalries in the area and in the Pacific, the unsettled situation in East Asia eventually entailed the convening of the Washington Conference in 1921–1922 to establish a regime of international order in East Asia.

Third, the story of how China refused to sign the Versailles Treaty was a clear indication of China's desire to be incorporated into the modern Family of Nations, but not in the Versailles fashion. To a certain extent, there was a mutual rejection: the Powers rejected the Chinese demands and China rejected the Powers' dictation. It was the beginning of a new phase in which China would play the role of a subject in international life, instead of being a mere object to be acted upon by power politics, as it had experienced in the past, especially since 1895.

Fourth, China's refusal resulted from an active diplomacy from a comparatively weak state. It was seen in China as the beginning of an end to the diplomacy of 'resistance at first and concession in the end' which the Chinese had regarded as one essential feature of the diplomacy of weak states, particularly China, in international relations.[298] It gradually gave the Chinese confidence that they could carry on independently with their own diplomacy. Chinese diplomacy of a nationalistic nature became the outward expression in the international arena of the heightening of modern Chinese nationalism at home.

3 Whither China in the East Asian International Order?

The three-year period between the Armistice in 1918 and the Washington Conference in 1921–1922 saw a 'blank', as it were, in the international order of East Asia. The old order was gone, a new order based on consent was yet to emerge. The pre-war balance of power and the *status quo* in East Asia had been totally destroyed by the defeat of enemy states, the defection of Russia, the expansion of Japan in China, and the ascendancy of the United States in world politics. There was also the growing national consciousness of the Chinese to be reckoned with. There seemed to be a recognition in world politics that East Asia was becoming a theatre in international politics in its own right. By the same token, East Asia was now left to work out its own salvation. The most interested Powers, Britain, the United States and Japan,[1] were each groping in their own ways for an order, a way to deal with the legacies of the war and the prospect of post-war development. China, on the other hand, was to assert its more independent standing in its external relations. The construction of an international system with the consent of all parties concerned was the central theme around which the development of international politics in post-war East Asia was to evolve.

Upon hearing the Big Three's decision on April 30, 1919 to hand over Shandong to Japan, E. T. Williams, adviser to the American Delegation on the Far Eastern affairs, promptly complained that it was 'an unsettlement'.[2] But he did not, probably could not, see what was unsettled in the broader perspective of post-war East Asian international relations. The 'Shandong unsettlement' at this predominantly European peace conference was in fact only of symbolic value, reflective of the unsettled issue of China's place in the international system. While the three Great Powers in East Asia, the United States, Great Britain and Japan, were trying to define how China could fit into their framework of a new international order, China took a number of diplomatic initiatives to assert its own role in international relations concerning China. The 'Shandong unsettlement' was virtually the beginning of a battle to search for a solution of the pending issue of a feasible international order in East Asia.

Both the Powers and China were responding to the changes in international politics. For the Powers, the pre-war balance of power in East Asia had gone. The defeated Germany and Austria-Hungary and the defected Russia were for the time being inactive in the China scene. France, too much occupied with internal and European issues, was almost impotent. Great Britain had managed to keep the British interests in China 'practically intact in spite of all risks [to which] they were exposed'.[3] Though exhausted in the war, it now intended to stage a comeback to the China market and to protect and expand its commercial interests. The predominance established by Japan in China during the war years had to be reconciled with the return of Western interests, and with the influence of the United States, which came out of the war as a world power with special interest in East Asia, particularly in China. The power relations there had to be redefined and regulated in accordance with the changed circumstances in world politics. For China, the war had exposed the Powers' inability to hold on to their own ground and had resulted in the crumbling of the 'united front' of the treaty powers *vis-à-vis* China seen in the pre-war years.[4] This offered China a chance to break the system of its 'unequal' treaty relations with the foreign Powers. On the other hand, the influence of Wilsonian idealism in China, as shown in the last chapter, could not be undone. It had made it legitimate and respectable in the context of national self-determination for China to make its intended efforts to win back its lost national sovereign rights and to demand total equality with other members in the Family of Nations. China's self-consciousness as a sovereign nation entitled to take an active and independent standing in its external relations constituted probably the most radical change in the milieu of international politics of East Asia after the war.

In the pre-war years, and even during the war, the power politics in East Asia was based on the assumption and the treatment of China as merely an object or a 'mere diplomatic appendage'[5] of the Great Powers' relations. Now that the Powers had to find a new basis on which to build a viable post-war international order in East Asia, they found themselves again confronted with the so-called China problem. What were the differences and concurrence of their respective visions of a new international system in East Asia? What would be, in their view, China's place in this system? And where and how would China itself stand? The search for an order in post-war East Asia was centred around the issue of China's place in the future international system. It began even before the convening of the Paris Peace Conference and continued well into 1920.

THE BRITISH PERSPECTIVE

At the end of the war there began a series of communications, frequent and frank, between the British Legation in Beijing and the Foreign Office in London on the post-war international problems related to China. From London, Macleay at the desk of the Far East Department of the Foreign Office sought advice from Jordan, the British Minister in China, on the British presentation of the issues concerned with East Asia at the Peace Conference. From Beijing, Jordan took the initiative to suggest some radical changes of British policy toward China as the basis for the new international order in East Asia.

On November 26, 1918, Macleay, in a private and personal telegram to Jordan in Beijing, informed him that he had been entrusted with the preparation of the British case in regard to East Asia at the Peace Conference. He further asked Jordan for assistance and advice on questions which appeared likely to come up for discussion at the Peace Conference. What was most telling of the British mind with regard to China's future relations with the European Powers was Macleay's suggestion that

> We propose to provide in the treaty of peace for the Far East that all extraterritorial rights and privileges previously enjoyed by Germany and Austria–Hungary in virtue of treaties, the Protocol of 1901 or otherwise *should be maintained* [my emphasis]. This will involve restoration of enemy concessions at Tientsin and Hankow as well as their rights in settlement of Shanghai.[6]

He went on to state that this was considered 'desirable' because 'we *assume* measures promised by Chinese Government ... have not been carried out effectively' and

> because [of] our fear that it would create a dangerous precedent to encourage Chinese Government to withhold or restrict extraterritorial and other rights previously enjoyed by all foreigners and thus weaken solidarity of foreign diplomatic and consular representations in defence of such rights.[7]

If Macleay was not speaking for the British Foreign Office in this case, his opinion expressed above at all events represented that of most Foreign Office officials looking at Far Eastern affairs from London. The reconstruction of order in East Asia simply meant a restoration of the old order and a return to old patterns and to old days. Jordan, an experienced diplomat on the scene, promptly disputed this view, however. He told Macleay that 'Revival of Treaties with enemy Powers would be strongly resented in China and would be a retrograde step' and Britain could not 'go back to pre-war conditions'. He was convinced that the 'time (?)has) come for a completely new outlook and for a revision of our policy in regard to China'.[8]

Jordan's 'very radical proposals'[9] for reshaping the British policy toward China and East Asia were first made in his dispatch to Balfour on October 23, 1918[10] and his telegram to Macleay on December 4. They were systematically finalized and presented in his lengthy letter to Balfour on December 23, 1918.[11] Summarized briefly, those proposals were

1. The unification, consolidation, and neutralization of all railways under an International Committee of Administration;
2. The abandonment of spheres of influence and surrendering of special privileges;
3. An appointment of an International Finance Committee to control expenditure so as to avoid corruption and bankruptcy;
4. Relinquishing and internationalization of leased territories and national concessions at the treaty ports;
5. Reform of customs tariff;
6. Reform of mining loans;
7. Agreement for the conditional abolition of extraterritorialities, including consular jurisdiction; and
8. Revision of treaties and protocols, including abandonment of Boxer Indemnity and Legation Guards.[12]

These were what Jordan called 'heroic measures' and fundamental principles which constituted 'a courageous policy of reconstruction, based upon a firm adherence to the principle of equal opportunity in a reunited China'. He had defined the new perspective which the end of the war brought into the situation in East Asia as 'the problem of Japan's position in China'. It was a problem because the imperial ambitions of Japan had caused a 'growing sense of insecurity' among the political and commercial interests of other nations in China and because the 'vigorous and unusual methods' favoured by Japan in pursuing its imperial ambitions had stirred 'the torpid polity of China from its traditional inertia'. China, Jordan further contended, 'is awakening from a long period of stagnation, realizing her latent powers and determined to find her place in the world' and was 'rousing herself from sleep and bidding fair to renew her mighty youth'.[13]

It is of interest to note that the drastic measures proposed by Jordan had considerable similarity to the Chinese demands raised in their memorandum entitled 'Questions for Readjustment' submitted to the Council of Four in April 1919. Jordan, 'who has devoted his whole life to the study of the problem of China',[14] had probably a rather unique perceptiveness of the basic issues for the reconstruction of the East Asian international order. He was clearly urging the cooperation of all Powers in their China policy to check Japanese expansion and to accommodate 'half awakened consciousness of this vast and virile country'.[15] In October, Jordan had argued that a change in Western policy in China was indispensable to give China an opportunity 'to work out their own salvation' and that

> International rivalry and competition as shown during the last twenty years in the acquisition of leased territories, the marking out of spheres of influence, the prolonged struggle for concessions, and in many other ways, have proved a very unsettling influence, and has much to do with the present state of China. Before, then, we set out to reform China, we must reform our own methods.[16]

Jordan envisaged an East Asian international system based on drastic changes in the Powers' China policies so that China would open up to the industries and commerce of all Powers in the true spirit of equal opportunity. Moreover this international system should be based on 'a strong free China, carrying her own burdens and responsibilities in the family of nations'. Great Britain, as the first country to open China to foreign commerce, Jordan urged, should continue to play a leading role in the rehabilitation of China for the construction of the post-war international system in East Asia. Only in this way could Great Britain 'look towards a broader and bright east horizon on which China will stand strong and self-reliant as a healthy and helpful partner in the comity of nations.'[17]

Such radical proposals for an overall change of Britain's China policy were quite unexpected by the Foreign Office in London. In particular, it shocked the Foreign Office and the Colonial Office alike that Jordan had proposed that the Powers give up all leased territories, which, in the case of Britain, would include Weihaiwei and the Hong Kong Extension. The Undersecretary of State at the Colonial Office observed that

> ... the suggested return of all leased territories to China would also affect the Territory known as the Hong Kong Extension. The Secretary of State [for Colonial Affairs] considers it essential that any agreement which may be come to as regards the return of leased territories to China should be so worded as not to include this territory.[18]

The British opposition to surrendering the Hong Kong Extension was clearly derived from their concern over the security and prosperity of Hong Kong.[19] Curzon, however, was also 'entirely opposed to the surrendering of Weihaiwei'[20] which, Jordan told the Foreign Office, had 'hardly any political importance' for Britain and was only a 'health resort for the British Navy'.[21] Curzon thought otherwise. The surrendering was only possible 'as part of a general settlement with China based on the abandonment by all interested Powers of their leased territories in North China'. The question of the Hong Kong Extension, he agreed with the Colonial Office, should not even be raised.[22]

Jordan firmly defended his position. He reminded the Foreign Office that all leased territories in China 'had their origin in imperialistic aggressions of Germany and Russia'. Efforts should be made by all interested Powers now to neutralize or internationalize all leased territories so as to 'bring America and Japan in line with the total abrogation of concessions' and 'render such terms as "Open Door" and "China's integrity" realities and not the meaningless expressions they too often are at present'. He had, he asserted,

> carefully considered the question of Hong Kong extension and fully realize that its retrocession would entail a considerable sacrifice for us. But without sacrifices on the part of all Powers who acquired or inherited leased territories of 1898, no solution of [the] China problem seems possible ... But if the United States and we are willing to attune our minds to the spirit of new principles which are to govern the world and to enforce application of these principles in China, it should not be impossible to devise a scheme which would guarantee economic freedom and military security of leased territories.[23]

The minute by Curzon on the above dispatch sent by Jordan was interesting and revealing. He wrote,

> I am not clear how far we have encouraged those altruistic speculations on the part of Sir John Jordan, but in my view they are misplaced.

> We cannot begin to dig up by the roots all previous cessions, perpetual leases, etc.

> To give back the Kowloon Extension[24] is in my view out of the question.[25]

Jordan's ideas and proposals might sound 'idealistic and impracticable'.[26] But his perceptiveness of and insight into problems of international relations in East Asia were undeniable. The Foreign Office in London, however, was simply not ready or prepared to overhaul its China policy. There was little evidence that their minds were attuned to the spirit of new principles to be applied to the postwar East Asia. In fact, it was the pre-war spirit of international competition and rivalry among the Powers that was dominant in their consideration of the East Asian affairs. Macleay suggested that

> we can only keep Sir John Jordan's views in mind when we discuss the question of China's future with the American and Japanese Delegates as affording very valuable suggestions for the solution of the problems to which the past policy of the Powers in China has given rise.

He maintained, however, that

> It would appear to be unwise for us to take the initiative in advocating a policy such as Sir John Jordan recommends until we know exactly what the United States Government have in mind and how far they are prepared to go. We must also wait to see in what spirit the Japanese Delegates will approach the question.[27]

This line of policy was repeated by Müller in London in April while Macleay was engaged in Paris during the Peace Conference. Minuting a memo about the Japanese willingness to discuss its China policy with the British Government, Müller remarked that it was still

> advisable to defer any discussion of the Chinese question with the Japanese Government until we know the result of the labours of the

Conference, and we are in a better position to judge of post-war conditions in the Far East.[28]

Later, Müller also tried to justify this postponement by referring to the Allies' preoccupation with other issues of more immediate concern. Commenting on one of Jordan's dispatches in June 1919, Müller noted that

> Sir John [Jordan] entertained rather exaggerated ideas of the amount of time and labour that would be devoted by that body [the Peace Conference] to the discussion of the Far Eastern questions not directly connected with the war, so now he leaves out of consideration the regrettable fact that the Governments of the Allies have their hands and minds more than fully occupied with questions nearer home and which seem to them – wrongly perhaps – to call for more immediate treatment than the relations between Japan and China.[29]

Now, half-way into 1919, Great Britain was still unable to develop a positive and clear policy towards China and the reconstruction of an international order in East Asia, although there had been heated debate among the Foreign Office officials and diplomats. Great Britain was still 'marking time' in East Asia, as it had during the war. Indeed it did not take any initiative at all at the Peace Conference as far as East Asian affairs were concerned. Britain honoured its war promise to Japan out of a sense of 'fair play' and gratitude, and served as a mediator on the Jiaozhou question between America and Japan when required. At the Peace Conference, Lloyd George's ignorance of China's problem and Balfour's sympathy to Japan were well known.[30] The decision to let Japan have Shandong, however, unexpectedly made the China problem 'a world one'.[31]

For the Foreign Office officials who still defined the British interests in China in terms of the rivalry of the Great Powers, Shandong was a problem only so far as Japan would use its position to prejudice the British trade. Müller made this clear. On May 1, 1919, having heard of the Big Three's decision on April 30, he noted

> We may be quite sure that so long as Japan controls the harbour and customs at Tsingtao, British trade will be subjected to the unfair treatment herein described, in spite of many assurances we may receive to the contrary.

If it is true, as reported in the papers today, that the Japanese have got their way in Paris in regard to Shantung, we are likely to experience in that Province the differential treatment that the Japanese have meted out to foreign trade in Manchuria. Our only hope now is that the conditions of the ultimate return of the German rights to China should be straightforward and above board and should not be rendered negative by all kinds of reservations.[32]

Macleay had foreseen the outcome of the Shandong controversy as early as the end of March. The Japanese, he observed,

> will retain such complete commercial control over the port of Tsingtao, over the existing and prospected railways and over iron and mining enterprises in the Province as to nullify the political value of the territory to the original owner.

> The only solution appears to be for us to endeavour in conjunction with the United States to prevent Japan from abusing the privileged position which she will obtain in the Province of Shantung by tying her down to the strict application of the principles of the Open Door and equal commercial opportunity.[33]

One cannot fail to read a sense of helplessness between these lines. Britain had to agree to transfer Shandong to Japan in spite of the fact that it was fully aware of the harm which would be done to the British interests in China in general and in Shandong in particular. Having handed over Shandong to Japan, Britain could only hope for the best and for cooperation with the United States to curb the Japanese ambition. But Macleay's minute did point out a general direction of British policy towards Japan in China: i.e., in order to protect the British interests in China, Britain would seek American cooperation in its East Asian policy and Japanese adherence to the principles of the Open Door and commercial equal opportunity.

Curzon executed this line of policy soon after the signing of the Versailles Treaty. In Alston's words, it was 'to convert Japan from a policy of which we do not approve to our own'.[34] On July 18, 1919, Curzon went out of his way to see the Japanese Ambassador, Viscount Chinda, in the Foreign Office for a conversation which, Curzon admitted, 'had already been more than once postponed'. Curzon virtually lectured the Japanese Ambassador on the whole question of Japan's policy in China, with special reference to the restoration of Shandong, which, Curzon claimed, 'I treated as of first-rate importance with regard to its effect not only on the relations between Japan and

China, but also on the relations of Japan and the Western Powers, including more especially ourselves, in the future'.[35]

Curzon began with a candid criticism of Japanese policy in China during the war. Japan had 'in the most systematic and unblushing manner' pursued a policy

> aimed at securing commercial and political supremacy in China, by many forms of pressure, particularly by a series of loans in return for valuable concessions ... The object of Japan for many years, and especially during the war, had been, if not to reduce China to complete dependence, at any rate to acquire a hold over her resources which would make Japan her practical master in the future.[36]

He went on to recall that twenty-five years before when he was Undersecretary in the Foreign Office, 'the policy of competitive partition had been followed with no great scruple by the European Powers ... while Japan was also extending herself on similar lines'. He warned Viscount Chinda, however, that

> The days had gone by ... when China could be cut up and divided into spheres of influence by foreign powers ... the future of China did not lie in this sort of subdivision. Neither did it lie in the assumption by Japan of the overlordship of the Far East ... the ideals and principles that were now moving mankind were incompatible with any such pretension.[37]

Curzon also challenged the validity of Sino-Japanese treaties and agreements concluded during the war.[38] He compared these agreements with the Treaty of London – 'an unfortunate agreement' – Britain and France concluded with Italy in 1915 and with the Sykes–Picot Agreement – 'an equally stupid and shortsighted arrangement with regard to Syria' – made between Britain and France. Since both these treaties had been swept out of existence by the force of events, he maintained, 'it was unwise of Japan to insist upon the technical rights secured by her agreements with China in respect of Shantung'.[39]

This is probably the most candid and straightforward criticism of Japan's China policy at the time by a top executive of the Foreign Office in front of the Japanese Ambassador.[40] Chinda was obviously astounded, while he was 'taking careful notes' of what Curzon said.[41] He was to come back four days later to see Curzon and ask whether the latter had expressed this opinion as an official statement of the views of H.M. Government. If that were so, did it mean that the British Government had changed their views? He asked this because the various agreements between Japan and China had been communicated at each stage to the Foreign Office and had, as far as he was aware, in no case been objected to by the latter.[42]

Curzon replied that, without any intention to disassociate himself 'from the line which had hitherto been taken by the Foreign Office', he had ventured

> not indeed to express official opinion on behalf of the British Government, but to offer advice to the Japanese Government as to the best method by which they could extricate themselves from a position which was doing no good to them and might end by doing great harm to much larger interests.[43]

In fact, during its alliance years, Great Britain had supported, sometimes reluctantly, Japan's China policy, not only because of the Anglo-Japanese Alliance, but more because of its recognition of Japan's legitimate expansion of its interests in China. Even after the war, the Foreign Office officials still recognized that 'Japanese expansion in China, commercial at all events, if not political, is an inevitable factor of future history with which we have to reckon, and though we must do what we can to check it, we must go slow and not risk another explosion in the Far East.'[44] Indeed Curzon himself would later tell the Cabinet that 'Japan herself was incapable of maintaining more than her present population, and it was natural that she should look to China.'[45] Britain also had its own reason to let Japan expand in the direction of China, as explained by Balfour:

> At different times he had talked a good deal to Earl Grey about the question, and the latter had always taken the view that His Majesty's Government must be very careful as to how far they tried to keep Japan out of China. It had to be remembered that the Japanese were not allowed to go to Australia or to New Zealand, or to California, or to the Philippines, or in fact to any place where there was a white population. It was, therefore, somewhat unreasonable to say that she was not to expand in a country where there was a yellow race.[46]

The British concern, as expressed by Curzon, was not over the fact that Japan was expanding in China, but over the way and the extent of the Japanese expansion, lest it should be done at the expense of the

British interests there. Curzon told Chinda that the whole policy of Japan was 'wrapped in a mist of doubt and suspicion which was creating very general alarm'. Chinda must realize that 'by judicious and conciliatory action now the position and aspirations of his country, so far from being imperilled, might in the future be made more secure'. On the other hand, 'Japan, if she practised too selfish or inconsiderate a policy, might find herself in a state of isolation in the Far East.'[47] By such an admonition in the capacity of an ally, Curzon urged Japan to engage itself in international cooperation in order to build up an order concurred upon and managed by the three most interested Powers, Britain, Japan and America, rather than in the rivalry of groups of interests or the ascendancy of an individual Power.

The Foreign Office were fully aware that any post-war arrangement in East Asia should be made in full cooperation with the United States.[48] The emergence of the United States as a world power after the war and its growing influence in Asia were new factors to be reckoned with. Great Britain, exhausted by the war and overstretched in its imperial interests, desired to have the United States on its side to restrain Japanese ambitions on the Asian continent so as to maintain a balance of power in China. The Foreign Office officials further saw the possibility of American cooperation in China not so much because there was envisaged a post-war *Pax Anglo-Americana* as because 'generally speaking the interests of Great Britain and the United States of America in China are similar whereas they are often in conflict with those of Japan'.[49]

The apparent irreconcilability between America and Japan was, in Curzon's words, that 'She [America] wants to rescue China from what she thinks the dangerous clutches of Japan, not merely for the sake of China, but with some due regard to her own trade and interests in the future.'[50] This could play into the hands of Great Britain. But it also constituted a dilemma. Britain had a commitment to the Anglo-Japanese Alliance. It continued after the war to recognize its need to have Japan as an ally because of its naval weakness in the Pacific and of its belief that any viable order in East Asia was also dependent on Japan's good will. It could not afford to go too far to antagonize Japan. It was hoped that Britain might even use the Alliance to hold back Japan, which, many believed, was still susceptible to international pressure.[51] It followed that it had to work jointly with these two seemingly irreconcilable Powers in East Asia. In a broader scene, Britain had to reconcile its long-term global imperial strategy with its short-term regional interests.

For Britain, which was now in a position of 'extreme difficulty and delicacy',[52] the manoeuvrability of the situation was indeed narrow. In 1920, sophisticated Foreign Office officials came out with a formula of British policy towards the United States and Japan in China. This formula was, in Wellesley's words, 'working in China with Japan as ally and America as friend'.[53] Furthermore Wellesley explicitly stated that 'the goal towards which we [the British] must strive' was 'alliance with Japan; intimate friendship and cooperation with the United States of America for the rehabilitation of China'.[54] But to implement this British formula of power relations in China, Great Britain was faced with one standing block and one uncertainty: the Anglo-Japanese Alliance, and the willingness of American cooperation.

The Anglo-Japanese Alliance, initiated in 1902 and last renewed in 1911, might have lived its day in 1920, yet it did not outlive its useful purpose for the contracting parties. When the Treaty was about to expire, in 1921, both Britain and Japan wanted it renewed. In American eyes, however, the renewal of the Alliance would be directed against the United States, as both Germany and Russia, the original notional enemies of the Alliance, were in eclipse in East Asia now. 'American opinion had developed a neurosis towards the Anglo-Japanese Alliance'.[55] For Britain, to have a friendly America, the Alliance must not be renewed, not at least in its present form. Parlett observed, in a minute on a Foreign Office Memo on March 23, 1920 on the renewal of the Alliance, that it was obvious that

> if it is a question of deciding between the U. S. and Japan our choice must lie with the former. In consequence whatever form any new undertaking might take it would be desirable to make the position clear to America & to take in advance every precaution to prevent suspicion or distrust on her part.[56]

The War Office expressed similar opinion on the Anglo-Japanese Alliance and its relations with the United States:

> Whatever difficulties might be encountered in the event of war with Japan are not to be compared with the dangers which would result were America actually hostile to us.

> Further, our situation in the Far East would be to a great extent independent of the attitude of Japan, could we rely on the support of the United States. It is therefore the importance of not antagonizing America which must be the dominating factor in considering the question of the renewal of the Japanese Alliance. Hence if some form

of understanding with Japan is to be continued, it must be done in such a way as not to embarrass in the smallest degree our relations with America.[57]

The new form, if any, of the Alliance, which Lord Hardinge believed 'require[d] much discussion',[58] was described by Bentinck earlier in another Foreign Office Memo in the following words:

If our friendship with the United States and our alliance with Japan should enable us to influence for good the relations between those two countries and to cooperate with both in the rehabilitation of China and the peaceful development of the Far East, we shall have attained the goal towards which we must strive. Some sort of Tripartite understanding in the Far East, to which France might also adhere, would indeed be an ideal situation.[59]

It hardly needs to be pointed out that this became the line of policy which Great Britain pursued towards the convening of the Washington Conference.

The British vision of the Great Powers' management of international relations in East Asia therefore depends heavily on the willingness of the United States to cooperate and to concur with Britain in their perception of Japan as a threat to peace. In 1920, and even in the first half of 1921, however, the Foreign Office seemed to have little confidence in the predictability of American foreign policy. The American Senate failed finally to ratify the Treaty of Versailles in March 1920 and, by so doing, seemed to be determined to play a lone hand in world politics. Curzon denounced the action of the American Senate as the American 'defection' from international politics following the war. He remarked, not without regret, that

this great country, which had shared in our sacrifices and helped to win our victory, became, by the foolish policy of her own President, nervous, useless and impotent at the critical period after the war was stopped.[60]

By the end of 1920, the Anglo-Japanese Alliance Committee in the Foreign Office[61] had completed an overall review of all arguments for and against the renewal of the Alliance. In a report submitted to Curzon, it speculated as follows:

In the regrettable event of America finding it impossible to enter into any sort of arrangement with us such as indicated above,[62] we would suggest as an alternative the conclusion of an agreement with Japan, brought up to date and in harmony with the spirit of the League of Nations, and so framed as not to exclude the eventual participation of the United States.[63]

With Wilson a lame-duck President and with the forthcoming Presidential election in the United States, Britain had to keep its options open. Meanwhile it had to bide its time and wait and watch for new initiatives from the new American Administration to implement its policy with regard to East Asia.

Britain was confronted with a complicated situation in East Asia, which was probably more than it was prepared to deal with. The British policy towards East Asia

> was not determined by mercantile considerations alone nor were they entirely absent; it was not wholly strategic though there was undoubtedly a strategic element; it was not political or ideological, though the British diplomats had to recognize the emergence of Chinese nationalism and the need for a sympathetic response to it.[64]

As a result, Britain envisioned an international system in East Asia on the basis of a balance of power through coordination and cooperation between the three Great Powers, the United States, Japan and Britain, to reconcile all those considerations. It continued to base its relations with China on its special rights and privileges acquired through the treaties, and insisted on these rights and privileges even though they encroached upon China's sovereignty. It still regarded China as an 'unwieldy and helpless country',[65] a potential market[66], and the legitimate direction of Japanese expansion. It showed some sympathy for China's demands but little understanding of the need to accommodate the emerging Chinese nationalism. The British response to the post-war East Asian international situation was, therefore, that to the power vacuum created by the war. Its policy towards China was not materially different from its policy before 1914. It differed only to the extent that it seemed more ready to advocate a policy of managing Chinese affairs and the Powers' relations with China by collective efforts, rather than individual rivalry, based on mutual understanding and reconciliation between the Powers. This policy was rendered necessary partly because Britain was exhausted and weakened by the war and over-stretched in its imperial interests. To the British, it was made more plausible because the war had left only three active Powers in East Asia, and Britain was in a position and in a mood to play its customary role of a 'balancer' or a 'mediator', this time in East Asia, for the construction of the international system it envisaged. The success of this cooperative policy in establishing the British vision of a new order in East Asia, however, was predicated upon the good will and readiness to cooperate of the other two Powers, in particular that of the United States.

THE AMERICAN PERSPECTIVE

At the turn of 1918–19, while Jordan was sending his petitions to London for a readjustment of Britain's China policy, Paul Reinsch, the American Minister in Beijing, was despatching, on his own initiative, numerous telegrams to Washington, entreating the State Department, and even directly President Wilson, to take advantage of the Peace Conference to find 'a thoroughgoing and permanent settlement of the Chinese question'.[67] 'There is no single problem in Europe,' Reinsch claimed, 'which equals in its importance to the future peace of the world, the need of a just settlement of Chinese affairs.'[68]

Reinsch defined what he called 'the Chinese question' or 'Chinese affairs' firstly in terms of the Great Powers' rivalries, political and economic, in China. In his words, it was

the localized preferences or spheres of influence which divide foreign action and policy and which threaten to develop rapidly into causes of the most serious friction ... Under the system of localized preferences, the influence and enterprise of foreign nations in China pull in different directions, spend half of their energy in blocking each other, fail to develop China constructively as a whole, act in a retarding, reactionary manner, and involve constant friction and danger of world conflict.[69]

He suggested the abolition of all local preferences and adoption of the principles of 'trusteeship and non-secrecy of agreements', which he elaborated in these terms:

The Powers engage themselves to give up mutually all claims to exclusive preferences in any part of China and to base their action here on the principle that China must be treated as a unit open to foreign commerce and enterprise under the provisions of general treaties. The Powers pledge themselves that they will insist that activities undertaken on behalf of the Chinese Government by their nationals shall be carried out in every detail in the spirit of trusteeship for China without an attempt to establish special national interests. The Powers will treat as invalid any agreements relating to China which are not made public upon their conclusion or which aim to establish localized preferences.[70]

Reinsch further remarked specifically that this system of trusteeship should include (1) commercializing all Chinese railways and putting them under the control of the Chinese Government with the assistance of an international commission of experts; (2) an international supervision of non-political character over China's national administration of finance, communications and police, etc.; (3) a liberal economic regime with equal opportunity open to all responsible competitors. Reinsch seemed to believe that, if the Powers could 'unite in a policy of self-denial and prohibition, undertaking to cancel and to forbid the creation of localized privileges in China',[71] they could find their interest identified with a unified China. He appealed to Wilson: 'Peace is conditioned on the abolition for the present and future of all localized privileges' and 'Slight sacrifices of special advantages already held by one or two European powers would be justified by the suppression of formidable danger to civilization.'[72]

Secondly, Reinsch defined the 'Chinese question' in terms of Japan's expansion in China during the war.[73] Like Jordan, while acknowledging the legitimate aspirations of Japan to expand, he strongly condemned the means and manipulations Japan employed to gain 'a position of predominance' in China at the expense of the interests of the other Powers and the rights of China. 'Divested of their political and military aims the economic activities of Japan [in China] would arouse no opposition.' Reinsch said, however, that

it must be remembered that every advantage is gained and maintained by political and military pressure and that it is exploited by the same means in a fashion taking no account of the rights of other foreign nations or of the Chinese themselves.[74]

Japan had used 'every device of corruption and coercion' to 'demoralize China', Reinsch told Wilson, and by the end of the war had further consolidated its special position in Manchuria and Eastern Mongolia and secured a foundation for its special position in Shandong and Fujian. It had also secured an extensive range of railway concessions, mining rights and other monopolistic rights through a series of loans. He urged that America, as well as European nations, now released from war pressure, 'must face the issue which has been created' because

> the methods applied by the Japanese military masters can lead only to evil and destruction ... they will not be stopped by any consideration of fairness and justice but only by the definite knowledge that such action will not be tolerated.[75]

Following this line of argument, Reinsch recommended a policy of non-recognition of the *status quo* at the time in China, created by Japanese manipulations during the war years. He contended that

> Only the refusal to accept the result of Japanese secret manipulation in China during the last four years, particularly the establishment of Japanese political influence and privileged position in Shantung, can avert the onus of either making China a dependency of a reckless and boundingly [boundlessly?] ambitious caste which would destroy the peace of the entire world or bringing on a military struggle inevitable from the establishment of the rival spheres of interests and privileges in China.[76]

Understandably, as America had fewer economic interests in China than Britain, Reinsch's apprehension of Japan dominating China did not mainly lie in the commercial rivalries between the two countries, as did Jordan's. It lay rather in another direction. As he explained later to Polk,

> ... the Far East question is not merely one of relations between China and Japan; in fact, whether China is to be left free to develop as a peaceful industrial state, or is to be made the material for supporting and strengthening the most reactionary militarist society now existing in the world: that is a question the solution of which will affect the future of our country fully as much as anything the Peace Conference can do.[77]

Finally, Reinsch defined the 'Chinese question' in terms of a chance for America to play a leading role in East Asian international politics. He was fully conscious of the growing influence of America as a new factor in world politics and confident that Wilson's words appealed to the Chinese from their President 'down throughout all the ranks of the people'. He claimed, therefore, that

Never before has an opportunity for leadership toward the welfare of humanity presented itself equal to that which invites America in China at the present time.

He noted at the same time that this was probably 'the last opportunity by which to avert threatening disaster by removing the root of conflict in China'. He warned, like Jordan, but with different reasoning, that, if the United States should not take any initiative to remedy the situation in China, as was expected by the Chinese, America,

> instead of looking across the Pacific towards a Chinese nation sympathetic with our ideals, would be confronted with a vast materialistic military organization under ruthless control.[78]

The policy which Reinsch was advocating was, like Jordan's, a liberal international cooperation of all Powers in China and a condemnation of Japan's intrigues in its imperial expansion on the Asian Continent. Both of them came to see this as the only way to save China, thus maintaining a peace in East Asia in the interest of all Powers. However, while Jordan emphasized the need to bring the United States and Japan in line with Britain to implement this policy, Reinsch envisioned a system of America championing the cause in China to carry this policy through.

In a sense, Reinsch's plea had a better fate than Jordan's. It had the full support of some State Department officials, especially Stanley Hornbeck of the Far Eastern Division and Professor E. T. Williams, an adviser to the American Delegation on Far Eastern Affairs.[79] Hornbeck, in forwarding Reinsch's dispatch to Wilson and the other American 'Commissioners to Negotiate Peace', stated that Reinsch's statements of fact 'are uniformly and absolutely accurate' and

> This message is worthy of the most careful consideration of the Peace Commissioners. The necessity for arriving at a just and practicable settlement of various outstanding Far Eastern questions is, in its bearing upon the problem of safeguarding the peace of the world, most urgent. The problems are vital.[80]

These messages seem to have had only little effect in diverting the American Delegation's attention to East Asia. There is little evidence from the archive sources that either Wilson or Lansing or other Peace Commissioners had seriously considered Reinsch's proposals, though, almost without exception, all of them had spoken on different occasions about the post-bellum world peace being endangered in

East Asia.[81] Again, timing was important. The Peace Conference was opening and the European problems were predominant. The American Delegation was engrossed in them. Indeed, as Polk told Reinsch in February, 'the Peace Conference has more important work than straightening up relations between China and Japan'.[82]

Timing was at best only a partial explanation. The essential questions were: did the United States, and more specifically, did Wilson, have a clear policy towards China? Could we identify an American version, if any, of a viable international order in East Asia? The answers to both questions were probably more negative than affirmative.

The Americans went to Paris with a series of general high-sounding principles and ideals as elaborated in Wilson's war-time speeches, in particular the Fourteen Points, but not a clearly oriented policy, to make peace. General Bliss, one of the American Commissioners, expressed his worries as early as December 1918: 'I am disquieted', he wrote,

> to see how hazy and vague our ideas are. We are up against the wiliest politicians in Europe. There will be nothing hazy or vague about their views.[83]

Wilson himself seemed from the very beginning obsessed with his idea of the League of Nations. Aboard *George Washington*, he told House and the others that 'the League is the centre of the American Programme, all else is secondary'.[84]

As for East Asia, Wilson's idea of a definite policy seemed even hazier. He once told Koo that he always felt 'sympathy' for China and had an 'interest' in the problems there. But when Koo expressed his hope that Wilson

> would see to it that the 14 principles would be made applicable to the Far East as well as to other parts of the world. He [Wilson] said that it was probably more difficult to apply them to the Far East, but that mere difficulty was no good reason for not applying them there.[85]

Wilson did not explain where the difficulty was. But it would not be difficult to see a clear ambivalence in his attitude toward East Asia. In the same conversation with Koo, he stated that 'peace was more likely to be endangered there [in East Asia] than in other parts of the world, in future'. He believed, however, that the League of Nations, once established, would provide international guarantees for the territorial integrity and political independence of all States ... This would prevent any particular nation from seeking selfish advantage.[86]

In the second half of April, 1919, when the Shandong issue was in contention and approaching a deadlock, he again appealed to the idea of the League of Nations. At the Council of Four, he told the Chinese that wrongs done to China would be redressed by the League of Nations. Indeed, as has been explained previously, it was his obsessive belief in these 'platonic guarantees of countries far from danger points'[87] that could partly account for his vacillations and final compromise in dealing with the Japanese. It also provided a convenient escape for his lack of a policy towards different specific areas of contending world politics. Some issues concerning East Asia were thus left to the League of Nations.

Wilson's policies, or lack of policies, for peace-making were inspired by 'the domination of morality and ideals', in Lansing's words. In considering the 'future basis of the foreign policies of the United States', half-way through the Peace Conference, Lansing wrote in a private memo that

> An idealistic conception of the universality of the wish and purpose of nations to be just in their relations prevailed in the United States and formed the cornerstone of the rudimentary place for a League of Nations. It was assumed that, excepting Germany and her allies, the nations were wholly devoted to justice, and the policies of the United States prior to, during and after the war have been and would be moulded on this assumption.[88]

The United States, Lansing contended, should realize that the world was 'back again to the old doctrine of force and the right of the strong to rule' and 'self-interest is dominant in international affairs'. The future foreign policies of the United States, therefore, 'should be formulated on the assumption that the League of Nations cannot properly function'.[89] The implicit argument of Lansing's criticism was that Wilsonian idealism based on this false assumption had cost the United States realistic foreign policies in the period of peace-making.

Indeed, except for a general framework for an idealistic world order embodied in so-called Wilsonism, it could hardly be said that the United Sates had any clear vision of what the international order in East Asia should be. The State Department officials, meanwhile, manifested an ambivalence in their attitude to China's standing in the post-war international system in East Asia. While they professed that they sympathized with China and would help it win back its lost rights, Polk, Hornbeck and Williams all categorically maintained in separate memos and dispatches before and during the Peace Conference that it was a 'foregone conclusion' that the Chinese demands for tariff autonomy and for friendly Powers to renounce their extraterritorial rights in China would not be granted.[90]

The greatest ambivalence in the American attitude could be seen, of course, in the Shandong transaction. The question, as posed in the Senate, was 'why should the United States have consented to a proposition which was in flagrant contradiction of the fundamental principles of political justice and right which, through President Wilson, had been so emphatically declared?'[91] A more pointed and relevant question would be: Why should Wilson have to give in? There must be more than his obsessive belief in the League of Nations as a panacea to redress the wrong and to guarantee the right. The rest of the answer lies elsewhere.

There had been, in fact, a continuity of ambivalence in American policy, if any, towards China, especially in the two Wilson Administrations. The Open Door doctrine had claimed as one of its principal purposes the guaranteeing of Chinese sovereignty and territorial integrity. However, at the beginning of the war, when China asked America to help maintain China's neutrality, Lansing told Reinsch that 'It would be quixotic in the extreme to allow the question of China's territorial integrity to entangle the United States in international difficulties.'[92] There were two other cases more illustrative of American ambivalence: the so-called Bryan Message of March 1915 and the Lansing-Ishii Agreement of 1917. The United States were believed, rightly or wrongly, actually to have recognized by virtue of the latter agreement Japan's special position in China, particularly in Manchuria, derived from its geographical propinquity.[93] Further ambivalence was to be found in the American response to the May Fourth Movement in China. There was little evidence to sustain the claim that 'The new Chinese nationalist movement which flared up in the summer of 1919 was supported by the United States.'[94] On the contrary, as W. Cohen argued, the State Department seemed to be bewildered and its reaction was slow. Wilson himself, the foremost champion of national self-determination, never showed anything beyond a sympathetic understanding of the May Fourth Movement and never considered the possibility of cooperation with Chinese nationalism in solving the China problem.[95]

Wilson's approach to the China problem was that of benevolent patronage. He was 'no deep student of the Far East', observed Li Tien-yi in his study of Wilson's China policy from 1913 to 1917. His knowledge of China

> was chiefly acquired through his contact with American missionaries and friends working in that country. With a sense of pride and superiority he thought that the United States as a leading Pacific Power should help to implant the basic principles of Christianity and democracy in Chinese soil. Out of profound sympathy for the weak, oppressed and underdeveloped peoples, he became benevolently inclined toward China as an independent nation.[96]

Wilson, to be sure, was not unique in this aspect. At the beginning of this century, many Americans came to see China as a vast country where the American ideal could be transplanted. They had developed a view of China as a great potential market not only for American goods but also for American culture and American democracy. It must be remembered that Wilson and his generation were heavily influenced by F. J. Turner's frontier thesis in American history. Turner's concept was that America's unique and true democracy was a product of an expanding frontier. By the same token, a moving frontier was the cause of American democratic success. He reasoned:

> Having colonized the Far West, having mastered its internal resources, the nation turned at the conclusion of the nineteenth century and the beginning of the twentieth century to deal with the Far East, to engage in the world politics of the Pacific Ocean.[97]

Combined with a belief that world civilization had progressed, following the setting sun, from Europe to America and now to Asia, Turner's frontier thesis instilled a spirit of international crusading into a generation of Americans.[98] Professing to have an anti-imperialist tradition, the Americans envisioned their mission in China as saving it from external aggression and oppression and internal decay. China in turn would provide a potential outlet for manufactured surplus American products and a field for the realization of American civilization, thus saving American democracy by keeping its momentum.

The American interest in China, in the final analysis, was more ideological than commercial, though more commercial than strategic.[99] As a result, up to the end of the second Wilson Administration, the United States had only a clear commitment to China, but not a clear policy towards China, whether it spoke from strength or from weakness. Whenever America had a stronger commitment than its general commitment to the American ideal in China, China would be abandoned.[100] The ambivalence of the American attitude towards China could probably be better seen in this light.

Interestingly, however, China was high on the agenda of United States domestic politics in the years 1919 and 1920, mostly because of the Shandong controversy in the Senate debate on the ratification of the Treaty of Versailles. The Shandong provisions in the Treaty became 'the Achilles Heel',[101] to be attacked by the opponents of the League of Nations in the American Senate. It stood as an irony that an East Asian issue was used by Wilson's opponents for political purposes to defeat the American ratification of the Versailles Treaty and to frustrate Wilson's programme for a new international order.

We may recall that Wilson's concern, when he was about to concede to the Japanese on the Shandong issue, was the public opinion of America, not that of China. What was at the back of Wilson's mind was the fact that the Democrats had become a minority in the Senate. What further worried Wilson was the campaign started earlier by Henry Cabot Lodge, the Republican Senator for Massachusetts, against total American involvement in and responsibility for European affairs in the form of the League and the Versailles Treaty. Already in May and June of 1919,

> One of the principle [*sic*] grounds upon which the opponents of the Treaty of Peace stand in arousing prejudice against the proposed League of Nations is the provision relating to the Province of Shantung, which is represented by the opponents of the Treaty as a gross violation by Japan of the rights of China in which the United States has participated by supporting Japan.[102]

After Wilson presented the Treaty to the Senate in July, 1919, the debate in the Senate on Shandong was more influenced by American party politics than by Wilson's China policy. Lansing noted in August that

> The purpose of the chief anglers, Johnson, Borah, Fall and Brandegee was to find something about which to criticize the President and not to elucidate the terms of the treaty.[103]

In October, he further observed that 'the treaty debate in the Senate continues with the usual political claptrap and oratorical fireworks'.[104]

In the Senate debate, the Republican Senators Lodge, Borah and Watson had made it clear that what they were concerned about most in the issue was not China but America itself. Lodge declared that '... I for one do not wish to see my country's name at the bottom of such an agreement as that ... which provides for the robbing of China'.[105] Borah followed a similar line. 'There is just one principle,' he said affirmatively, 'that guides me in this treaty transaction from beginning to end, and that is to protect the United States. I want to vote so as to put her in an honourable position.' In other words, he wanted to keep the American record 'clean'.[106] Watson was more straightforward. When asked by Senator Hitchcock what practical benefit China would have gained if the United States should eliminate the Shandong provision from the Treaty, he replied,

> My answer is very simple. Whatever the result might be to China, the result in which I am interested is to the United States, for we would not give our approval to such an act as that; we would not condone that and permit Japan to hold Shantung. Then it became our act, and whatever the future might hold for us that is our act. I say to the Senator that is why I object to it ...[107]

As regards this line of argument, the Democrat Senator MacCumber questioned: 'Is it an act of true friendship toward China or a mere political move to defeat the treaty?'[108] A statement by Democrat Senator King was more indicative of partisan politics in the Senate debate. Senator Watson, he claimed,

> is expending all his condemnation upon a Democratic administration for attempting to write a treaty that will in the future protect China against aggression while he apparently forgets the wrongs which a Republican administration condoned and approved a number of years ago.[109]

The net result was that, although the Shandong issue was heavily debated, the debate did not lead to the formulation of any American policy towards the situation in East Asia consequent to the Versailles Treaty. The Republicans, however, had virtually, by so debating, made an implicit commitment, i.e., should the Shandong issue be raised again before a future Republican Administration, the American Government would help China to regain its sovereignty.

In March 1920, the American Senate finally rejected the Treaty of Versailles and in April Wilson vetoed a separate peace with Germany. By then, he was bedridden, but still insisted on the idea of the League of Nations.[110] Henry White remarked in April 1920 that, for the United States, international affairs were

> still so chaotic and in so far as we are concerned, involved in domestic questions, chiefly political. It is unfortunate that this should be our 'Presidential Year' when Party passions run high.[111]

With the Presidential campaign already under way, it was almost impossible for either Party to pay more attention to the conditions of East Asia. The second Wilson Administration, in its peace-making years, drifted in this fashion to its end without either a clearly-defined vision of the post-war international system in East Asia or a definable policy towards China.

The uncertainty of the Presidential campaign certainly accentuated the uncertainty about future American policy towards East Asia.[112] The Harding Administration inherited the general American commitment to China and the specific commitment to Shandong made implicitly during the Senate debate on the League of Nations and the Treaty of Versailles. The new Administration had also inherited all unsettled issues in world politics the United States had to face. Two of them required immediate consideration: the possible continuance of the Anglo-Japanese Alliance, which 'was inevitably regarded as prejudicial to the interests of the United States' as both of the Alliance's *objet d'être* – Russia and Germany – no longer constituted any threat,[113] and the naval armaments rivalries between the United States, Great Britain and Japan which added to the state of tension in East Asia and the Pacific. For the Americans, 'Back to normalcy', in the realm of international politics, may be interpreted as a reaction to Wilsonian idealism in American foreign policy. It meant a return to the traditional American isolationism, a refusal to be entangled in the Old World in any form of alliances. As to East Asia, however, 'normalcy' meant the 'Open Door' and commercial equal opportunity guaranteed by a balance of power in China. This called for a readjustment of the Powers' relations in East Asia in the spirit of realism and for an involvement of America in East Asian international politics. The Harding Administration, with Charles Evans Hughes as its Secretary of State, had to take up the formidable task of reformulating America's foreign policies, especially its policy towards East Asia and the Pacific.

As noted earlier, the Harding Administration practically inherited every legacy of the Wilson Administration in regard to American policy towards East Asia, excepting Wilson's consent to the Shandong settlement but including the absence of a definable policy towards

China. The state of affairs was not materially changed until the beginning of the Washington Conference at the end of 1921. Most revealing of this was an 'Especially Confidential' memorandum originally prepared for the Chief of Staff in October 1921 but immediately transferred to the American Delegates to the Washington Conference. The memorandum was entitled *A Pacific Policy for the United States*. While urging 'the need for a Pacific Policy' because of the coming Washington Conference, the Memorandum affirmed that

> the interests of the United States lie in republicanizing the world and it is probably true that the United States has, in effect, adopted the policy of favouring the establishment and maintenance of governments under the republican form.

Commercially, 'As the development of the United States progresses the need for markets in the Far East will increase' and 'The market and raw materials of Central and South China indicate one important economic objective of American policy.' In the long term,

> With a population of 350,000,000 people, coal reserves estimated to be sufficient to keep the world going at its present rate for a thousand years, and iron reserves estimated at a half billion tons, it needs no argument to prove that China offers a potential market of importance to future generations of Americans.

It followed that it was 'the future trade of China that all the great nations have in mind when they treat of the Chinese problem'. Consequently,

> economic advantages are sought by the Powers in the Far East, particularly in China. Political advantages are also sought usually with a view to aiding the economic policy.

In particular, 'the Japanese Asiatic policy is in direct conflict with the future interests of the United States'. That was because

> Japan desires to provide for her security and the industrial future of the nation by gaining political control of China and Eastern Siberia. In other words, Japan wishes to control politically the raw material and markets of China so her nationals may be given a preferential treatment.

The Memorandum concluded:

> But give Japan control of the iron of China, the power to exploit the
> industry and intelligence of the Chinese as well as the resources of
> Eastern Siberia, and there will be erected in the Far East a political
> and economic unit so strong that no power can say it nay. It would,
> in the words of another, '*Make the world safe for autocracy for a
> thousand years*'.[114]

It is not difficult to see that in America under the new
Administration there continued the same sentiment for China, the
same image of China, and a similar definition of the China question in
terms of rivalry between Japan and America.[115] The American interests
in China, political and commercial, remained the same. As we will see
later, the clashes of American interests with those of Japan in China
were to some extent the outcome of the conflict between the American
ideal and the Japanese mission in the Middle Kingdom.

In 'the fateful Spring of 1921',[116] the new Secretary of State, Charles
Evans Hughes, was seeking a common ground upon which to build the
new power relations in China and was groping for a realistic solution of
America's East Asian and the Pacific problems. It is hardly necessary
to say that a package of deals was made at the Washington Conference
which initiated the so-called Washington System, a new pattern of
power relations in East Asia and the Pacific.

THE JAPANESE PERSPECTIVE

While the British and the Americans mostly defined the post-war East
Asian problems in terms of Japan's entrenched position in China, some
Japanese leaders had predicted that the post-bellum problem for Japan
would be a revival of pre-war imperialistic rivalries between the Powers
in East Asia. Not long before the end of the war, Yamagata Aritomo,
the most powerful surviving *genrō*, warned that the Allied victory
would bring Great Britain back to East Asia. Britain was expected to
expand its interests with its full power, and Japan should realize that

> whichever side wins [the war], post-war Asia will be exposed either to
> the aggression of Germany and the United States, coming from east
> and west, or to that of Great Britain and the United States, from
> south and north; and Japan will have to face at least one of the two
> combinations.[117]

Prime Minister Hara held a similar view. He believed that, if Japan wanted to develop its national strength after the restoration of the peace, it would be engaged in fierce competition with other Powers, especially in the economic field. This, he claimed, the Japanese leaders had realized during the war.[118]

It is probably because of such a prospect that the Japanese leaders greeted the Armistice 'without enthusiasm'[119] and were immediately preoccupied with matters concerning Japan's share of the spoils and the terms Japan was to seek at the forthcoming peace conference.[120] Little attention was paid to the other issues, not the least to the reconstruction of an order in East Asia where the pre-war power equilibrium had been destroyed beyond recognition. There was only a belated discussion in the Gaikō Chōsakai (the Advisory Council on Foreign Relations)[121] about Wilson's Fourteen Points, not on their merits as the basis of the peace, but with a view to making reservations to them.[122] There seemed to be, among the members of the Gaikō Chōsakai, widely held confusions and suspicions about the intentions of Wilson's Fourteen Points. Naturally the decision taken at the meeting was to make extensive reservations to all the points concerning the future of Japan, such as the abolition of secret diplomacy, the freedom of the seas, the abolition of economic barriers, the disposal of German colonies, the limitation of armaments, and the League of Nations.[123]

Hosoya has contended with this piece of evidence that the Japanese leaders had 'shown no appreciation' of Wilson's idea of a new international order embodied in his Fourteen Points.[124] It is probably just to the contrary. It is because the Japanese leaders fully understood what Wilson advocated that they refused to adopt it as their own policy guideline. Moreover it was precisely because the Japanese leaders had perceived that this 'Anglo-American order', if initiated, would be irreparably detrimental to Japanese interests in East Asia that they first delayed any response, and then tried to make broad reservations, to Wilson's scheme.

The more extreme reaction to the Wilsonian new order was expressed vocally by younger members of the Japanese political elite. Of these, Prince Konoe Fumimarō, who was to become Japan's Prime Minister in the 1930s, with the intention of 'reordering the international system',[125] was most notable. Before going with Marquis Saionji to the Paris Peace Conference as a member of the Japanese Delegation, he had published in a fortnightly – *Nihon oyobi Nihonjin* (Japan and the Japanese) – an article entitled *Ei-Bei hon'i no hewa shugi o haisu* (Down with the Anglo-American Peace Principles). Konoe was emphatic that Japan did not want what he termed an 'Anglo-American peace' which, he claimed, was based on Anglo-American interests alone and had nothing to do with either justice or humanity. Peace and humanitarianism, he wrote, did not necessarily harmonize with each other. The British and American statesmen only desired to maintain conditions convenient to themselves. The proposed League of Nations by which some Japanese had been enchanted was in fact an instrument in the hands of the two Powers – Great Britain and the United States – with which to carry out their economic imperialism. He envisioned a confrontation between Great Britain and the United States, the 'Powers in being', desirous of maintaining the existing conditions, and Japan, the 'Power to come', bent on destroying the *status quo*. He believed that Japan should endeavour to assert its legitimate right to existence and prepare to fight to the last.[126] This is particularly worth noting because Konoe was here not only speaking his mind but also expressing the public sentiment of some Japanese people towards the coming peace at the end of the war.[127]

These rejections and reservations notwithstanding, the Japanese leaders did not seem to have their own vision of what a post-war East Asian international system should be. Underlining the manifested Japanese rejection of and reservation to this *Pax Anglo-Americana* was Japan's primary concern over its paramount position in China, secured while the interested Western Powers were preoccupied with the distress of the war. Implicitly, the Japanese leaders harboured a desire that the Powers should let Japan get away with its broad expansion and incursions in China during the war, and that order in East Asia, if any, should now be based on Japan's hegemonic position in China. During the war, Japan became less restrained and was more successful in seeking its hegemony politically, financially and economically in China and had attempted to prevent the interference by any 'third country' in its China policy.[128] At the same time, by signing secret treaties with European Powers and the Lansing–Ishii Agreement with the United States, Japan had meticulously secured recognition or acquiescence by the Powers to its special relations with China. At the end of the war, its war-time prosperity and its expanded military strength gave Japan an illusion of power. It was with a mixed feeling of fear of post-war resurgence of Western domination of Asia and confidence in Japan's illusive power that Japan sought at the Paris Peace Conference to protect and consolidate its newly acquired territorial rights and economic interests in East Asia and to pit itself against any attempt by the Western Powers to clip Japan's entrenched position in China in the name of a new order. That Japan had a stronger commitment to the maintenance of its predominance in East Asia than to any other type of international order could best be seen in its contention on the Shandong issue and in former Prime Minister Okuma's remark that

> if in all the important decisions reached at the Peace Conference the Powers were only acting in their selfish interests the Japanese delegates need show no hesitation in withdrawing from the League.[129]

It is ironic that Japan, as one of the five 'Big Fellows' running the show, should come out of the Paris Peace Conference as a 'dissatisfied' nation. The Peace Conference seemed to have more than proved the Japanese hunch, much to the frustration of the Japanese, that the Western Powers, especially Great Britain and the United States, were determined to stage a comeback in East Asia. Not only the United States 'were not disposed to acquiesce quietly in Japan's aggression',[130] but Great Britain, the ally of Japan, as observed by Nish, had shown a fixed determination to reassert its interests in East Asia and would not 'wish to continue after the war the pusillanimous policy towards Japan which she had followed inevitably during the war years'.[131] The Japanese leaders, according to the British Ambassador to Tokyo, had appreciated by then, not without a feeling of apprehension, the fact that 'the attention of the West was focused again on the Far East' and that

> the policies of Great Britain and the United States with regard to affairs in this part of the world were rapidly converging, and that in future Japan must be prepared either to abandon her own exclusive ambitions or, failing this, to confront the united strength and prestige of the two most powerful nations in the world.[132]

Sir Conynghame Greene had probably put the two alternatives for Japan too crudely. Japan was not to abandon its ambition, nor could it confront in isolation the 'combination' of two Anglo-Saxon Powers. The Hara Cabinet would try to 'get the best of both worlds',[133] i.e., to fulfil carefully its ambition in East Asia while securing the understanding and even cooperation of the Powers. For Japan, the 'lessons' at the Paris Peace Conference would not change its mind, but they did dictate a necessity to change its methods. Japan had to adapt itself to the realities of the changing configuration of international politics in East Asia.

Before departing for Paris as one of the Japanese Plenipotentiaries, Baron Makino had made his celebrated speeches at the Gaikō Chōsakai, renouncing the 'old diplomacy' in favour of the 'new diplomacy'. He criticized Japan's 'high-handed, selfish and conspiratorial' means and measures. Japan should do away with 'private diplomacy', and 'military diplomacy', especially in its China policy. His was then rather a lonely voice.[134] Now in mid-June 1919, he was joined by Matsui, the Japanese Ambassador to France, who sent a lengthy telegram on behalf of the Japanese Delegation in Paris, urging upon the Government a 'grave and profound reconsideration' of its foreign policy. He emphasized that

> The Far East today is completely different from what it was yesterday ... To indiscreetly regard ourselves as the overlord in the Far East and to strive for excessive monopoly of economic and territorial rights in China are not the right way to comply with the changing international situation.[135]

Some studies have identified a period of transition in Japanese foreign policy between the Paris Peace Conference and the Washington Conference, when the so-called 'old diplomacy' was gradually replaced by the 'new diplomacy'.[136] There was a certain departure from Japan's war-time practices of Army-sponsored Asianism – the unrestrained expansion on the Asian Continent – towards cooperation with the European Powers and the United States as advocated by Gaimushō, the Foreign Ministry.[137] There was more emphasis on conciliation, not confrontation, between Japan and the Powers. There could be seen some restraining of Japan's forward policy in China. Japan seemed to be coming gradually into line with Great Britain and the United States in its international policy.

However these were changes of Japan's tactics, not of the purposes of its overall foreign policy. They were initiated partly because, after the war the influence of Gaimushō in foreign policy-making had been increasing as the Hara Government was committed to a unified diplomacy under him, particularly in its China policy.[138] And Gaimushō veered more towards a policy of harmonization with the Western Powers. These changes were effected, however, to consolidate Japan's established position in China rather than to weaken it. The Hara Government was pursuing an international policy which would serve the purpose of furthering its China policy, a China policy which, it was hoped, would not stand in the way of its international policy. General Ugaki of the Japanese General Staff put this point bluntly. In

his words, 'the time for Japan to take new initiatives has passed ...
Now is the time for us to consolidate what we have and protect the
position of the Japanese Empire'.[139]

The Hara Cabinet and the Japanese military in 1919 had a
commitment to Japan's continental policy as strong as that of their
predecessors. The difference was that they had to operate in a 'radically
different international environment surrounding Japan'.[140] The
Japanese leaders seemed to have realized that Japan had to
accommodate itself to the changing pattern of power relations in
East Asia and to be adjusted to the new international power
configuration. If there was anything new in Japan's foreign policy
after the Peace Conference, it was that Japan was moving from a
strategy of confrontation-rivalry to that of cooperation-rivalry. Japan
was to fulfil its 'old' ambition with its 'new' diplomacy.

Among the Japanese leaders, there was a slow realization of the fact
that the post-war international system was to be dominated by the
United States and Great Britain. Early in August 1919, Itō[141] was
speaking in Gaikō Chōsakai of the 'Anglo-American-dominated
international order' and 'an era controlled by American omnipo-
tence'.[142] With his own wisdom, Prime Minister Hara remarked earlier
in May in his diary that

> ... the world is now controlled by two powers, Britain and the
> United States. However, as far as the Far East is concerned they
> cannot exclude Japan ... As I have always maintained, Japan's
> security rests upon the cooperation of these three nations: Japan,
> Britain and the United States. We must take advantage of the
> present situation and adopt the proper measures to achieve our
> goal.[143]

Hara thus identified two levels of order: a global order dominated by
Anglo-Saxon Powers and a regional international order collectively
managed by the three most interested Powers. Japan could accept the
dominance of the world by the Anglo-American Powers, yet it would
insist on being accepted as the leading Power in East Asia and as one of
the triumvirs of the future East Asian international system. This
version of the international order would not compromise Japan's
paramount position in East Asia but could possibly reconcile Japan's
world-wide and special interests with those of other Powers. This later
became the general framework within which Japan was to pursue its
foreign policy.

Hara had advocated a policy of cooperation with the United States and Great Britain ever since the war.[144] Now the changing international power configuration and domestic political and economic exigencies reinforced the necessity for Japan to cultivate the goodwill of the other Allied Powers, particularly the United States.[145] As Prime Minister, Hara reaffirmed that reconciliation with America was 'the cardinal principle and basic framework of the foreign policy of the Imperial Government',[146] while the alliance with Great Britain had long been 'the main feature of Japan's foreign policy'.[147]

What about Hara's China policy? It is probably more of a myth that Hara had a liberal China policy. There were immediate and ostensible modifications of the Terauchi Government's China policy when the Hara Cabinet started to function in the beginning of October 1918. For example, it decided to adopt an attitude of impartiality in China's civil strife between the North and the South, to cooperate with other Powers for an embargo on ammunition imports into China and for North–South reconciliation, and to stop political loans to China.[148] This must be seen, however, in the context of Hara's overall policy of cooperation with the West and against the fact that the war had ended. Even if the Hara Government had had the will, it would not have had any 'divine opportunity' to continue its predecessor's China policy. It was time for consolidation, not for aggression. Hara himself believed and privately observed that

> It is all superficial diplomatic rhetoric to say that we should make China a unified, civilized and prosperous country ... So far as Japan's interests are concerned, even if China could not be civilized and made economically prosperous and militarily strong, it is of little consequence to us.[149]

Hara was less critical of Japan's war-time policy than insistent on Japan's treaty rights in China. In 1920, he still maintained that the Shandong question 'which all the world is now agitated about' should be solved on the basis of the Versailles Treaty and treaties between Japan and China concluded during the war.[150] He was rhetorical about the Japanese–Chinese friendship yet emphatic that Japan, or at least his Government, had done nothing wrong to China and that the nationalist agitations and anti-Japanese boycott in China were brought about, not by Japan's China policy, but because of Chinese misapprehension of that policy. He believed, therefore, that the relations between Japan and China could be improved only if this Chinese misunderstanding could be properly dispelled.[151] His Cabinet, on the other hand, was still contemplating an armed intervention in China, to put to an end to China's internal dissensions.[152]

A more telling evidence is the Hara Cabinet's insistence on Japan's special position in Manchuria and Mongolia. Early in the century, in the aftermath of the Russo-Japanese war, Japan had identified its 'line of interest' there, the defence of which was believed to be vital to Japan's strategic security and economic prosperity.[153] Before World War I, it had established an exclusive sphere of influence there through a series of alliances and ententes with other Powers. Mitani has contended that, although Hara himself was willing to modify Japan's China policy, he 'could not override the restrictions of history' in regard to Japan's interests in Manchuria and Mongolia.[154] But there was little evidence that either Hara or the Hara Cabinet was willing to break these 'restrictions of history'. In the summer of 1919, Foreign Minister Uchida virtually asked the Gaikō Chōsakai to reaffirm a notion that Manchuria was a vassal state outside China itself and 'should come back to the administration of the Empire [of Japan]'.[155] In the negotiation for a Four-Power Banking Consortium to finance China in 1919–1920, the Hara Cabinet repeatedly insisted that Manchuria and Mongolia should be excluded from the operating field of the Banking Consortium and reserved for the Japanese interest only.[156] 'Japan could never agree to open its regional interests in China to exploitation by international finance, as finance is the surest form of conquest.'[157] Hara himself once told a Chinese journalist that Japan was not to be satisfied with 'maintaining the established rights' in Manchuria and Mongolia.[158] The Hara Cabinet had actually decided that Japan's 'basic policy towards Manchuria and Mongolia is to further strengthen our influence there' and that 'even in the future, [Japan should] make more efforts to secure Japan's special position and special interests in Manchuria and Mongolia', which 'were essential to Japan's national defence and national economy'.[159]

There were other dimensions, it must not be forgotten, of Japan's foreign policy-making context. Traditionally, the Army had assumed a position independent of the Cabinet and was directly responsible to the Emperor, especially for Japan's continental policy. There had been constant and bitter conflicts between Gaimushō and the Army with regard to Japan's China policy. Even as late as June 1919, the Ministry of the Army, in a document on its proposed China policy, stated:

Whether in view of the geographical relations, or of the racial and linguistic relations, or of the political, economic and defense relations, Japan is bound up much more closely with China than are Britain and the United States which are thousands of miles away ... Therefore, it is recommended that the Empire should pursue an independent China policy rather than to conciliate with Great Britain and the United States.[160]

In addition to this, the influence of the Opposition party was to be taken into consideration, particularly in the post-war years. Banno argued that the major political Parties, Seiyukai and Kenseikai, began to exert great influence in foreign policy-making in the period of Taishō Democracy and this was particularly true in orientating Japan's post-war foreign policy.[161] Viscount Katō, formerly the author of the Twenty-One Demands and now leader of Kenseikai, the Opposition party, was particularly vocal in criticizing the Government's 'weak diplomacy' at the Peace Conference, indecision about insisting on Japan's treaty rights, and failure to convince the Chinese of the sincerity of Japan's China policy.[162] These criticisms, Sir Eliot observed intelligently, 'were obviously due not to a different and clearly defined policy, but to a desire to weaken the other side by any criticism likely to appeal to the public'.[163]

There was, in fact, a solid common ground where the Government, the Opposition, and the Army could and did stand together. The Japanese leaders had long accepted that Japan had 'left Asia' to join the imperialist club. They had the same image of China as Japan's market, source of raw materials and defence perimeter. They had developed a sense of superiority over and contempt for the Chinese, which had helped to inspire a sense of Japan's mission: to lead the Yellow race against the White domination and to protect the Oriental civilization, and to 'harmonize the Oriental and the Occidental civilizations'.[164]

Moreover there seemed to be a general concurrence on Hara's notion of Japan's position in the global and regional international systems. As to the premises of Japan's China policy, Katō also emphasized Japan's special relationship with China and maintained that Japan could not and would not give up its special position in South Manchuria, for which it had sacrificed £150,000,000 and 100,000 lives. Japan must have a 'dominant' position in China – dominant not meaning absolute control but 'predominance' in China's affairs.[165] General Tanaka, the Army Minister, stressed the Army's desire to secure a recognition of an Asian Monroe Doctrine, especially with regards to Manchuria and Mongolia, on the ground of Japan's national defence.[166] He was also reported to have insisted on the exclusion of Manchuria and Mongolia from the operation of the Four Power Banking Consortium 'at any cost'.[167]

On the legitimacy of Japan's expansion in China, both Katō and Tanaka, like Hara, maintained that Japan, with its growing population, had to expand and it had done nothing wrong in .its imperialist policy towards China. Katō told the British chargé d'affaires that

> Japan had done nothing that had not been done by other Powers, and that in every respect his country had steadily copied her European preceptors.[168]

Tanaka had the same vision. He told the British Military Attaché in Tokyo that Japan had only been following the examples set by other countries in its policies towards China. He remarked, not without regret, that if only Japan had started its development earlier it would have had the whole of China. He reasoned that the logical solution of Japan's expansion would be in the direction of Manchuria, Mongolia and Siberia where it was least likely to clash with other Powers.[169] In a farewell conversation with Alston, who was leaving Tokyo to become the British Minister in China, Tanaka emphasized the existence of an unfortunate misunderstanding between the Japanese and the British representatives in China and left an impression that 'he felt the need of enlisting British sympathy or co-operation in immediate Japanese policy in China'.[170]

Of course all this did not mean that the military meant to renounce totally its China policy. It did seem that there was an underlying consensus on readjusting Japan's foreign policy in the direction Hara had decided. On top of that, the fact that both Katō and Tanaka went out of their way to cultivate British sympathy and understanding of Japan's continental policy· indicated their realization that the cooperation of the Anglo-Saxon Powers was indispensable in rebuilding the East Asian international order. On August 8, 1919, Hara wrote with relief in his diary that 'The present Minister of the Army is not of the militarist opinion. He complies entirely with my policy.'[171]

This was probably where Hara's success lay. The consensus ensured a general support of his international policy. By mid-1920, Hara had secured a pattern of residential ministers and ambassadors in major countries favourable to carrying out his version of Japan's foreign policy. 'Bluffing' Obata had been placed in Beijing as the Japanese Minister. In May, Baron Hayashi, who was regarded as in favour of a policy of international harmonization, replaced Viscount Chinda in London. And Baron Shidehara, who was known for advocating a policy of conciliation with the United States, was appointed the Japanese Ambassador to Washington.[172] The Hara Cabinet was embarking on its way to the reconstruction of the East Asian international system. Somewhat *à contre-cœur*, Japan would fall into line with the Anglo-Saxon Powers without renouncing its ambition of hegemony in East Asia.

Beneath the ostensible differences and conflicts in their visions of an East Asian international order, there was still much in common among the three most interested Powers in East Asia, in whose hands, it was assumed, lay the responsibility of shaping the world order there. All of them recognized the necessity and urgency of readjusting their power relations and responded actively to the power vacuum left over by the war. All of them addressed the question of reconstructing East Asian international order in terms of their own national interests and of international rivalries between Great Powers. All of them regarded China as a market or a source of raw materials and defined the 'China problem' as that of their conflicting interests, endangering their relations in the area. And they all talked about 'international control' over China's finance and railways. None of them, however, questioned the legitimacy of Japan's expansion into China. None of them was ready to reckon with the growing national consciousness of the Chinese and the 'awakening of China'. If some of their diplomats on the scene had realized this radical change, their voice was either too remote to be heard or deliberately neglected. None of them was willing to give up its treaty rights and to concede to China its full sovereignty. None of them could conceive any order other than a reconciliation of their respective interests in East Asia. And in none of their visions of the post-war East Asian international system was China treated as a positive factor.

This was exactly where they could and did eventually find common ground to strike compromises in the spirit of a 'united front' and 'cooperativeness'. The reconstruction of the East Asian international system as was to be completed at the Washington Conference was 'to remove causes of misunderstanding and to seek ground for agreement as to principles and their application'. By implication, China, around which 'international rivalries, jealousies, distrust and antagonism were fostered to the utmost degree',[173] was still regarded very much as an object or at most a passive spectator of international power politics.

East Asia was drifting, in this fashion, to the Washington Conference of 1921–1922.

THE CHINESE PERSPECTIVE

The three most interested Powers in East Asia, in pursuing their respective visions of the post-war international order in the area, had thus assigned China a place in Eastern Asian international relations which not only fell far short of the Chinese nationalist aspirations but was also totally inappropriate to the changing realities of the international politics in the region. As indicated above, they went over China's head and addressed to each other the so-called 'China problem', which all of them took as the key issue of the reconstruction of the post-war East Asian international order. There was little evidence, however, that the Chinese would silently accept this. Its rejection by the Chinese was evident in various manifestations of China's self-conscious exertion of its independence and sovereignty, with China's concern about its future position in the international society as the underlying tone. The war and China's disappointment at Paris

> impressed more strongly on the Chinese the necessity for seeking their salvation through their own exertions rather than through reliance on the support of foreign Powers, more often than not accorded merely in order to obtain advantages over political or commercial rival.[174]

It not only awakened the Chinese national consciousness but also effected a singleness of purpose in Chinese foreign policy which had been lacking before, i.e. to assert and to recover its sovereignty whenever and wherever possible, and to eliminate piece by piece the Western political domination and economic control when opportunity arose. China was determined, it seems, to put itself on an equal footing with other nations and to take its own place in international society in spite of the treaty limitations on its sovereignty. This was more because the Chinese believed now that it was a recognized right of an independent nation to do so rather than because they felt that China had fulfilled the standard of 'civilization' set for membership of the 'Family of Nations'. The Shandong diplomacy of China at the Paris Peace Conference could be seen as the beginning of a series of consistent Chinese efforts to adjust to the profound changes in world politics and to readjust China's relations with foreign nations. Notwithstanding the Powers' refusal to heed China's pleas at the Peace Conference for a readjustment of its foreign relations, China went on with its own initiatives in the post-war years, especially with regard to the two 'most disliked and exploited'[175] questions in its treaty relations: extraterritoriality and conventional tariff.

In 1919, China's treaty relations with foreign nations witnessed both the end of a period and the beginning of another. On October 8, 1919, China exchanged with Switzerland ratifications of a Treaty of Amity signed on June 13, 1918. This was the last time China entered into relations with a foreign nation on an unequal basis, granting unilaterally privileges of extraterritoriality and of most-favoured-nation treatment.[176] On December 3, 1919, China signed a Treaty of Friendship with Bolivia. In Article II of the Treaty, it was stated explicitly that the diplomatic representatives of the two countries would 'enjoy the same rights, privileges, favours, immunities, and exemptions as are or may be accorded to the Diplomatic or Consular Agents of the most favoured nations'.[177] In a supplementary exchange of notes, it was specified that the most-favoured-nation clause of Article II did not include the right to extraterritorial jurisdiction in China.[178] This was the first treaty in the history of modern Chinese diplomacy by which China entered into regular relations with a foreign nation on a totally equal footing as a sovereign and independent state. It was followed by a Treaty of Friendship with Persia which China signed at Rome in the same spirit six months later, on June 1, 1920.[179] More significant was the fact that (1) both Bolivia and Persia had initially asked for the grant of the consular jurisdiction and other extraterritorial rights; (2) the Chinese had on both occasions firmly rejected the proposal; (3) the Chinese rejection had been accepted. Meanwhile, the Chinese Government had rejected unyieldingly the demands from the Governments of Chile, Czechoslovakia, Greece, Lithuania and Poland for a commercial or a friendship treaty which would grant consular jurisdiction.[180] For China, extraterritoriality was no longer a matter of administration of justice. It became a matter involving questions of national sovereignty and independence.

China's determination to regulate its foreign relations as a sovereign state had found verbal expression earlier in a Presidential Mandate issued in Beijing in the heat of the Shandong controversy at Paris. China had already expressed its intention at the beginning of the Peace Conference to end the consular jurisdiction and extraterritorial rights possessed by the enemy states. At a meeting on April 26, 1919 the

Cabinet decided to request the President to issue a mandate declaring that enemy subjects in future would be subject to Chinese law in all aspects, as would the subjects of newly formed states.[181] Two days later, a Presidential Mandate declared:

Hereafter, all non-treaty countries[182] wishing to enter into treaty relations with China should do so on the basis of equality. Those severing their connection with their parent countries and establishing new independent states should not be allowed to succeed to the rights and privileges secured in the treaties signed by their parent countries. The peoples of these races now living within Chinese territory in large numbers should all obey and respect Chinese laws and orders in matters of taxation and litigation. If any Third Power should demand the privileges of protecting them, such demands, one and all, must be rejected by quoting the authority above referred to.[183]

Consequent to this Presidential Mandate, in the Summer of 1919, a Cabinet decision was made that thenceforth any new treaty with any non-treaty country should be based on total equality and should not grant either conventional tariff or consular jurisdiction.[184]

With respect to the existing treaty relations, the post-war international situation seemed to have favoured China with opportunities for breaking the structure of foreign rights and privileges in China created and perpetuated by the common action of the Powers in the past. The division of the Powers into the victors and the vanquished and the ostracism of Russia broke the myth of European unity in the expression of a 'united front' *vis-à-vis* China. In Beijing, the Diplomatic Corps, insistent as it was on treaty rights such as consular jurisdiction and conventional tariff, was no longer able to speak with one voice. Before long, China would have its first success in recovering its lost sovereignty which was to be followed by other successes. On the afternoon of May 26, 1920, the Chinese House of Representatives at Beijing ratified the St. Germain Treaty with Austria.[185] Two days later, the Senate did the same.[186] Austria became the first treaty Power to renounce its treaty rights and privileges in China.

Another breakthrough in China's treaty relations was that with Germany. China's refusal to sign the Versailles Treaty and its unilateral declaration of the end of the state of war had put Sino-German relations in suspension. By March 1920, however, there had been reports from both the Chinese Minister in Copenhagen and Chang, Secretary of the Chinese Legation at Berlin, that Germany was

> most eagerly and anxiously hoping to resume commercial relations with us, offering on her part to declare publicly her recognition of all the rights and privileges accorded to China by the clauses in the Versailles Treaty which China has not yet signed.[187]

The Cabinet promptly authorized the Foreign Ministry to instruct Chang to reply to the Germans that China was not 'averse to resuming trade relations with Germany if Germany will make a formal and binding declaration to the effect as offered'.[188] Negotiations between China and Germany which followed first at Tokyo and later in Beijing resulted in an agreement on May 20, 1921 between the two Governments for the re-establishment of friendly and commercial relations. The Agreement was preceded by a unilateral declaration by Von Borch, the German Plenipotentiary. The German Government undertook to declare formally that the friendly and commercial relations between China and Germany 'should be based on principles of complete equality and absolute reciprocity in accordance with the rules of international law' and that 'Germany hereby consents to the abrogation of consular jurisdiction in China'.[189] The Agreement also stated that both Governments recognized that

> the application of the principles of respect for territorial sovereignty, of equality and of reciprocity is the only means of maintaining good relations between peoples.[190]

China's attempts to shake off its traditional treaty burdens were also directed at the conventional tariff in an effort to restore as much as possible its tariff autonomy. It should be remembered that China had raised the question of revising the 5 per cent standard treaty tariff of 1902 to an effective 7½ per cent as a *quid pro quo* for joining the Allies early in 1917.[191] On December 25, 1917, the National Customs Ordinance was promulgated, introducing a national customs tariff for all merchandise produced or manufactured in non-treaty countries, irrespective of the nationality of the importer. In the summer of 1919, the Chinese Government showed its serious intention to enforce the general tariff. In mid-June, regulations were promulgated by the Chinese Government that

> subjects of non-treaty Powers would not enjoy the privileges of the treaty tariff, of inward or outward transit passes, of transportation

taxes for goods manufactured by machinery, or of the tacitly-accepted (extra-treaty) privilege of acting as agents in the interior.[192]

On July 23, the Chinese Foreign Ministry addressed an identical note to the Diplomatic Corps, proposing to introduce a system of certificates of origin in order to protect the interests of the treaty Powers. The note stated: 'It is requested that this matter may be laid before the Diplomatic Body with a view to obtaining their consent thereto.'[193]

The consent that the Chinese had hoped for was not forthcoming. The proposed general tariff and the system of certificates of origin met strong opposition from the Diplomatic Corps representing the treaty Powers and specifically from British commercial interests in China. The joint note presented on October 8 by the Diplomatic Corps in Beijing in reply to the Chinese Foreign Ministry's note of July 23 objected to the procedure proposed by the Chinese. It argued that the procedure would affect adversely the trade of Chinese and foreigners alike; that there was no precedent for such action in the practice of other countries and that by virtue of the most-favoured-nation clause, all treaty Powers had the right to claim that the duties enumerated in the tariff should be imposed upon articles shipped or imported into China by their nations, without regard to the countries from which they came. Therefore,

> the general tariff can only be made applicable to those goods which were originally manufactured in non-treaty countries, and imported from non-treaty countries by the nationals of those countries.[194]

The rejection by the British Chamber of Commerce seemed to be more straightforward and more revealing. It was against the proposed general tariff mainly for two reasons:

> (a) That it was impracticable, as it would require most careful specific rates and would involve objectionable certificates of origin regulations;

> and

> (b) That it would force non-treaty countries to abandon ex-territorial [extraterritorial] rights in order to secure equality of treatment *re* tariff.[195]

These rejections of the general tariff by the treaty Powers, it can be seen, were based on their own commercial interests. They were largely based on matters of technicality concerning its implementation. This clearly showed the treaty Powers' disregard of China's sovereignty in this matter. Among the treaty Powers, there could be found little sympathy with and understanding of this move as China's initial efforts to regain part of its lost sovereign rights.

To the arguments cited above for the rejection of the Chinese general tariff by the treaty Powers, the Chinese provided some counter-arguments in a reply by the Foreign Ministry on December 22 to foreign legations in Beijing. They contended that the system of certificates of origin did exist in the practice of other countries, according to the Inspector-General of Customs. The application of the general tariff was in accordance with the principle of equity, and

> If, acting in accordance with the contents of your Excellency's note, goods imported into China by Treaty Power nationals, irrespective of the country of their origin, are all to be subject to the treaty tariff, the effects of the treaties will be extended to all non-treaty countries; which is, it is to be feared, hardly consonant with the original meaning of the treaties; while the general tariff proposed by the Chinese Government will have been established in vain.[196]

Pending the reply from the Diplomatic Corps on the application of the general tariff, the Chinese Government had in September 1919 instructed the Superintendent of Customs at Shanghai not to apply the newly revised treaty tariff to imports from non-treaty countries. The instruction asserted that the treaty tariff was 'both prejudicial to our national rights and detrimental to our revenue receipts' and that it should be understood

> that our country has full right and freedom to fix and impose a national tariff or duty on imports from those countries without let or hindrance ... This is very important, constituting as it does our first step toward the retrocession of our full right to fix and impose a national tariff of customs duty ultimately.[197]

One can hardly fail to read in the quotes above China's consciousness of its sovereign rights and a strong determination to assert these rights, which were largely lacking previously in China's national life and its external relations.

Chinese nationalism also found its expression in other issues involving China and related to the reconstruction of the post-war East Asian international order. An illustrative example was the renewal of the third Anglo-Japanese Alliance. In the 'rights-recovery' movement early in the century,[198] the Chinese had come to look upon the diplomatic engagements between third Powers concerning China with a critical eye, and regarded them as an 'interference with China's sovereign rights'.[199] In 1917, when the Lansing–Ishii Agreement was published, the Chinese Government had made an official announcement that China was not to be bound by an agreement concluded by two foreign Powers relating to China's own territory, and to which China was not a party.[200]

The renewal of the Anglo-Japanese Alliance of 1911, as shown previously in this chapter, was a vital concern in 1920 for the three most interested Powers. It concerned China as well, but in a somewhat different way. In Section B of the preamble of the Alliance, in the text of both the 1902 and 1911 agreements, it was declared that one of the purposes of the Alliance was the maintenance of China's independence and territorial integrity. Yet it was in those years that China had been greatly encroached upon by Japan territorially, politically and economically. When the issue of the renewal of the Alliance was about to come up for review, the Chinese Minister in London was instructed to make formal inquiries at the Foreign Office about the British policy and to point out that

> the treatment of China merely as a territorial entity in the written text of any such agreements would no longer be tolerated by the public opinion of the country and would, indeed, be viewed by all as an unfriendly act.[201]

In May, an *aide-mémoire* handed to the British Minister in Beijing by the Chinese Foreign Ministry further stated that

> it has been an International usage that when two friendly nations conclude a Treaty it can only cover those rights and interests which legitimately belong to the nations party to the Agreement. This usage has acquired fresh strength as the result of the Great War, in that international equality has become a watchword with the nations.[202]

Chinese public opinion as expressed in the press was very much behind the firm attitude of the Government towards the renewal of the Anglo-Japanese Alliance. The memory of the Powers' deal at Versailles on Shandong was still fresh and the Japanese encroachment on China was deeply and bitterly felt. Clive, British chargé d'affaires in Beijing, reported that the Alliance was widely regarded as 'the stepping stone' for the accomplishment of Japan's expansion in China and 'the instrument of Japan's encroachment'.[203] If it were continued without modification, 'China would perish under the policy of the Japanese party of encroachment and become an Eastern Balkans'.[204] Moreover, with growing national consciousness, the Chinese could not but look back at the treatment of China in the international system in the past twenty years with apprehension and resentment. In a memo on China and the Anglo-Japanese Alliance handed to Alston and signed by Huang Yanpei[205] and other influential Chinese representing eleven Chinese organizations in Shanghai, it was bitterly resented that in the second and the third alliance treaties, 'matters affect [*sic*] China's international standing and relations were specifically treated' without China being consulted. With regard to China's general position in the international system, it was observed that

> During the last two decades there has developed the practice among the powers of treating China as a semi-dependent country. Instead of treating directly with China concerning her affairs and welfare, they treated among themselves as if China were a mere diplomatic appendage. The Chinese people cannot but regard such practice with apprehension and resentment, especially in the case where a certain Power assumes a paternal diplomatic relationship to China and pretends to exercise a right to intervene in the diplomatic intercourse between China and any other countries.[206]

China would now, it went on to state, 'refuse to be treated except as an independent nation exercising full sovereign rights'.[207]

In another open letter addressed to Alston and published on June 12, 1920, China's rights as an independent and sovereign nation were firmly defended. It would be 'a violation of the principles of international law, as well as of the spirit of the League' to continue the Alliance in its present form, noted the open letter, because China as an independent nation 'has, according to international law, the right to be treated with respect and to preserve her dignity'. It was also because

> China has now formally ratified the Austrian Treaty and thus joined the League of Nations, according to the 10th article of which members of the League undertake to respect and preserve as against external aggression the territorial integrity and existing political independence of all members of the League.[208]

Also in June, the Foreign Ministry made public an official statement against the renewal of the Alliance along similar lines. China 'had suffered enough from its [the Alliance's] operation during the World

War in the matter of Shantung', declared the statement. It was further pointed out that, as a full member of the League, China considered that

> a contract regarding her affairs between other members of the League cannot be entered into without her prior consent having been obtained, Article 10 being a sufficient guarantee that her territorial integrity will be respected.[209]

The recognition of the force of China's contentions also found its expression in a report to the Foreign Office by the British Legation in Beijing. China had realized, the report said, that

> The renewal of this alliance, which was supposed to stand for the maintenance of the *status quo*, the open door, and the territorial integrity of China would be of little use to China. She was tired of these high-sounding phrases which meant so little, and if in the future other countries wished to enter into engagements affecting her, she intended to be consulted.[210]

Naturally, when the joint declaration by Great Britain and Japan on the Alliance signed by Curzan and Chinda was published on July 8, 1920, it was aimed partly at public opinion in China. It declared publicly that, 'if the said Agreement be continued after July 1921, it must be in a form which is not inconsistent with that Covenant [of the League of Nations]'.[211]

How much the Chinese diplomatic initiatives had succeeded was probably hard to tell. However the messages conveyed by China's initiatives in those two years could hardly be mistaken. Neither could the Middle Kingdom be ignored any longer in the settlement of issues concerning the reconstruction of the East Asian international system. Nor could China shut its eyes to the changing world politics. China was, as declared by Dr. Wang Chonghui, the Chinese Chief Justice, bent on 'setting to work through the whole network of her international relations to preserve her rights'.[212] As an independent nation, China had an inalienable right to determine its affairs related to its external relations, and its participation in world politics should be based on total equality with other nations in the world.

There was an acquiescence by the Powers in China's equality in the emerging international society. It acquired full membership in the League by signing the St. Germain Treaty. In selecting the first non-permanent members of the League Council during the Paris Peace Conference, Miller had talked with Cecil about selecting China in place of Greece. The idea was given up because they believed that 'one

Asiatic Power [Japan] on the Council was enough'.[213] In December 1920, however, China was elected with a considerable majority into the League Council with the support of Powers such as Britain and France.

It is important to note the tension between theory expounded by international jurists and practice in international politics in the issue of China's status in the international society. As late as 1927, some international jurists still held that China was not a state 'in the full sense of international law' because it was not 'allowed to exercise certain rights over foreigners within their own jurisdictions'.[214] They maintained that 'The entrance of the state into international statehood ... depended entirely upon the recognition by those states already within this circle' and 'as to the proper qualifications for admission in each case the states already within the family claim and exercise the right to judge'.[215] Yet, while the Powers were not prepared to grant China full sovereignty and full international status, they accepted China's full membership in the League of Nations and further elected China in December 1920 one non-permanent member of the League Council.[216] This amounted to a *de facto* recognition of China as a full member of the international community. If, by invoking the niceties of international law, it was still possible to deny that China was a state in the full sense of international law, it would be difficult to maintain that the Powers' insistence on their treaty rights was the evidence that they did not accept China in the emerging international society. It can be argued that China's membership in the League and its election to the League Council were strong evidence that it was being accepted by the original members into the emerging international society. As with the Ottoman Empire, China was admitted to the Family of Nations, not as a fully sovereign nation, but with treaty limitations on its sovereignty. The differences were that, whereas the admission of the Ottoman Empire was explicitly written in the Paris Treaty of 1856 after the Crimean war, the admission of China was implicitly embodied in a series of international policies of the Great Powers.

4   Russia Breakthrough

In Chapter 3, we have approached the issue of China in the reconstruction of the international system in East Asia from the perspective of China and of the three most interested imperial powers, Britain, America and Japan. Russia, a traditional imperialist power in East Asia, has been conspicuously left out. This is not because Russia emerged after the October Revolution as an anti-imperialist state and therefore was irrelevant to this study. Rather, it is because the emergence of Soviet Russia and the Bolshevik revolutionary diplomacy meant that Sino-Russian relations constitute an independent aspect in the post-war reconstruction of an international order, and need to be examined separately. In other words, the emergence of the revolutionary state of Soviet Russia not only produced another cleavage among the imperialist powers but also marked the end of the exclusive management by the imperialist powers of the East Asian international system, thus adding a new dimension to the development of that system. For China, the Bolshevik revolutionary diplomacy and the Russian weakness resulting from the civil war opened up possibilities to break its 'unequal' treaty relations with another imperial Power–Russia.

Scholarly studies of Sino-Russian relations in the period which this study concerns are still very few. The existing literature has either approached the subject largely from the Soviet perspective and depicted China as a victim of the Narkomindel (People's Commissariat of Foreign Affairs) or the Comintern intrigues,[1] or over-emphasized the Soviet ideological impact upon the founding of the Chinese Communist Party.[2] Only a comparatively recent study by S. T. Leong has a detailed account of the Sino-Soviet diplomatic relations of the period. While it is an important complement to the previous studies in this field, it has some serious omissions and lacks an analysis in the broader context of China's search for its place in the post-war international system in East Asia.

This chapter studies some principal Chinese initiatives to roll back the Russian encroachments on China's sovereign rights, and argues that in the two years 1918–1920, the ex-Middle Kingdom was not a passive and incompetent object to be worked on by Soviet policies. On the contrary, there were as many Chinese initiatives to take advantage of the Russian weakness for China's rights recovery as Soviet initiatives to capitalize on China's internal and external situations for its revolutionary purposes. Both the Central Government in Beijing and the local authorities along the borders readily capitalized on the situation in Russia, and in spite of the opposition from other treaty Powers, took initiatives to shake off treaty limitations on China's sovereign rights in an attempt to assert China's independence and sovereignty. They achieved a certain degree of success. This constituted an important part of China's consistent efforts to break down the structure of foreign rights and privileges and to recover its lost sovereign rights from the treaty Powers whenever and wherever possible. It also indicated a new direction in which China's assertion of its place in the international system might be more effectively made. By the end of 1920, most Russian treaty rights in China were suspended and China had put itself on a *de facto* equal footing with Russia.

OPPORTUNITIES UNDREAMED OF

Russia, as one of the principal imperialist Powers in East Asia, had from the 1860s secured extensive treaty rights and spheres of influence in China. The former comprised extraterritoriality, trade privileges, concessions and the Boxer indemnities, whereas the latter concerned two parts of the Chinese territory, Outer Mongolia and northern Manchuria, with predominant Russian influence. It has been argued by E. H. Carr that the Peace Decree and other broadcast appeals of the first days of the Bolshevik regime, though addressed to belligerent nations, were not aimed at China.[3] However the Bolshevik regime itself, with its anti-imperialist stance and its revolutionary diplomacy of the early days, did hold out for China a chance that further Russian erosion of China's sovereignty might be stopped and that China's rights lost to Russia might be recovered.

The first practical opportunity for China to reassert its sovereign rights presented itself soon and unexpectedly. Ever since the abdication of Tsar Nicholas II in March 1917, Russian domestic political struggle had its reverberations in the Russian-managed Chinese Eastern Railway (CER) Zone[4] which, though nominally still part of Chinese territory, was actually an extension of the Russian Empire into North Manchuria. Immediately following the Bolshevik seizure of power in Petrograd, the local Bolsheviks made their bid for power in the CER Zone and their attempt to take over the Railway from its Russian president, General Horvath. This resulted in a situation at the end of November where

> ... due to the almost complete breakdown of the police system in Harbin, lawlessness and crime had increased to such an extent as to seriously threaten the lives and property of foreigners resident there.[5]

As the crisis in Harbin grew acute in December, Jordan visited the Foreign Ministry in Beijing on the morning of December 5 to make an informal request that the Chinese Government send troops to Harbin to quell the disturbances. He told the Foreign Ministry officials that he was speaking for the Japanese Minister in Beijing as well.[6] During his visit to the Foreign Ministry in the afternoon, the Russian Minister, Prince Kudachev, who still represented the toppled Tsarist government, also stated that Russia would like to ask China for help and would resent seeing any other third country interfering in Harbin.[7] On December 6, the Allied Ministers, after much consultation, decided to 'call on [the] Chinese Government to support with troops the authorities established under the treaties in Manchuria'.[8] On December 7, Jordan, in the capacity of Dean of the Diplomatic Corps in Beijing, formally requested that, in the event of the Russian Soviet in Harbin taking over the Railway, the Chinese Government would 'act in accordance with the Sino-Russian Agreement of 1909 and send troops to protect the Railway Administration and to maintain law and order in the railway zone'.[9] On the same day, the Chinese Cabinet meeting resolved after deliberations to meet Jordan's request.[10]

The dispatch of an international police force to protect foreign residents and their property was first proposed by Jordan in November. However he excluded at the same time the possibility of sending the British Indian troops stationed in Tianjin for service in Harbin because they were obviously 'not suitable'. He sounded out the possibility of America sending a detachment to act as military police but did not get a favourable reply.[11] In later talks at Beijing between Legation Ministers, it was clear that, whereas the Anglo-American Powers would oppose any suggestions to send Japanese troops to Harbin, Japan was against the idea of an international police force in general, for fear that its special interests in Manchuria as a whole would eventually be challenged.[12] Strategically, the Allies were considering the possibility of blockading the Trans-Siberian Railway with Chinese troops in the event that the continuing Soviet–German negotiations should result in a separate peace between Russia and Germany. The options were indeed limited.

The decision of the Allied Ministers to ask the Chinese Government to send troops to the CER Zone was probably the best compromise possible at the time to transcend individual Powers' interests in the area. China seemed to be the state least capable of challenging seriously the balance of power in Manchuria. It was now an Allied nation and had sovereign rights over the area involved. To use its troops to control the situation in the area was logical and legitimate. It is interesting to note, however, that by asking the Chinese Government to act 'in accordance with the 1909 Sino-Russian Treaty', Jordan had hoped that this Allied invitation would serve the purpose of the Allied Powers and at the same time restrict the freedom of action of the Chinese Government by treaty limitations in regard to the railway and the railway zone.

Quite unwittingly, however, the invitation from the Allied Ministers provided China with an undreamed-of opportunity to reassert China's sovereignty and regain China's control over the railway and the railway zone. Ironically, as it turned out, the Chinese, who were supposed to be there to support the treaty authorities of the CER Administration, began immediately to dismantle the Russian authorities and to reassert their own sovereignty, which had long been suspended.

As early as the end of November, the Chinese local authorities in Harbin had already dispatched Chinese police into the Railway Zone to 'protect the Chinese merchants'.[13] Before the formal request from the Allied Ministers, the Chinese Government had also contemplated the possibility of dispatching troops to deal with the deteriorating situation in Harbin. This was based on two considerations: to protect the Chinese residents in the railway zone, and to preempt any Japanese move to interfere.[14] Now, upon the formal request from the Allied Ministers, the Foreign Ministry invoked both the Sino-Russian Treaty of 1881 and the Sino-Russian Agreement of 1909, and promptly instructed the Military and the Civil Governors of Jilin, General Meng Enyuan and Guo Zongxi, to dispatch massive forces to suppress any violence and disturbance in the railway zone.[15] By December 20, about 4,000 Chinese troops were deployed along the railway.[16] In the early hours of December 26, the Chinese soldiers moved in to disarm the Harbin Soviet and expelled them from Manchuria by the end of the year.[17] General Horvath and the Russian CER Administration survived under the Chinese military protection, only to find themselves faced with another serious challenge to their authority from the Chinese.

The Chinese military moves would have had limited significance if they had not been followed by other measures to reassert Chinese sovereignty in the railway zone. In fact, underlying the Chinese Government's decision to take the military actions as requested by the Allies was China's desire to recover its rights over the CER Zone. In the early stage of the Chinese military 'intervention', frequent communications between Beijing and the local authorities were exchanged as to how to proceed with the recovery.[18] The Chinese Government had to operate within a number of constraints. Three complications had ruled out any possibility for China to take over the Railway Zone directly by denouncing unilaterally the Sino-Russian Treaties: the Allied request of China to abide by the treaties, the precarious political situation in Russia, and the Japanese presence in South Manchuria. Consequently, China had to manoeuvre within the treaty provisions by broad interpretation of them and was to 'recover its rights to the Railway by effecting the treaties'.[19] Interestingly, this move of 'rights recovery' by the Chinese Government was not to recover Chinese sovereign rights which were lost in the Sino-Russian treaties but rights which were there legally guaranteed for, yet practically denied to, China. The move was embodied in China's speedy appointment on December 29, 1917 of Guo Zongxi, the Civil Governor of Jilin, as the Chinese President to the board of directors of the CER.[20] As the Chinese frankly admitted, it was the first time since 1900 that China had exercised this right of appointing the CER President.[21] Soon, China would begin to take unilateral action to take back the administration of the entire railway.

On January 7, the Cabinet instructed Guo Zongxi to 'assess the situation and draw up appropriate plans to recover [our rights] according to the treaties and contract'.[22] Acting on the instructions from the Cabinet, Guo, in the capacity of President of the CER, together with General Meng, held on January 11, 1918 a meeting of senior military and civil officials of the two provinces of Jilin and Heilongjiang and drew up a six-point programme for the administration of the CER Zone. The resolution of the meeting again asserted that China had the right to deploy troops along the railway and to establish and expand its police in Harbin and other areas within the CER Zone. Only on the management of the railway itself did the Chinese seem less insistent on their control. They decided to let the Russians have their way before the authority of the President was further clarified by the interpretation of the treaties. The two most interesting decisions were, however, those on the tariff and the judicial system applied to the CER Zone. On the tariff matter, the meeting approved the establishment of customs offices along the railway by the Finance Department of the two provincial administrations involved and decided that 'there is no need to inform the Russian Company about it' because 'it had nothing to do with the treaties'. On the more sensitive matter of the judicial system, they decided to keep the change to a minimum but, at the same time, that the President should be empowered to effect any change in the future, if need be.[23]

There was a clear mixture of assertion and caution in the proposed programme. The Chinese seemed to be prepared to go only as far as their interpretation of the treaties allowed them to do. In Meng and Guo's report to Beijing after the January 11 meeting, it was explicitly stated that, except that on the tariff question,

all the proposals were based on treaties and contracts [between China and Russia] so as to put ourselves in a legally unassailable position. We must steadily and cautiously expand our real power [over the CER Zone] to recover our lost rights and to prepare ourselves for further changes in the future.[24]

While the Russian Minister, Prince Kudachev, protested on January 23, to little avail, in the Foreign Ministry against 'extensive interpretation of China's rights and excessive use of power by the military governors of Jilin and Heilongjiang in the CER Zone',[25] the Cabinet sanctioned the proposed programme on January 24, 1918.[26] In this manner, China took, within the early months of the Bolshevik Revolution, the first step of its long journey to recovering its sovereign rights from the Russians.

In Petrograd, meanwhile, the Harbin affairs prompted the first direct contacts between the Chinese Legation and the Narkomindel (People's Commissariat of Foreign Affairs). It was during these contacts that the Soviet Government first offered to abolish the Russian extraterritoriality in China and to return the Russian concessions to the Chinese. On January 18, 1918, the Narkomindel addressed its first note to the Chinese Legation, declaring that

the former Russian Minister to China cannot represent the present Government and General Horvath has been dismissed from his post as Russian President of the CER. The Commissariat hereby informs the Chinese Government of its hope that a joint Sino-Soviet Committee would be organized to deal with the CER question.[27]

At almost the same time, A. N. Voznesensky, Head of the Far Eastern Department of the Narkomindel, called the Chinese Legation and pressed to see the Chinese Minister for an informal discussion of the questions addressed in the above note.[28]

It must be noted that, like all other Allied governments, the Chinese Government neither immediately withdrew its diplomatic mission after the October Revolution nor officially recognized the Bolshevik regime. The Chinese Legation, in concerted action with other Allied missions in Petrograd, declined any official representations with the Bolshevik regime while maintaining informal contact with the Narkomindel.[29] On January 19, Voznesensky was received in the Chinese Legation, not, however, by the Minister but by Li Shizhong, a legation secretary. Voznesensky's proposition seemed quite generous. If China could remove General Horvath and organize a Sino-Russian joint committee to run the CER before China's official recognition of the Soviet Republic, the Soviet Government would do its best to satisfy the Chinese interests. Furthermore, if China accepted Voznesensky himself as the Soviet diplomatic representative in China, the Soviet Government would first renounce the Russian extraterritoriality in China and then propose to return the Russian concessions in Tianjin and Hankou. Li told Voznesensky that what China did in Harbin was completely within its sovereignty and the limit of the 1896 Sino-Russian Contract on the CER. He dismissed any possibility of a joint Sino-Soviet committee before official recognition and insisted that the CER was legally but a business enterprise and that any other rights it enjoyed previously were simply usurped. Voznesensky's request to go and represent the Soviet Government in China was also declined.[30]

On January 24, Li paid what seemed to be a return visit to Voznesensky at the latter's home. Unexpectedly, he met there Polivanov, a Deputy-Commissar of the Narkomindel, and the talk lasted five hours. Li again defended China's action in Harbin and declared China's intended neutrality in Russia's civil war. He argued that the Imperial Russian Government had used the railway as an instrument to carry out its aggressive policy in East Asia and that the new regime, a revolutionary opposition to the Monarchists, should not attach any political importance to the CER. When Polivanov talked about the doctrine that 'China belongs to the Chinese' and repeated the Soviet offer on Russian extraterritoriality and Russian concessions, Li made an interesting proposal: 'If the Soviet Government is to abolish Russian extraterritoriality in China and return the Russian concessions to the Chinese, why not make this policy public?' Before the official recognition, Li suggested, this Soviet policy might as well be made known by the Chinese Government to the Chinese people, who would definitely welcome the overture. Li explained, however, that it was difficult for China to enter into any official talks with the Bolshevik regime because China was one of the Allies and must act in concert with other Allied governments on the recognition issue.

The informal yet official contacts in Petrograd between China and the Soviet authority were partly a continuation of the CER affair and constituted the initial stage of Sino-Soviet relations on a state-to-state basis. Three observations can be made on these Petrograd contacts. First, they were not one-way traffic. The Chinese and the Soviets took their respective initiatives in approaching each other to feel out the other's policies. Secondly, the Chinese showed clearly their concern with China's sovereignty over the CER and their readiness to cash in on the situation. Particular interest on the Chinese part in the Soviet overture on Russian extraterritoriality and concessions was also expressed. The Chinese seemed to have spotted another opportunity open to them to assault Russian rights and privileges in China. Thirdly, the Chinese Government was aware of the Soviet offer to abrogate Russian consular jurisdiction in China as early as January 1918 when the messages from the Narkomindel officials were relayed to Beijing. While the Soviet offer did not have immediate impact upon the Chinese policy towards Soviet Russia, the Chinese government's knowledge of the offer was, as will be seen later, always at the background of China's future decision-making as regards its Russian policies.

ALONG THE BORDERLANDS

The Sino-Soviet official contact was brought to an abrupt end when the Chinese Legation withdrew from Petrograd to Vologda, together with the American and the Japanese missions at the end of February 1918 just before the conclusion of the Brest–Litovsk Treaty on March 6, 1918.[31] The Allied intervention in Siberia and the Allied policy towards the Soviet regime would further make impossible any direct contact between the Chinese Government in Beijing and the Soviet authorities in Petrograd and later in Moscow for the next two and half years. Legally, China continued to recognize the Russian Legation in Beijing headed by Prince Kudachev which now represented no Russian Government yet still acted as the guardian of the Tsarist rights and interests in China. These complicated the picture of continued border contacts between China and Russia, which had the longest land frontier in the world. Russia was bordered by China in three areas: Manchuria, Outer Mongolia and Xinjiang. China was left to deal with whatever Russian authorities were extended over each border area, whether they were the Monarchists, the White Russians or the Bolsheviks. A closer examination of those border contacts in the years 1918–1920 reveals a remarkable degree of consistency in China's efforts to recover its lost rights. In all three areas, China seemed to have launched, taking advantage of the situation as it arose, what amounted to an overall attack upon the Russian rights and interests in China.

Leong in his study has dealt at length with China's actions in Manchuria and Outer Mongolia.[32] Suffice it here to recapture briefly the themes of the two cases. In Outer Mongolia, China had gone as far as claiming at the end of 1919 its sovereignty over Outer Mongolia. It did this by literally forcing the Mongols to give up their autonomy patronized by the Russians and by unilaterally cancelling the Russian–Mongolian Commercial Treaty of 1912 and The Sino-Russo-Mongolian Treaty of 1915.[33] In Manchuria, 1920 opened with China's renewed efforts in its rights recovery in the CER Zone. Direct appropriation of the railway was proposed,[34] but more cautious measures were taken to put the Chinese moves on a sounder legal basis and to avoid international complications. In February, the Chinese proposed a reorganization plan for the board of directors to ensure an equal joint management as interpreted by the Chinese. In March, General Horvath was removed by the Chinese Government in Beijing from his post as Managing Director and Vice-President of the CER.[35] With him out of the way, the Chinese authorities proceeded to strip the Railway Administration of any political and judicial rights so as to reduce the railway to a purely commercial corporation. To legalize the Chinese moves, the Ministry of Communications in Beijing pressed the Russo-Asiatic Bank, the private enterprise entrusted to build the railway, for negotiations for a supplementary agreement to the original contract of 1896. Several months had passed before an agreement – the 'Supplement to the Agreement for the Construction and Operation of the Chinese Eastern Railway' – was signed by both the Chinese Ministry of Communication and the Russo-China Bank on October 2, 1920, whereby the Chinese Government was

> to assume provisionally, pending such arrangement concerning the railway as the Government may reach with the Russian Government

that may be recognized by China, the supreme control exercised over the said railway.[36]

Article VI further explicitly stated that

The rights and the obligations of the Company will henceforth be in every respect of a commercial character: every political activity and every political attribute will be absolutely forbidden to it. To this end the Chinese Government reserves the right to prescribe restrictive measures of any character and at any time.[37]

It must be noted that, in both areas, China was dealing diplomatically with the defunct Kudachev mission in Beijing, at which China began to look askance from 1919 onwards.[38] It was the political disintegration of Imperial Russia which provided the Chinese with these opportunities to reassert Chinese sovereignty. In Manchuria, where the international power configuration was complicated, China was cautiously insistent. In Outer Mongolia, however, it was unilaterally assertive. It is true, as Leong argued, that both the Outer Mongolian and the Manchurian cases are illustrative of China's bold attempts to reassert its sovereignty. They do not, nevertheless, seem to have affected the entire structure of treaty Powers' rights and privileges in China.

The Xinjiang case, however, carried immediate implications for the treaty Powers in China. Advantage was taken by the Chinese authorities of the consolidation of the Bolshevik regime and the Soviet anti-imperialist overture to dismantle the structure of the Russian treaty rights and interests in the region. It was with the Bolsheviks that the Chinese local authorities in Xinjiang, sanctioned by the Central Government in Beijing, concluded a prototype treaty – the Yili Protocol – as early as May 1920, four months before China formally ceased to recognize the Russian Kudachev mission. It amounted to a *de facto* recognition of the Bolshevik regime and the Protocol carried provisions which explicitly abolished the Russian extraterritorial and tariff privileges in the area covered by the agreement.

Interest was early expressed by the frontier military authorities in approaching the Bolsheviks for a favourable response to China's rights recovery attempts. On April 29, 1919, the Office of Army's Chief of Staff forwarded to the Cabinet and the Foreign Ministry an intelligence report from Yu Yixi, the Chief of Staff of the Chinese Army residing near Vladivostok, on the situation in Russia and the Bolshevik

Government in Moscow. Yu firmly suggested that China should immediately send a capable official to Moscow to open talks with the Bolsheviks 'so as to be able to recover some of its lost rights'. The listed reasons for this policy suggestion were (1) the Moscow Government had been gradually consolidating itself; (2) the other Allied nations were approaching the Bolsheviks; (3) judging from the policies, if any, of the White Russians towards China, it was difficult for China to regain from them any Chinese rights and interests.[39]

There was little doubt that rights recovery was at the back of the Chinese Government's mind, too, in its considering the recognition of any Russian regime. When Liu Jingren in Vladivostok informed the Chinese Government in May 1919 that the Allied Governments were considering recognizing conditionally the Kolchak regime at Omsk,[40] the Cabinet decided to act in concert with the Allies and instructed the Foreign Ministry to 'prepare China's conditions for the recognition' and to 'seize the opportunity to recover our lost rights'.[41]

Xinjiang, like Outer Mongolia and Manchuria, had seen relentless penetration of Russian interests since the Russian conquest of Turkestan and the expansion of the Russian Empire southward from Siberia in the 1860s. Like Outer Mongolia, it was inhabited mostly by non-Chinese and non-Russian peoples; yet, unlike Outer Mongolia, it did not come under the Russian protectorate and remained a Chinese province, though highly autonomous.[42] Like Manchuria, largely owing to Great Power rivalries in the area, Xinjiang did not fall a victim to a particular Power;[43] yet, unlike Manchuria, Xinjiang was no longer involved in the mainstream of major imperialist rivalries.[44]

From 1912 to 1928, Xinjiang was under the comparatively effective rule of Yang Zengxin, a Chinese who was both the military and the civil governor of the province.[45] Distance and history had made Xinjiang more autonomous than any other province and the warlord politics added itself to that dimension. On foreign relations, however, Yang consulted Beijing on almost every important issue, received instructions, and acted accordingly. Yang's period, if anything, would certainly defy any generalization that Xinjiang's autonomy 'has been carried so far that governors have conducted their own foreign relations with Russia and India and have even treated the National Government of China almost as if it were a foreign power'.[46]

The Bolshevik military victory and its approach to the Chinese border areas were followed with intense interest in Beijing. In November 1919, the Cabinet had already warned that the Bolshevik successes in the East should be closely watched because of China's common borders with Eastern Russia.[47] Early in December, President Xu Shichang went out of his way to suggest clearly in a presidential memorandum that,

> if the White Russians in Irkutsk collapse, we will be bordered by the Bolsheviks. It would be advisable to entrust the Foreign Ministry to conduct a special investigation on the principles and the leadership of that Party [the Bolsheviks] so as to be prepared to deal with them ... If it is true that the European Powers would let Lenin's regime have its own way, we may as well get in contact with them when they actually border with us.[48]

On December 31, 1919, the Foreign Ministry advised the Ministry of War, the Office of Army's Chief of Staff and the Frontier Defence Bureau that there was, reportedly, fierce fighting between the Bolsheviks and the White Russians in Irkutsk and Tashkent. The matter not only concerned China's frontier defence in the Northwest in general and in Xinjiang in particular, but also had important bearing on future Sino-Russian relations.[49] It was certainly fair to observe that because China had some thousands of miles coterminous with Russian territory, 'the question of relations with the Bolsheviks has for her therefore an even more vital importance than in the case of most other nations'.[50]

In Xinjiang, there had been some *démarche* from both sides in 1918. Early in April, Yang was instructed by the Foreign Ministry to continue to recognize the Russian consulates in Xinjiang commanded by the Kudachev mission in Beijing, while at the same time getting into informal contact with the Bolsheviks 'with a view to protecting the Chinese residents and the Chinese trade across the border'.[51] Late in the month, the Soviet Government at Tashkent relayed to Yang a telegram from the Narkomindel, demanding the dispatch of the Soviet consuls to Xinjiang.[52] In forwarding the Soviet demand to Beijing on May 25, Yang strongly suggested that the proposed Soviet dispatches to Xinjiang be accepted before China's formal recognition of the Soviet regime in Petrograd. The acceptance, however, should be based on the conditions that, first, the Soviet representatives to Xinjiang were to deal with consular affairs, but not in the name of the Russian consulate before Soviet Russia was recognized by the Powers; secondly, the correspondences between the Chinese authorities and the Soviet representatives were of unofficial and informal nature; and thirdly, the Soviet representatives should be denied any consular jurisdiction and consulate guards.[53] On June 20, at the insistence of Yang, his proposal in the form of a Foreign Ministry memo was discussed at a Cabinet meeting.[54] Meanwhile Soviet trade missions were allowed to operate in Xinjiang with little interference. In August, a Soviet trade agency was even permitted to be set up at Yining to handle trade matters.[55]

Yang's considerations were mostly pragmatic. First, Xinjiang was now bordered by the Bolsheviks who were winning what seemed to be an overwhelming victory in the whole of Russia; secondly, trade across the border in Russia was essential to Xinjiang's economy; thirdly, there was the problem of protecting the Chinese emigrants and the Chinese labourers living and stranded in Soviet Turkestan;[56] fourthly, Xinjiang had to deal with a large number of Russian refugees seeking asylum from the Russian civil war in Xinjiang who numbered 50,000 by August 1918 in Yili region alone; last but not least, Yang believed that, by taking advantage of the situation, China could secure some not insignificant *quid pro quo* from the Soviet authorities in exchange for accepting the Soviet representatives.[57]

The changing situation in the Russian civil war in the Autumn of 1918 was not favourable to Yang's proposal, however. The anti-Bolshevik military forces regained some of the initiatives and practically cut off the Turkestan Soviet Republic from both the central regions of Soviet Russia and Xinjiang. On top of this, China was participating in the Allied military intervention in Siberia. Any acceptance of Soviet agents in Xinjiang was practically and politically out of the question. Yang, however, tried to maintain Xinjiang's neutrality in the Russian civil war. While rejecting any further demand from the Bolsheviks to be allowed to send Soviet consuls to Xinjiang, he disarmed the White Russians who fled into Xinjiang and quelled the efforts of the Tsarist consuls to recruit an anti-Bolshevik brigade to engage in raids across the border into Russia.[58]

1920 started with a succession of events on the Russian scene which opened new vistas for Sino-Soviet relations. On January 5, the Kolchak regime at Omsk collapsed completely. Four days later, the Americans withdrew from the Allied intervention, followed by other Western intervening powers. The Allies were also to lift their economic blockade against Soviet Russia. By the end of January, following the fall of Irkutsk, Bolshevik power had extended to Vladivostok and the whole Maritime Province. The Chinese found themselves adjacent to the Bolsheviks along the entire borderlands. Meanwhile, in early February, an agreement on the exchange of prisoners of war between Britain and Soviet Russia was signed in Copenhagen. The Western Powers were moving towards closer relations with Soviet Russia.

Along the Xinjiang borders, in early 1920, there seemed to be a repetition of the same situation as in early 1918. The Tashkent Soviet made the same *démarche* as it had to the Xinjiang authorities and Yang moved to respond positively.[59] It must be noted, however, that the overall international situation was now materially different. The World War had ended and the Versailles Treaty had been signed and ratified. Unlike the situation two years before, the Allies were now disengaging themselves from Russia and were lifting the economic blockade, and Soviet Russia had now firmly established itself as a viable state and was actively seeking recognition by other states. The Bolsheviks military victory had eliminated any possibility of Soviet contact with Xinjiang being interrupted by the White Russians. In China, the first Karakhan Manifesto was to be received officially by the Foreign Ministry for the first time on March 26, which would make the Chinese Government at Beijing more readily responsive to any Soviet *démarche*.

There was one more reason which made negotiations in Xinjiang with the Soviet representatives not only necessary but also imperative: the revision of provisions concerning Xinjiang in the Sino-Russian Treaty signed at St. Petersburg on February 2, 1881. The Treaty granted duty-free privileges to all imports from Russia through the land frontier into China via Xinjiang on an experimental basis, i.e. until such time as increased trade warranted a levy by China. It was to be reviewed every ten years and China was to propose any revision six months in advance.[60] In the first three successive decades, however, the Tsarist Government had successfully blocked the Chinese attempt to effect any revision.[61] Now the fourth decade was coming to an end in February 1921. On December 3, 1919, Yang urged the Foreign Ministry:

> We lost a number of sovereign rights in the 1881 Sino-Russian Treaty. Of these, the duty-free privileges granted [to the Russians] were particularly harmful ... The ten-year period had passed three times and we could not effect any revision because the Russians were so coercive. Next year is the end of another ten-year period. I sincerely hope that the Foreign Ministry will get prepared in advance and propose revision to the Russian Minister (especially that of the duty-free provision) in time so as not to miss again the opportunity for another ten years.[62]

At approximately the same time, the Ministry of Agriculture and Commerce and the Beijing and Shanghai Chambers of Commerce also sent their propositions to the Foreign Ministry, urging them to propose to the Russians the intended revision of the 1881 Treaty.[63] The Foreign

Ministry felt, however, that the situation in Russia was such that China was yet to find a legal Russian government to negotiate with.[64]

The *démarche* made by the Soviets in late January and February to the Xinjiang authorities for talks on reopening trade along the borders and repatriation of White Russian soldiers and Russian refugees in Xinjiang provided an opportunity to bypass the vexing question of the Russian negotiating authorities. In late March 1920, the Sino-Soviet talks between the Yili authorities and the Turkestan Soviet Republic on the above-mentioned questions were well under way in Horgos.[65] While these talks were taking place, Yang made fresh efforts to suggest explicitly to the Foreign Ministry that

> The old Russian Government has now been wiped out and the Bolsheviks have repeatedly approached the Xinjiang authorities for establishing trade relations. We may as well take this opportunity to send officials to the Russian provinces of Tashkent, Qihe and Xiemi to negotiate with the Soviets for the abolition of the Russian tariff privileges and for a new tariff. If this can be done, we may recover some lost rights ... If not, it would also give us room for manoeuvring when in the future the Foreign Ministry is negotiating a revision of the Treaty.[66]

Yang also had his own reasons to regard the matter as urgent, as he frankly admitted later that,

> if we do not take advantage of the situation then to abrogate the duty-free provisions in the old treaty, it is very hard to say whether the Russians would give in to our demands when Russia is again unified and strong.[67]

The sanction from the Foreign Ministry of Yang's propositions above could not have been more encouraging. On May 2, Yang was given a go-ahead for his rights-recovery proposal and, more specifically, he was told that, because the Bolsheviks believed in equality among nations, he was

> to take the opportunity to negotiate [with the Soviets] for the application to all the Russian imports of the general tariff promulgated in December 1917.[68]

There were clear indications in the above-quoted instruction that the Foreign Ministry was encouraged by the Karakhan Manifesto, which they had officially received not long before, and that China intended to strip Russia of its treaty Power status and to treat Soviet Russia as a non-treaty country.

In May, at the Sino-Soviet talks in Yili, the Chinese side turned its attention from questions such as the repatriation of White Russian soldiers in Xinjiang and the protection of the Chinese nationals in Russia to questions of its tariff autonomy. On May 3, the Foreign Ministry message was transmitted to Xu Guozeng, the Intendant of Yili, who was negotiating with the Soviets.[69] On May 18, Yang was more specific in his instructions to Xu. At the Yili talks, China would insist on two demands which were for China matters of rights recovery. First, any trade agreement between the two nations should be based on equality and justice, which meant that Russia's unilateral privilege on tariff exemption secured by the Imperial Russian Government in the 1881 treaty should be abolished. Second, it followed that, after the abolition of Russia's privilege on tariff exemption, taxes would be levied on the Russian goods imported into Xinjiang. This would be done in accordance with the Xinjiang Combined Tax Regulations before the two national governments concluded a formal agreement on the matter.[70]

Concurrently, in Beijing, there were some developments favourable to Yang's *démarche* to the Soviets. On May 20, the Senate approved a motion proposed on May 13 by Senator Wang Xuezeng on the revision of the Sino-Russian 1881 Treaty.[71] Moreover the Chinese Government seemed to have been prompted to consider seriously the prospect of negotiating with the Soviet Government in Moscow. The President wrote to the Cabinet in mid-May that, according to Reuter, there was ample evidence that Britain, France and Italy were negotiating through their diplomatic representatives with the Soviets for the reopening of trade with Russia, and that the League of Nations was also dispatching its officials to Russia. As China's policy towards Soviet Russia was to act in concert with the Allies and that Britain and other Powers were negotiating with the Bolsheviks, the Cabinet should now

> instruct the Chinese diplomatic representatives in Denmark to enter into talks with the Soviet officials there for re-establishing trade relations and for the protection of the Chinese residents in Russia. On the other hand, the Cabinet should instruct the Foreign Ministry and the frontier defence authorities to prepare proposals as to how to conclude treaties with Russia in the future, which old treaties were to be abrogated, which to remain, and what new treaties to be concluded; or alternatively, whether we should take the Soviet

Government note [the Karakhan Manifesto] as the basis for negotiation and prepare ourselves for opening talks.[72]

On May 24, 25 and 26, full approval of Yang's action in tariff matters in Xinjiang was expressed by the Presidential Secretariat, the Cabinet, the Foreign Ministry and the Frontier Defence Bureau.[73]

In Xinjiang, the Chinese demands on tariff autonomy, when raised, seemed to have been readily met by the Soviets.[74] The Yili Protocol was signed on May 27, 1920 at Yining. Of all the provisions, there were two which were of historical significance to China. Article 3 provided that

The Russian organization for commercial and foreign affairs and common Russian nationals, transporting merchandise from Russia to Ili [Yili] or transporting merchandise from Ili [Yili] to Russia, must alike pay duty to the customs offices of China in accordance with the Sinkiang [Xinjiang] Combined Tax Regulations.

Article 5 stipulated:

In case of disputes arising out of trade between the nationals of the two parties and in all civil and criminal cases, the matters will uniformly be decided and disposed of in accordance with the law of the country in which they reside.[75]

These two articles at once regained for China its tariff autonomy and its full jurisdiction in Xinjiang. This was another treaty through which China had secured restoration of its lost rights in an agreement with a foreign nation. The two provisions practically brought to an end the Russian tariff privilege and consular jurisdiction in Xinjiang four years before the Soviet Union formally relinquished in 1924 all special rights and privileges acquired by the Tsarist Government in China. Yang in his report to Beijing hailed the Protocol as 'internationally a rare achievement' because China had thus recovered its tariff autonomy and abolished the Russian consular jurisdiction in Xinjiang.[76] He was certainly right. Early in June, the Cabinet approved the Yili Protocol[77] and on July 1, the Yili Customs Office came into operation.[78] In the following four years, before the Sino-Soviet Friendship Treaty was signed in 1924, during which Sino-Soviet relations were kept in suspension, the Yili Protocol remained operative.

Three salient features made the Xinjiang case radically distinct from the Outer Mongolia and Manchuria cases. First, China's efforts to assert its sovereignty were directed at the destruction of the basis of the treaty power structure: conventional tariff and extraterritoriality.

Secondly, China's reassertion of its sovereignty was embodied in an agreement properly negotiated with an effective authority. Thirdly, it was with the revolutionary regime of Soviet Russia that China had negotiated and entered into this agreement. It was little wonder that, in Beijing, the Xinjiang agreement with the Soviets caused considerable anxiety within the foreign diplomatic community. Both the British Minister Alston and the French Minister Boppe made immediate inquiries on June 3 in the Foreign Ministry to ascertain the truth and content of the agreement.[79]

A SPECIAL MISSION

On June 20, 1920, in the remote Mongolian border town of Kiakhta, two missions, one Russian and one Chinese, encountered each other.[80] The Yurin mission was on its way to Beijing, seeking the formal recognition by China of the newly established Far Eastern Republic. The Chinese mission headed by General Zhang Silin was dispatched by Beijing, ostensibly to 'console the Chinese nationals' suffering in the Russian civil war, but actually 'to study the situation [in Russia]' and 'to get into informal contact, when opportunity arises, with both the Soviet Government and the Government of the Far Eastern Republic'.[81] By September, both missions had reached the capital of their designated nation. In September and October, when Yurin was cold-shouldered in Beijing, Zhang was meeting Chicherin and Karakhan in the Narkomindel in Moscow. The second Karakhan Manifesto was formally addressed to 'Lieutenant General Zhang Silin, head of the Chinese Military Delegation' on September 27. Zhang was even received by Lenin on November 2 before he left Moscow for Beijing.[82]

Historians seem to have rather cold-shouldered the Zhang Silin mission. While the Yurin mission has been subjected to detailed studies in almost every scholarly work on the Sino-Soviet relations in this initial period, the Zhang Silin mission remains an unrevealed chapter, receiving little more than a casual mention, if any at all.[83] Yet the Zhang mission, with its apparent success, merits more intense attention, particularly in the context of China's post-war efforts to assert itself in the reconstruction of the international system. What was the Zhang Silin mission? How and why was it dispatched? What authority did it have in approaching the Soviet Government? What did it do in Moscow and what did it accomplish? Answers to these questions would indicate the position which the Mission occupied in the overall puzzle of China's initiatives to tear apart the structure of the Russian treaty rights and interests in China.

As has been noted previously, China's Russian policy seemed to have been undergoing a review at the end of 1919 and the beginning of 1920. There were a number of reasons for China to have this policy review at this particular moment. First and foremost were the Bolshevik military victory in Siberia and the changing policies of the Allied Powers towards the Soviets. These changes consequently held out an implicit prospect for China to face the Bolsheviks on its own along its long and vulnerable frontier. Hovering on the horizon, there was also a danger of Japanese aggression and a possibility of a Soviet–Japanese *rapprochement* following the Allied withdrawal.[84] Moreover it must be remembered that the Chinese Government had all along regarded the chaotic situation across its northern borders as a good opportunity to at least initiate a demand for the revision of the existing treaties with Russia[85] and that the Bolshevik offer of July 1919 in the form of Chicherin's address to the Fifth Congress of the Soviets was known to the Chinese Government, though not officially received by the latter.[86] Not insignificantly, the rising Chinese nationalism after the May Fourth Movement had also made itself felt in China's official attempt at rights recovery. Now that constraints were released as the Powers were talking with the Soviets, the Cabinet meeting in mid-December 1919 readily decided to 'act in concert with the Allies', i.e. to enter into intercourse with the Bolsheviks.[87]

In early 1920, contact with the Bolsheviks was going on in Xinjiang and in Vladivostok;[88] and in Copenhagen, Cao Yunxiang, the Chinese Legation secretary, opened talks with the Soviet representative Maxim Litvinov.[89] A series of events in the Spring of 1920, however, moved China towards more direct and closer contact with the Soviet Government. On March 26, the Chinese Government officially received the first Karakhan Manifesto and its authenticity was soon after confirmed.[90] On April 6, the Far Eastern Republic was declared established. On April 11, the All-China Student Association published a circular telegram, advocating the establishment of diplomatic relations with Soviet Russia. On April 30, the Chinese Government began to pull back its troops in Siberia. On May 18, the President proposed to the Cabinet that China 'should prepare itself to open with the Soviet Government negotiations based on the proposals in the Soviet Government [Karakhan] Manifesto'.[91]

However Beijing's freedom of action in its Russian policy was still rather limited. First, the declared policy of the Chinese Government towards Russia was 'to act in concert with the Allies'. Though many Allied governments had made contacts with the Soviet authorities, they were centred on matters such as the exchange of prisoners of war and trade relations. Likewise China had to refrain from entering into any 'political' relations with Soviet Russia.[92] Secondly, China still officially recognized the Kudachev mission which had also the support of foreign diplomatic community in China. Any open diplomatic overture from China towards Soviet Russia would bring about international complications. Thirdly, the Chinese Government had practically no direct knowledge of the Bolshevik regime in Moscow after direct official contact had been disrupted more than two years before.[93] Even after they had received the first Karakhan Manifesto, they were still not sure of their own ground and of the intent of the Soviet Government. China wanted to explore further the opportunities created by the Bolshevik military victory and the Karakhan Manifesto for its rights recovery, yet it could not afford to do this by entering formal diplomatic negotiations independent of its Allies. The best solution of this dilemma seemed to be the despatch of an unofficial mission to Russia to investigate the situation there and to get into informal contact with the Soviet Government. The Zhang Silin mission was then launched in June.

According to Zhang's own account, the Cabinet had decided as early as January 1920 to send officials to approach informally the Bolsheviks who were winning an overwhelming victory in Russia. He was then in Beijing reporting to the Frontier Defence Bureau and was ordered to go to Russia immediately to enter into informal talks with the Soviet Government. He was delayed, however, in Harbin when he was re-ordered to assist General Bao Guiqing in dealing with the CER general strike breaking out in March and with the dismissal of General Horvath from his CER post. In May, he returned to Beijing to report on his work at CER and urged upon the Frontier Defence Bureau that the Karakhan Manifesto by the Soviet Government had provided the best opportunity to recover China's lost sovereign rights. He was then ordered again by the Frontier Defence Bureau to go to Russia and get in touch with the Soviets in the name of China's military representative and to console the Chinese nationals in Irkutsk. On his way to the border town of Manzhouli he received several telegrams from the Frontier Defence Bureau which was instructed by the President to order him to investigate the principles and conditions of the Far Eastern Republic and to get into direct contact with that government when appropriate.[94]

The choice of Lieutenant General Zhang Silin as China's special envoy was probably only natural. He had been appointed on April 5, 1919 as China's military representative in Russia to observe the situation of Kolchak's Omsk government.[95] His despatch, therefore, was unlikely to excite suspicions from the Allies and could avoid harassment from the White Russians, particularly the Semenov forces, still active in Chita and some other areas of Siberia. Diplomatically, it would be easier for the Foreign Ministry to deal with representations from other Allies. More important, Zhang had connections with the Bolsheviks in Harbin[96] and was reported to have sympathy with the Bolsheviks.[97] This would enable him to cultivate the goodwill from the Soviet side on his official mission, bearing no government credentials.[98] Moreover Zhang was educated in Japan and enjoyed the complete trust of the military authorities and the Government which were both controlled by the Anfu Clique at the time.[99] This, however, proved rather costly for him and his mission when the Government under the control of the Anfu Clique collapsed later in July.

On June 27, Zhang reached Verkhne Udinsk, the capital of the Far Eastern Republic. Before then, he had already cabled both the Far Eastern Republic and the Soviet governments, 'making clear my mission to them'.[100] At Verkhne Udinsk, Zhang met Chevony, Foreign Minister of the Far Eastern Republic, and other important officials on several occasions in July and told the latter that he was sent on a special mission to enter secretly into informal talks with both the Verkhne Udinsk government and the Moscow government on questions of mutual concern and of mutual relations.[101] The Verkhne Udinsk government seemed to have reacted with guarded enthusiasm and at first withheld at Irkutsk Zhang's cipher telegrams to Beijing. There was the question of Zhang's credentials, as Zhang reported that 'the Verkhne Udinsk government can not formally recognize my mission, as our Foreign Ministry has not consulted with them about it in advance'.[102] The suspicion of the Verkhne Udinsk government was deepened when Yurin reported from Kiakhta that a Chinese Foreign Ministry official, Niu Binwen, denied in a talk with him in early July that Zhang had any other special mission except to console and to send relief to the Chinese nationals at Irkutsk.[103] For all this, Zhang was delayed at Verkhne Udinsk for about a month, trying to clarify the situation with Beijing and to dispel the suspicions of the government of the Far Eastern Republic. He seemed to have succeeded in both by late July.[104]

Meanwhile Moscow had shown great interest in Zhang's mission and had instructed the Verkhne Udinsk government to send Zhang west to Moscow. Zhang was told then that

> The Far Eastern Republic, though an independent nation, had to take orders from the Soviet Government on questions of international significance, as it has to follow the same policy as that of the Soviet Government. Moscow has by now sent here seven telegrams, inquiring as to the whereabouts of the representative and reasons for the delay and instructing us to urge you to proceed on your journey to Moscow.[105]

He was also advised at the same time by the Commander-in-Chief of the Far Eastern Republic that the Verkhne Udinsk government was incapable of dealing with the questions he had raised concerning mutual relations and, that he had better go to Moscow to talk with the Soviet Government there for their solution.[106]

On July 22, Zhang met Chevony again and asked the latter about the Verkhne Udinsk government's stand on the Soviet offers in the Karakhan Manifesto. He was told that the Verkhne Udinsk government saw eye to eye with Moscow on the matter. The Far Eastern Republic was especially pleased that China had sent its special envoy to Verkhne Udinsk. Zhang was also told that Moscow had instructed Chevony to entertain Zhang as best he could and Chevony's ministry would send a secretary to accompany Zhang on his westward journey.[107] Zhang suggested, while reporting to Beijing the situation described above, that

> The Government of the Far Eastern Republic today is so incapable that the real power is transferring. The Soviet government, which has total control of the Russian Far East, is virtually what concerns us most. There will not be any solution of the problems concerning the Chinese nationals residing in Russia unless I go west [to Moscow] to make representations. Moreover, we had better take this opportunity to enter into contact and to have mutual consultations [with the Soviet Government] as early as possible so as to be prepared for concluding a treaty in the future. The recovery of our lost sovereign rights depends on this move.[108]

In the same telegram, Zhang asked to be given full written credentials so that he could pursue his mission in Moscow smoothly.[109] Zhang's suggestion was sanctioned by the Frontier Defence Bureau.[110] He was instructed that

Since the Soviet Government have shown their readiness to receive you, you must go immediately westward and carry out on-the-spot investigation. You can properly enter into informal contact [with them], if need be and when appropriate, to find out the real situation [in Russia] so that we get prepared to deal with it.

The matter of his credentials was referred to the Ministry of War and in turn to the Foreign Ministry.[111]

There is little record in the Chinese archives we have seen about Zhang's journey from Verkhne Udinsk to Moscow. He started his westward journey most probably in early August with Zhu Shaoyang, the Chinese consul at Irkutsk, whom Zhang himself picked up at Verkhne Udinsk.[112] The two of them were said to have arrived in Moscow either at the end of August or at the beginning of September.[113]

By September 18, Zhang had had two talks with Karakhan, one at Karakhan's residence in Moscow and the other in the Narkomindel. Karakhan repeated the Soviet offers to relinquish Russian extra-territorial rights in China and to renounce all Russian treaty privileges in China. He asked Zhang to clarify the purposes of his mission and the questions he would like to discuss. If Zhang had plenary powers, Karakhan said, the Soviet Government would like to enter into negotiations with him for the conclusion of a preliminary treaty so as to restore the friendship between the two countries. The Narkomindel, however, would like to have a confirmation of Zhang's plenary powers from the Chinese Foreign Ministry.[114]

In reporting this back to Beijing, Zhang again asked to be made China's plenipotentiary to Soviet Russia. The Soviet Government, Zhang told Beijing, had consolidated its international position, for Italy, Denmark and other European nations had either accepted its representatives or opened trade with it as a preliminary step for formal recognition. For China,

because the newly-established Soviet Government was bent on restoring mutual friendship and establishing trade relations [with China], it would not hesitate to stoop to all kinds of compromises. We should take advantage of this opportunity to regain our lost sovereign rights.[115]

Zhang went on to ask the Cabinet to consult with the Foreign Ministry and decide whether he could be appointed China's envoy with full powers to 'conclude a friendship treaty as demanded by the Soviets'.[116] He further warned that

> China stands every chance to gain from the Soviet offer to cancel all old Russian treaties. If we refuse [to accept the Soviet offer], not only will we let slip a golden opportunity but the Soviets will think we are too cowardly. Then, they will change their policy. They will make an ally with Mongolia and conclude a treaty with another country[117] to plot against China.[118]

The Cabinet seemed to have taken Zhang's proposals quite seriously. On September 20, it instructed the Foreign Ministry that propositions in Zhang's report were very important and the Foreign Ministry should study them carefully for further decisions.[119]

Zhang was not, however, to be empowered as China's plenipotentiary, but to be recalled by the Foreign Ministry on September 23, as 'his services were required in Peking in connection with certain questions between the Peking and Russian Governments'. This telegram was published in the vernacular press on September 25.[120] The best possible explanation for this unexpected development could be found in the drastic changes in China's warlord politics. General Duan Qirui, the head of the Anfu Clique, had resigned on July 19 after the military defeat of the Anhui Army earlier. The Anfu government accordingly collapsed. As pointed out earlier, Zhang had connections with the Anfu Clique and was initially sent out by, and reported directly to, the Frontier Defence Bureau with Duan Qirui as its director. Though Zhang had been reporting to the Foreign Ministry after the Frontier Defence Bureau was abolished in August, the newly constructed Foreign Ministry with Dr. Yan Huiqing in charge presumably resented having an 'Anfu emissary' in Moscow who was not a Foreign Ministry official and was not sent by them. What was most difficult to explain was that the Foreign Ministry did issue the recall in spite of the fact that Zhang's mission had the blessing of President Xu Shichang and of the Cabinet, which was kept informed of every detail of the mission.

In Moscow, the move to recall Zhang and Zhu produced confusion and alarm. As Zhang reported on October 6, both Chicherin and Karakhan, informed of the recall of the mission, told him that they were rather shocked because the two governments had only recently been able to get into direct contact through Zhang and they were expecting to talk with him on many important matters concerning bilateral relations. They urged Zhang to stay and said they would hand him an important manifesto[121] for him to transmit to Beijing. Zhang advised Beijing that the Soviet Government felt honoured that of all the nations, China was the first to send its representative to Moscow and reassured him that, the Soviet Government would renounce all old Russian treaties. China should follow the situation closely so as not to lose any opportunity because of temporary separation between China and Russia and consequent misunderstandings. He further stated that

> it is fortunate that since I came here, I have received warm welcome from many important people of the Government and they desire to establish relations [with China]. If I suddenly leave [for Beijing] with the mission, not only will it hurt the international feelings between the two nations, but all our previous efforts will be wasted and it will be difficult for us to make this achievement in the future, even if we desire to.[122]

Without any explanation from the record in the Chinese archives, it remains a mystery how the Foreign Ministry changed its mind a few days later. Between October 6 and 9, Zhang received a telegram in Moscow from the Foreign Ministry, instructing him to stay on for talks with the Soviet government until he finished his mission. Zhang reported that when he broke the news, the Narkomindel was pleased and thankful that, the Chinese Government had shown the sincerity of its desire to restore good relations with Russia.[123] Meanwhile Zhang and Zhu had translated into Chinese the second Karakhan Manifesto which they received on October 2 and sent it back to Beijing.[124]

By this time, China had made a unilateral decision to withdraw its recognition of the Tsarist Minister Prince Kudachev and was encountering tremendous pressure from the Allies not to violate the Russian treaty rights. Beijing did not, indeed could not, respond readily to the second Karakhan Manifesto and Zhang did not receive from the Foreign Ministry any comments on the Manifesto about which he could make representations to the Soviet government.[125] Zhang's remaining days in Moscow were, as he wrote, 'busy talking with government officials of various ministries'.[126]

By the end of October, Zhang seemed to have finished his business in Moscow. On October 31, the Narkomindel held a formal farewell party for him, and Chicherin made a speech, emphasizing the similarity in the situation and the external problems the two countries were faced with. On November 2, Lenin received Zhang.[127] Zhang's mission was completed when, on November 28, 1920, he arrived back in Beijing with the original copy of the second Karakhan Manifesto.

There have been a number of haunting questions about Zhang's mission. Was General Zhang merely 'an emissary of the dispossessed Anfu government' sent out by Duan Qirui?[128] Or did Zhang go to Moscow without authorization, as the Foreign Ministry claimed?[129] Was Zhang's mission only a 'scouting body' without any political significance?[130] Or was it a Military–Diplomatic Mission 'charged with the task of negotiating with the Commissariat of Foreign Affairs'?[131] Evidence from the record in the archives disputes rather than proves all the assertions implicit in these questions.

It must be remembered that, by virtue of its common borders and historical relations with Russia, China had a great stake in its future relations with Russia. It had followed closely the changing policies of the Allies towards Soviet Russia ever since the Russian Revolution, particularly after 1919, and had shown great anxiety lest it should 'fall behind in [its] diplomacy' towards the Soviets.[132] Beijing's Russian policy review at the end of 1919, coupled with the Soviet offers in the Karakhan Manifesto, had further pushed China to adopt a 'multi-dimensional diplomacy'[133] and a flexible policy towards Soviet Russia.

As indicated above, Zhang was initially dispatched by the Frontier Defence Bureau headed by Duan. Perhaps the Foreign Ministry was bypassed.[134] But this could not and should not make him an 'Anfu emissary'. The dispatch had been decided by the Cabinet and had the blessing of the President. The Mission had the full approval of the Government. Moreover, after the collapse of the government controlled by the Anfu Clique and the abolition of the Frontier Defence Bureau in August, Zhang had been reporting directly to and was instructed by the new Cabinet and the reorganized Foreign Ministry. Secondly, Zhang did have explicit authorization from the Frontier Defence Bureau to go westward to Moscow. The President, the Cabinet and the Foreign Ministry were all duly informed of the authorization. While in Moscow, he was authorized in early October, when the Foreign Ministry seemed to have second thoughts on its earlier decision to recall the mission, to stay on for informal contact with the Soviet Government. Zhang himself later defended his action vigorously, arguing:

My mission was at first ordered by the Frontier Defence Bureau. Later, I have been sending telegraphic reports [to the Government] on my journey and have received no word of disapproval [of the mission]. It is therefore clear that I am not taking unauthorized action. How could I treat such important state affairs as a trifling matter?[135]

Thirdly, whereas to investigate the situation in Russia was one of its purposes, Zhang's mission was much more than a 'scouting body'. Under instruction, it had made informal approaches to both the Verkhne Udinsk Government and the Soviet Government to sound out their attitudes towards the abolition of all old Russian treaties and the establishment of full diplomatic relations on the basis of mutual equality and reciprocity. Yet Zhang did not head an official Chinese 'Military–Diplomatic Mission' as the Soviets had hoped and was never, even when this was demanded by the Soviets in Moscow, delegated with plenary powers to negotiate with the Soviet Government for re-establishing normal relations.

This is probably just what had made Zhang's mission special: the way in which it had been dispatched, how it had approached the Soviet Government, and how it served as a direct communication channel between Beijing and Moscow. It was an officially approved and dispatched unofficial diplomatic feeler sent off in the first instance by the military authorities which seemed to have greater say in Sino-Russian relations concerning China's northern frontier defence. Launched after the Chinese Government had received the first Karakhan Manifesto in March, 1920, it was to explore further the revolutionary situation in Russia for the total denunciation of old Russian treaties with China. The fact that the mission was entrusted to approach the Soviet Government informally and that it had all the way received broad instructions from the Chinese Government had enabled Zhang to take some initiatives in his own hands. While in Moscow, he had exercised his power so extensively as to be very close to exceeding it. Zhang was not, however, China's plenipotentiary to Moscow and was only authorized to have informal intercourse with the Soviet Government.

Nevertheless Zhang's mission had accomplished what could be regarded almost as 'unaccomplishable' in 1920. Its frequent reports to Beijing from Russia had acquainted the Chinese Government with the situation in the Far Eastern Republic and Soviet Russia by providing them with much needed information. It had also provided a direct contact between Beijing and Moscow. In particular, by his personal contact with Chicherin and Karakhan in the Narkomindel, Zhang had successfully established a channel through which the Soviet policies towards China could be transmitted directly to Beijing. It was only because the Karakhan Manifestoes were exciting too much international concern that Beijing did not take any advantage of the opportunities.

In spite of all the controversies around the Zhang mission at the time and ever since, the launch of the mission was a Chinese initiative pure and simple to cash in on the situation in Russia in an attempt to make a break in the structure of treaty Powers *vis-à-vis* China. It is a clear indication that the Chinese Government had seen in the Russian Revolution the opportunity which it intended to take for recovery of China's lost sovereign rights from Russia. It constituted the first independent approach Beijing made to the Soviet Government in Moscow. If the Soviet revolutionary diplomacy could be said to be 'self-denial',[136] the Chinese certainly showed their readiness to cultivate the Soviet 'denial' to fulfil its nationalistic aims for rights recovery from Russia.

THE BREAK

Commenting on changes in Sino-Russian relations in 1920, Alston observed:

> Faced with innumerable and urgent problems along her long and undefined Russian frontier, China is forced to stave off complications as best she may by unofficial missions and pourparlers, but it is unlikely that she will enter into serious negotiations until the anxiously awaited lead has been given her by one of the powers.[137]

If this observation by the British Minister was an accurate description of China's approaches to Soviet Russia, it certainly could not be used to describe what he did not mention here: China's bold decision to withdraw its recognition of the Tsarist Russian diplomatic mission in Beijing. China made this long-awaited move in September 1920, in spite of the anticipated foreign complications, mostly from its closest Allies, and without awaiting any lead from any one of them.

The Foreign Ministry had long regarded the position of the Russian Legation in Beijing headed by Prince Kudachev as 'anomalous and embarrassing'.[138] It was anomalous because it represented a government which no longer existed and could not discharge its responsibilities as a resident diplomatic mission. China's recognition of Kerensky's Provisional Russian Government established in March 1917 had already cast a doubt on Kudachev's creditability as the Russian envoy accredited to China. After the Bolshevik October Revolution, Trotsky, in the capacity of Commissar for Foreign Affairs, had twice called on Kudachev, on November 30 and December 17, either to support the Bolshevik government or to resign.[139] On January 18, 1918, the Chinese Legation in Petrograd was also formally informed by Polivanov, a deputy Commissar of the Narkomindel, that the Soviet Government did not recognize Kudachev's mission in Beijing.[140] China, however, continued to accord full diplomatic recognition to Kudachev as part of the Allied policy of withholding their recognition of the revolutionary regime of Soviet Russia. It was embarrassing because, while the Kudachev mission could not discharge most of its responsibilities, it acted as the watchful guardian of Tsarist interests in China and had raised protests directly or through the Diplomatic Corps in Beijing against whatever Chinese Government acts it considered prejudicial to the Russian treaty rights and privileges in China.[141] It constituted a standing obstacle to China's attempts to recover its sovereign rights by steadily undermining the treaty structure on which the Russian rights depended and to profit by political changes in Russia so as to put Sino-Russian relations on a new footing.

As early as January 1919, a British diplomat in Kashgar observed that the Chinese were becoming less and less accommodating to the Russian consul there.[142] China's changing attitude towards the Tsarist mission in Beijing was recorded by Prince Kudachev himself in May 1919. The Chinese Government

> has lately changed its attitude toward the Russian Legation in Pekin and has exposed certain intentions to restrict its rights. Such intentions on the part of China is [sic] caused by the desire to free itself from obligations existing under treaties with Russia and to hinder the activities of the Russian Legation aiming to guard the Russian interests.[143]

The observation by the Russian Minister might partly refer to an interview which the French Minister, Boppe, had with the Acting Foreign Minister, Chen Lu on April 14. Asked about the status of the Russian treaties with China, Chen explicitly told Boppe that, because of internal disorder and anarchical conditions in Russia, the Russian treaties with China should be regarded as having been annulled. The Chinese Government would not, therefore, be bound by the previous treaties with Tsarist Russia.[144]

The changes in the attitude of the Chinese Government were gradually crystallized after its Russian policy review at the end of 1919. In the second half of January 1920, the Cabinet and the Foreign Ministry were instructed by President Xu Shichang to study carefully the memorandum on the Russian questions presented by Lenox

Simpson, one of the foreign advisers to the Chinese President. At the Cabinet meeting of February 26, 1920, six proposals in Simpson's memorandum were all in principle accepted, including the repudiation of the Tsarist diplomatic representatives in China and the suspension of payment of the Boxer Indemnity to Russia.[145] Nevertheless no immediate actions were taken to carry out the accepted proposals. The Chinese Government seemed to be only treading its way to the implementation of the agreed lines of policy. In early April 1920, the Foreign Ministry refused to accept an official note presented by Prince Kudachev protesting against the Chinese reception of the First Karakhan Manifesto, insisting that the Chinese Government could only accept Prince Kudachev's correspondence addressed in his private capacity.[146] In May, it advised the Finance Ministry on the matter of levying taxes on Russian imports via the north Manchurian borders, maintaining that

At present, the Bolsheviks have expanded their influences far and wide and the old regime has been swept away. All the treaties with Tsarist Russia can be regarded as having lapsed of themselves. The present Russian Minister in Beijing was commanded by the old regime and has no real power now. There is no need to make representations to him on the matter.[147]

On July 2, the Foreign Ministry addressed an identical note to the Russian Legation and all other Allied Legations in Beijing, informing them that

The Chinese Government now finds, upon consideration of the disturbed conditions in Russia, that there is no justification for any further payments of indemnity money and the Cabinet have decided that such payments be discontinued as from July.[148]

In vain, the French and the Japanese Ministers made representations to the Chinese Government to the effect that they hoped that payment would not be stopped, as there was no material difference between the Russian situation now and in the summer of 1918 when the Chinese Government agreed to continue the payment.[149] The British did not take any action, though Curzon later confirmed that Britain was also in favour of continued payment.[150]

The suspension of payment of the Boxer Indemnity was a prelude to the final withdrawal of China's recognition of the Old Russian diplomatic mission. It deprived the Tsarist diplomatic and consular establishments in China as well as in East Asia of the financial source which had paid their maintenance ever since the downfall of the Tsar in March 1917.[151] It also seemed to have served as a test case of the Powers' endurance of China's unilateral action in its Russian policy. The new Cabinet and the reorganized Foreign Ministry after the Anfu–Zhili War[152] in July continued implementing China's Russian policy. The differences were that the new administration seemed to be more determined and less restrained. This resulted rather from the changing internal and international situations favourable to the Bolsheviks in Russia than from the changes of the Cabinets as a result of warlord politics in China. There is little evidence to sustain the assertion that 'there was a volte-face on the part of China on its Soviet Russia policy in July 1920, after the downfall of the Anfu Club'.[153]

From late August, with Yurin on his way to Beijing, the reorganized Foreign Ministry stepped up its implementation of China's policy towards the Tsarist diplomatic mission in China. In August and September, the question of the status of the Kudachev mission in Beijing was given top priority in the Foreign Ministry. On August 19, the Ministry inquired of the Chinese ministers in the Allied countries about the official attitudes of their resident nations towards the Tsarist diplomatic representatives.[154] On August 24, Dr. Yan Huiqing, at his first meeting with Prince Kudachev after he was appointed Foreign Minister, intimated to the latter that the Chinese Government would desire his voluntary resignation as the Russian Minister in Beijing. Yan told Kudachev that the anomaly of his status and the Russian mission was not only an embarrassment to himself but also had caused difficulties for the Chinese Government in dealing with daily Sino-Russian intercourse.[155]

Meanwhile, in the Foreign Ministry, it was the question of how to, rather than whether or not to, proceed to bring to an end China's relations with Kudachev and the Russian consular jurisdiction in China that was the principal subject of both the sixth meeting of the Committee for the Study of Russian Treaties on August 24 and a meeting of councillors and department heads on August 30, 1920. The prevailing mood was one of determination and caution. China's policy was to draw close to the Bolsheviks while at the same time estranging itself from the Monarchists and White Russians. There was an urgent need for a basic solution of the anomalous status of the Russian diplomats and consular officials in China. Of the first importance, Russian consular jurisdiction must be stopped, if not legally abrogated. China's professed policy was still, however, to act in concert with the

Allies in regard to the Russian questions. Actively breaking relations with the Russian Legation was likely to evoke Allied opposition and to lead to international misunderstandings. Moreover, either to stop or to abrogate the Russian consular jurisdiction, China had to be prepared to deal with its impact upon other treaty Powers and with the enormous task of administering justice to a large number of Russian residents in China. If the Kudachev mission could not die a natural death, the Chinese Government had to find a way in between continued recognition and complete break so as to effect 'a *de facto* discontinuation of relations without giving the impression that anything has changed'.[156] The consensus reached was to start the process of withdrawing China's recognition by making representations to Kudachev on the Kalmykov case.[157] Kudachev should be advised that the Chinese Government believed that he had abused its goodwill and felt that it had to stop conducting any official affairs with him and his consuls because they had been long since incapable of dealing with problems arising out of Sino-Russian intercourse.[158]

This consensus was incorporated into the Foreign Ministry proposition on the treatment of Russian diplomatic representatives in China presented to the Cabinet on September 2. The break with Kudachev, it suggested, should be carried out 'step by step'. As the first step, the representations on the Kalmykov case should make it clear to Prince Kudachev that it was out of the goodwill of the Chinese Government that he and his legation and consular establishments in China were still recognized. Now that he and his consular officials had abused this goodwill and were unable to function properly, the Chinese Government had to stop any official transactions with the Russian Legation. On the other hand, provincial military and civil governors should be addressed by a circular telegram to the effect that, since the Russian consuls were no longer capable of fulfilling their functions and had occasionally committed actions inappropriate to their position, the local authorities could from then on take into their own hands the handling of problems concerning Sino-Russian intercourse. They must, however, report to the Foreign Ministry about their handling. The Foreign Ministry document further suggested that, if the first step encountered no difficulties, China could proceed to announce officially its break with the Russian Legation. Great care should be taken, it was advised, to assure the Allied Powers that China's neutrality in the Russian civil war and its common policy with the Allies towards the Bolsheviks remained unchanged. As for the Russian consular jurisdiction, the document stated that China 'naturally could not allow it to continue' after the Russian consuls were deprived of their status, and that the Ministry of Justice should take over the matter.[159]

Meanwhile, encouraged by the reports from the Chinese Legations residing in the Allied countries which confirmed no uniformity of the Powers' treatment of the Tsarist diplomats,[160] the Foreign Ministry had sent off, on September 1, telegrams to military governors of China's border areas with Russia, the Manchurian provinces and Xinjiang, to enlist their support for its proposed move.[161] The prompt replies were all in favour of the move.[162] The Foreign Ministry felt doubly assured when the Cabinet readily approved its plan.

On September 7, the Russian Legation was first denied the right to communicate by cypher with its consulates when a cypher telegram Kudachev addressed to the Russian consul in Harbin was returned to him. On his requesting explanations, Kudachev was summoned to Dr. Yen's private residence on September 8 and advised that the Chinese Government considered that the Russian Legation in Beijing and the Russian consuls in China had lost their status and, therefore, could no longer be allowed exchange of cypher telegrams between Russian officials in China. The Chinese Government expected that Kudachev would resign voluntarily and the Russian diplomatic institutions would be closed forthwith at his initiative.[163] Meanwhile the Chinese Government intimated to the Allied Ministers in Beijing its forthcoming decision to withdraw recognition of Kudachev and his consuls.[164]

The Russian Minister refused to resign of his own accord, arguing that his recognition did not depend on his own desire but on the Chinese Government.[165] Two weeks elapsed before the Foreign Ministry submitted its request on September 23 that a Presidential Mandate be publicly issued to suspend the recognition of the Russian Legation and consulates now functioning in China.[166] That request was immediately accorded and a Presidential Mandate was published on the same day.[167]

The official break with Imperial Russia, one of the original treaty Powers, marked the culmination of China's efforts to assault Russia's treaty rights and interests in China. The last paragraph of the Presidential Mandate read

> In the matter of the Russian concessions, the land utilized by the Chinese Eastern Railway, the Russian citizens residing in different parts of China, and all subjects connected therewith, the ministries

controlling these matters and the high provincial authorities are instructed to devise and execute appropriate measures.[168]

Couched in general and vague terms, it showed, nevertheless, China's intention and determination to take into its own hands Russia's privileges and interests in China, including the Russian extraterritoriality and concessions.

The provincial authorities were clearly and instantly instructed to take over the Russian consulates and the functions of the Russian consuls and put the provincial commissioners of foreign affairs in charge of those responsibilities. It followed that the Russian consular jurisdiction was to be abrogated forthwith and that Russian residents would be subject to Chinese laws and regulations henceforth. The Ministry of Justice was to devise a *modus vivendi* to govern the trials involving Russians in the Chinese courts which were to hear all Sino-Russian criminal and civil cases and Russian criminal cases.[169] The Russians, when applying for a passport to travel in the interior of China, would be subject to the procedures controlling the applications from nationals of non-treaty nations.[170] Special instructions were sent to civil governors of Zhili and Hubei Provinces to recover the Russian concessions in Tianjin and Hankou and to military governors of the Manchurian provinces to regain China's administrative rights as well as judicial rights within the CER Zone.[171]

There followed a storm of forceful Chinese actions to carry out the instructions elaborated above. The Russian concession in Tianjin was taken over on September 25 by local authorities with Chinese police and the Chinese national flag was hoisted over the municipal council.[172] In Hankou, a similar but less dramatic transfer of the Russian concession there was effected on September 28. In Harbin, the Chinese authorities had ordered the abolition of the Civil Department of the CER and prohibited any further issue of passports to Russians by September 30.[173] The Russian Consul-General was called upon to surrender by September 30 'all files of cases in Russian courts failing which they [the Chinese authorities] would proceed to seize them by force'. On the morning of October 1, Russian court officials 'were turned out of [the] court building' by a Chinese official 'accompanied by armed and mounted police with a machine-gun'.[174] Wherever the Chinese authorities could reach, the Russian consulate premises were either taken over forcibly, as in the case of Urga and Jilin, or transferred peacefully into the custody of the Chinese local authorities.[175]

To the other treaty Powers, it was not the Chinese breach with Imperial Russia's diplomatic representatives which was disconcerting. Anyway, as Dr. Yan later argued, to deny the Tsarist diplomats recognition as such was the policy which 'was put into effect in the different countries of Europe at a much earlier date'.[176] And the American Secretary of State Colby had to admit that the Chinese Government was 'free to continue or withdraw its recognition of the official status of Russian diplomatic and consular officers'.[177] It was, however, what was to follow and did follow that breach which was not only disconcerting but also threatening. Before the official break by the Presidential Mandate, there was already talk in Beijing of a French proposal of internationalizing the Russian concessions.[178] The American Minister in Beijing, Crane, was instructed by Washington on September 21 to invite the attention of the Chinese Government, in the eventuality of a break with Kudachev, 'not to make use of the present disability of Russia in order to invalidate or impair its own obligations to Russia' and not 'to violate or ignore the treaty rights of the Russian people'.[179] On the very day of the official break, representatives of the five Great Powers, America, Britain, France, Italy and Japan, were meeting in the Legation Quarters to discuss measures available to them to forestall the anticipated Chinese attack on the Russian treaty rights and interests following the break. The French, Italian and Japanese Legations, but not the American and the British, were already in possession of their governments' instruction to propose a joint international commission for the administration in trust of the Russian interests. According to Crane,

> No conclusion reached but French, Italian and Japanese made clear that exclusive Chinese control distasteful to their Governments and urged united and prompt action so that Government might not be faced with accomplished fact of Chinese control.[180]

No united action was possible in a divided house, however. While the French continued to 'agitate for international control',[181] the British were more concerned with their own interests and showed 'no concern about Russian rights and property'.[182] Asked by the French Ambassador in London for British collaboration in Beijing to protect Russian interests, Curzon, however, advised Clive that His Majesty's Government held that 'the disposal of the concessions is a matter for the discretion of the Chinese Government'. Clive should only point out to the Chinese Government that in the event of the concessions being taken over, British interests in them must be safeguarded, and China would be regarded as a trustee for a future recognized Russian Government.[183]

Clive duly communicated this message to the Chinese Government on September 29. He told Yan that the British Government did not reprove recent actions of the Chinese Government. It was bound to watch closely the Chinese actions if only on account of large British interests in Russian concessions and would have the assurance from the Chinese Government that China was acting as the trustee of Russian interests.[184] For the Japanese, decisions on the Russian questions were always based on its overall policy in East Asia. Obata was instructed on September 26 that

> In all your actions regarding consideration of present Russian questions where they concern, directly or indirectly, the interests of France, kindly support the opinion and desires of her representative. By this means we may be able to paralyze American efforts respecting that line.[185]

The ambivalence of America's China policy was again clearly manifest in its actively posing as a guardian of Russian treaty rights and interests in China after the official Chinese break with Imperial Russian diplomatic representatives. At the legations meeting on September 23, Crane, with no definite government instruction, was

> indicating view that, Russia, being helpless, [principal] Allied [and] Associated Governments are interested in seeing that rights and property of Russia in China are not wantonly sacrificed, and suggesting international guardianship.[186]

The next day, Crane personally made the proposal to Foreign Minister Yan and intimated that the international guardianship he proposed would prevent the Japanese from using the opportunity to fulfill its ambition in Siberia and Manchuria. He was, however, instantly rejected.[187] In spite of this, at the beginning of October, the State Department was still considering

> the question of having foreign countries take part in administering the concessions of Russia in various Chinese cities and of exercising judicial power in regard to the interests of Russia in China.[188]

There did seem to be one thing which united all treaty Powers: the fear that China would unilaterally abrogate the Russian extraterritoriality in China. In the words of Secretary of State Colby, 'the Government of China is in special danger of placing itself in a wrong position regarding extraterritorial rights, a matter in which the leading nations all have an interest'.[189] It was true that, as China's action constituted only a suspension of diplomatic relations, it should not, according to principles of international law, affect the treaty status of Russia *vis-à-vis* China. With this, the Chinese themselves agreed.[190] Nevertheless, in September 1920, extraterritoriality had become 'in the eyes of the Chinese, a matter of sovereignty', though 'in the eyes of the Europeans it was still a shield to protect their interests' and a matter of administration of justice.[191] It was plainly the Chinese intention to make use of the occasion to abolish practically, if not theoretically, the Russian extraterritoriality in China at one stroke. The Chinese had now created a situation where they could 'steal' the Russian rights. They had no intention of forgoing it.

The accentuated fear of the treaty Powers was that China's action was directed at dismantling the whole structure of treaty rights, the basis of which was foreign extraterritoriality. From Paris to Washington, this apprehension was expressed publicly in the press and secretly in official documents. A warning was given, on September 27, 1920, in *Le Temps* in Paris that China's break with Imperial Russia would be a forerunner of its unilateral abolition of all foreign extraterritoriality in China.[192] Washington shared the same sentiment. Koo reported that the *Washington Morning Post* stated on October 1 that America could not agree to China's abolition of Russian extraterritorial rights as it was the 'preliminary step' to the total abrogation of foreign extraterritoriality, including the same American rights. It was feared that China's action was instigated by the Bolsheviks against foreigners in China to attack the economic and political system of the capitalistic states.[193] If so, the State Department suggested, the interested Powers might take drastic actions against China. Colby believed that the Chinese Government should be given a serious warning that,

> By merely appearing to be subservient to the influences of the Russian Communists, China would, it is to be feared, lose the friendly regard of such nations, and also give an excuse for aggressions, justified with a show of reason as being necessary to keep the rights of Russia from being confiscated on behalf of the Russian Reds who possibly would try to make use of them as a weapon against the interests and rights of other countries.[194]

When the united action was taken belatedly on October 11, in the form of a note presented by the Dean of the Diplomatic Corps, Chinese control of the Russian interests in China was a *fait accompli*. With the closing-down of all Russian consulates in China, the Russian extraterritoriality also came actually, if not legally, to an end. The note seemed to have acknowledged the fact and asked only the assurance of the Chinese Government that the measures taken in executing the Presidential Mandate

ne sauraient, à aucun titre, constituer une dérogation permanente au régime des droits russes reconnus par traités, mais doivent être considerées seulement comme des mesures prises à titre provisoire et sous réserve du règlement à intervenir avec le prochain Gouvernement Russe reconnu.

Meanwhile, the note proposed

qu'un modus vivendi provisoire, pour l'administration des intérêts russes, soit recherché d'accord entre le Gouvernement Chinois et le Corps Diplomatique.[195]

The Foreign Ministry reply to the Diplomatic Corps on October 22 tried to get across the message that the Chinese Government did not intend to put itself officially and legally outside international law. The measures taken were temporary, it confirmed, subject to agreement with a recognized Russian Government in the future. The Russian concessions, on the other hand, were to be managed with the least possible change by the Chinese Government for the time being as Russia's trustee and the Russians in China would continue to enjoy treaty rights. The Foreign Ministry insisted, however, that the judicial authority of the Russian consuls had to be stopped thenceforth. It conceded only that for the trials in the Chinese courts of cases with Russians as defendants and other nationals plaintiff, Russian laws would be applied so far as they did not contradict Chinese laws and that experts in Russian laws could be employed as advisers to the Chinese courts. On this ground, it flatly rejected the idea of negotiating with the Diplomatic Corps for a *modus vivendi*, but intimated that

If any individual Power's interests in China should be affected as a result of China's withdrawing recognition of the Russian Legation, the Foreign Ministry is always ready to talk with its Minister in Beijing for a proper solution of all problems.[196]

It should be remembered that, from the very beginning, what the Chinese Government strove for in its break with Kudachev was not a *de jure* but a *de facto* abolition of Russian extraterritoriality in China. As early as August 24, the Committee for the Study of Russian Treaties in the Foreign Ministry had already discussed a draft version of *Provisional Regulations Governing the Lawsuits of Russian Residents in China Before Concluding New Treaties with the Future Russian Government*, prepared by the Department of Political Affairs.[197] The Presidential Mandate of September 23 had showed that 'the Chinese are determined to go ahead with the Russians on their own lines'.[198] Now, while the Foreign Ministry was dealing with the representations from the Powers, the President issued Mandates on October 30 and 31 respectively. The former promulgated 'Rules Governing the Administration of Russian Residents in China' and the latter established three grades of Chinese Courts of Procuration having jurisdiction in the CER Zone.[199] For all practical purposes, the Russians in China were reduced to the status of non-treaty nationals, though the Sino-Russian treaties remained in force until 1924.

The actual abrogation of Russian extraterritoriality and the restoration of Russian concessions in China marked the culmination of China's rights recovery efforts in the immediate post-war years. Following China's abolition of German and Austro-Hungarian extraterritorial and other consequential rights by an act of declaration of war, it constituted the second breach in 'the dike of foreign rights in China'.[200] More significant, probably, was that it set a precedent of China's taking unilateral action to abolish foreign rights and privileges in China in disregard of anticipated opposition from the treaty Powers.

By its break with the old regime of Imperial Russia, China also removed an obstacle in its way to approaching the victorious and seemingly generous Bolsheviks. With a sense of freedom of action, Yan held a private interview with Yurin at the end of November. Meantime, informal talks were to follow in the Foreign Ministry between members of the Yurin Mission and the Foreign Ministry officials on preconditions for formal negotiations on restoration of normal relations between China and the Far Eastern Republic.[201] A new vista was to be opened for China to have its impact felt in the reconstruction of the international system in East Asia.

Conclusion

By the end of 1920, China as a peripheral member of the international system seemed to have come a long way towards emerging from its subjection in world politics. Active Chinese diplomacy after the end of the war resulted in cracks of the treaty system in China. Extraterritoriality, the basis of that system, was doomed. Austria formally relinquished its extraterritorial rights in the St. Germain Treaty to which China was a signatory. Germany was to do the same in May 1921 in its treaty with China which also regulated Sino-German relations in other aspects in accordance with principles of equality and reciprocity. *De facto* abrogation of Russian extraterritorial rights was effected by China's withdrawal of its recognition of Russian diplomatic and consulate officials in September 1920. The Russian treaty structure in China had been practically dismantled, only to be legalized in the Sino-Soviet Friendship Treaty in 1924. China had rejected the verdict of the Peace Conference on Jiaozhou and was actively campaigning for its recovery. A number of other initiatives had also been taken by China to put its relations with other states on the basis of equality and reciprocity. The Chinese representative was taking China's seat at the Council of the League of Nations.

This study has given a detailed account of principal events of China diplomacy and of international diplomacy concerning China from 1918 to 1920 in the reconstruction of East Asian international system. It has also sought to analyse those events in the light of the development of the post-war international system and of China's entrance into the emerging universal international society.

In Chapter 1, we saw how the two Families of Nations – Chinese and European – met, and how the two incompatible world orders clashed in the mid-nineteenth century. We described how the Middle Kingdom was involuntarily yet inexorably incorporated into the expanding European international system and how China had undergone a series of political and cultural metamorphoses to adapt itself to the 'new world' it was faced with. We noted that a series of Imperial political and social reforms at the beginning of this century and the change of the Middle Kingdom's body politic had narrowed down the differences between China as a political community and other Western states. We also noted that China possessed one of the most important attributes of a modern nation: nationalism, which began to assert itself in China's nation-building efforts in the first decade of this century. By 1914, China, still a peripheral member of the global international system had become a prospective member of the emerging international society.

We argued that neither 1880, nor the turn of this century, nor 1911 could be seen as the point of entry of China into the Family of Nations or the emerging international society. The limited introduction of Western institutions to regulate China's external relations from 1860 to 1880 did not signify its acceptance of the European international order. Indeed even if, as was claimed, 'By 1880 China had realistically, if also painfully, assumed her place in the world community of nations',[1] it would still be difficult to explain what was this 'place' and whether or how members of the European Family of Nations would accept China's assumption of this 'place'. Further, it must be pointed out that it was in the same period that the subjection of China in world politics was taking shape, particularly in the form of a treaty system. In historical perspective, this period can be more aptly described as a process of the European states system expanding to incorporate China as a factor in its calculation.

There are, equally, difficulties with the suggestion that China's participation in the two Hague international peace conferences in 1899 and 1907 marked China's entrance into the emerging society of states. It is true that there were notable changes both in China's attitude towards international affairs and in geographical expansion of the European Family of Nations. China signed and ratified a number of international conventions and acts concluded at the Hague, and Japan became the first Asian nation to be accepted into the emerging society of states in 1899.[2] Yet, for the European states, China remained one of those political communities which had 'all the attributes of states, in the sense of public law and from the point of view of political science, and yet lack[ed] full international statehood' because they were not yet 'recognized by the "family of nations" as states in the full sense of international law'. It was invited, therefore, to the international conferences not 'as of right' but 'from courtesy'.[3] We may also question how much the European states would conceive themselves bound by a common set of rules with China in their relations with one another. Moreover neither the Chinese perception of common interests and common values nor its share in the working of common institutions with other European states, nor its participation in world politics was such that China no longer just acted 'as part[s] of a whole'.[4] In other words, although China was more closely integrated into the European-dominated international system, there was no material change of the status of China, which belonged to the expanding international system, yet not to the emerging international society. Similarly, the change of China's body politic in 1911 only nominally made the Middle Kingdom a nation-state. This single change did not and could not obtain for China membership in the emerging society of states.

However it is against this background of China's gradual integration into the expanding international system that the significance of China's assertive diplomacy of 1918–1920 is to be evaluated. By the end of the first decade of this century, the ancient Middle Kingdom had undoubtedly been further integrated into the global international system. China's changing perception of itself and of world politics, the making of a new society, the rising of nationalism and the change of China's polity – all worked to prepare China to behave as a nation in the now world-wide 'Family of Nations'. It must not be forgotten, however, that China was still totally subject to the capitulations system in its external relations and its existence was still endangered by imperialist encroachments. The double thrust of the rising tide of nationalism was to urge that China must carry out the duties and obligations of a nation in order to obtain the rights of a nation and to insist that China as a nation must have its inalienable full sovereignty and equal rights as a member in the Family of Nations. Both were directed at the treaty system in China and aimed at winning for China an equal international position among the nations. The most assertive and vigorous expression of this Chinese nationalism, as described in the main body of the text, was to be found in China's diplomacy in the peace settlement and the reconstruction of an international order in East Asia in 1918–1920.

From China's preparations for and participation in the Paris Peace Conference to its overall attack on the Russian treaty rights and privileges in China, the Chinese diplomatic history of the period was characterized by multiple assertive activities of Chinese initiative and by the singleness of their purpose and firmness of their determination. The war had further involved China in world politics. After the war, China participated in the Paris Peace Conference and presented to the international community the problems of its position in that community. It refused to sign the Versailles Treaty, but signed the St. Germain and other treaties,[5] joined the League of Nations as one of the original members and was elected in December 1920 a non-permanent member of the League Council. At home, it declared its policy to enter into treaty relations with foreign nations on the basis of equality and reciprocity and signed the first equal treaty with a foreign nation: the Sino-Bolivia Friendship Treaty in December 1919. It decided to apply the general tariff to goods imported from non-treaty nations in spite of the opposition from the treaty Powers, and raised a strong voice against any involvement of China's rights and interests in the renewal of the third Anglo-Japanese Alliance without prior consultation with China. It negotiated independently with Germany for the end of the war and for the renunciation of the latter's extraterritoriality and other synchronous privileges in China. It launched at the same time an overall assault on the Russian treaty rights and interests in China and approached the Soviet authorities for recovery of its rights. This series of intensive diplomatic activities was not systematic, yet their purpose was unmistakably simple and clear. It was to win or to assert for China a rightful place in the reconstructed international order after World War I.

The changing power configuration in world politics and the reorganization of the international order after the war provided a general background for China's assertive diplomacy. The United States was rising as a world power and Soviet Russia emerged as a revolutionary state. The defeated Germany and Austria–Hungary were excluded from the Powers' club. In China, this was seen in the general collapse of a pre-war 'united front', an international collective authority of the Powers *vis-à-vis* China, and in the cracks in the treaty system which used to be seen as formidably unassailable. On the other hand, democratic ideals of the post-war international system embodied in Wilsonian principles and actual democratization of international regimes during and after the war not only undermined the legitimacy of the pre-war international order, but also found their impact in the reconstruction of a new order in East Asia. It is abundantly clear that China drew great inspirations from democratic transformations of the international system, as can be seen in China's aspirations and demands to have an equal place in international society and in its diplomacy to strive for that place. The other change, of equal significance, must also be mentioned. In the reconstruction of the post-war world, there was an emerging consensus that there should be constructed an international order distinctly East Asian yet related to Europe. This consensus led to the convening of the Washington Conference in 1921–1922 and the establishment of the so-called 'Washington System'.

In 1918–1920, it was around issues of China and reconstruction of the East Asian international system that the conflict between China and the Powers was centred. Whether in such specific issues as the Jiaozhou question at the Peace Conference or in the general consideration of China in the reconstructed international order, the central theme of the conflict was China's place in the future international system. Whereas the most interested Powers in East Asia, Britain, Japan and the United States, continued to base their different versions of East Asian international order on the premise of China's subjection, China rose to claim its rights to be a positive actor in international politics. Whereas the Powers continued to deny China full international status, China insisted that it should by right have an equal position with other sovereign states and asserted itself to obtain that position. Whereas China regarded extraterritoriality as a stigma of its inferiority and impairment of its sovereignty which should be abolished, the Powers insisted that it should continue to operate ostensibly as a protection of life and property of their nationals, but virtually as the structural foundation of their treaty rights and privileges in China. It was through its resistance to and revolt against its continual subjection in world politics that China's impact was most keenly felt on the reconstruction of the international system in East Asia after World War I. It was made doubly so by the fact that China had become after the war the only area where all major Powers – Britain, Japan, United States, Soviet Russia and to some extent France – were involved and their interests clashed.

There was in the Chinese diplomacy of this period a radical departure from the past. This can be found at least in the following three aspects. First, it was extremely nationalistic, not only in rhetoric but more important, in action. The watchword of 'recovery of sovereign rights' in the first decade of this century was transferred into action of the Chinese official nationalism in the second. Whether China's claims at the Paris Peace Conference or its policy towards the Russian treaty structure in China – all aimed not only to resist the imperialist aggression but, more urgently, to roll back the imperialist encroachments on China's sovereignty and territorial integrity. Secondly, the Chinese diplomacy was no longer China's passive 'response' to the 'impact' of the West, but China's active participation in world politics. As one Chinese official communique in April 1919 frankly admitted, before the institution of the Republic, China 'had no very definite foreign policy beyond seeking to curtail the political ill effects of her increasing contact with Western nations'.[6] It is still arguable whether China could be said to have a well-defined foreign policy, even in 1920, yet there is little doubt that, whether at Paris or in

Beijing, and whether on the issue of China's membership of the League of Nations or that of China's new treaties with other states, the Chinese Government took a number of initiatives, not to ward off the West but to seek to take its part in international politics dominated by the West. Thirdly, it was principles universally acknowledged by the European Family of Nations in international law as governing their mutual relations that were mostly evoked to justify the Chinese diplomatic actions, whether it was an assault on the treaty system or an assertion of China's equal status in the comity of nations. China's claim to recover Jiaozhou was based on the principles of self-determination and territorial integrity. Its decision to reject any further demand on extraterritoriality in its treaty relations with foreign nations was vindicated by the principle of equality and reciprocity. Even its overall assault on Imperial Russia's treaty rights in China was defended on the ground that it was operated within the limit of international law.

To elaborate this point further: there could be seen in Chinese diplomacy a substantial degree of advance from using ideas 'learned from the West ... in argument with the West'[7] to staging a revolt in action against the Western domination of China in the form of a treaty system. This revolt was justified by the ideas present in the Western liberal political tradition and the principles embodied in international law, such as national self-determination and equal sovereignty. This posited a general acceptance by China of rules and institutions of international law as means to regulate inter-state relations. There was, however, a rebellious nature in this acceptance: it was predicated on the condition that they must be equally applied to China. What China now insisted on was the application by the West in their relations with China of the common set of rules which the West had in theory professed should be binding universally in international relations, but had in practice only applied to the relations among the founding and accepted members of the European Family of Nations. It must be pointed out that, in the process of its expansion, Europe did not export straightforward rules and institutions shaped in its own cultural framework to culturally heterogeneous systems. Thus,

> the rules and institutions which the Europeans spread out to Persia and China in the nineteenth century were those which they had evolved with the Ottomans (e.g. capitulations, consulates with jurisdictions over their nationals) rather than those in use within Europe itself (e.g. free movement and residence virtually without passports).[8]

In China's external relations, the embodiment of those rules and institutions was the treaty system. The revolt of the 'awakening China' against the treaty system was, therefore, a revolt against these 'regulatory arrangements'.[9] It was demanding that Sino-foreign relations be conducted in a manner similar to that in regulating relations between European nations rather between European and non-European nations. It was entirely justified by the common values accepted in the European international society and its demand was based on principles which, as was proclaimed then, should govern international relations.

China, then, interacted with the outside world in an unprecedented manner. But could this be regarded as the point of entry of China into the emerging universal international society? Or, in other words, did China now possess enough attributes not just to be regarded as a member of the international system but also as that of the international society? Was China now one of the states which, 'conscious of certain common interests and common values, form a society in the sense that they conceive themselves to be bound by a common set of rules in their relations with one another, and share in the working of common institutions'? Our answer is affirmative.

First, China's perception of common interests and common values and its cooperation in the working of common institutions with other members of the international system were unmistakable. China's participation in the war on the Allied side, its presence at Paris for the peace settlement, its representatives working in various committees of the Peace Conference, its ratification of peace treaties, and its joining the League of Nations were all strong evidence. Even China's assertion of its sovereign rights in a form of revolt against its subjection in world politics was vindicated by the Chinese with the notion that their relations with foreign states should be bound by a common set of rules, as among the European states.

Secondly, from the European perspective, there was a clear, though tacit, recognition that China and the existing members of the European Family of Nations had common interests and shared common values and that they could also cooperate in the working of common institutions. This recognition could be seen in the Allies' request for China to join the war and their invitation to China, certainly not from courtesy but as of right, as a member of the victorious Allied and Associated Powers, to participate in the work of the Peace Conference. It was more eloquently found in China's membership of the League of Nations with the consent of all other members and in its election as one of the non-permanent members of the League Council with the support of such Powers as Britain and France.[10] With regard to the common set of rules regulating each other's relations, the treaty Powers, pushed by China, also made a step forward, though somewhat reluctantly. They agreed to review China's complaints about treaty encroachments on China's sovereignty, which was eventually done at the Washington Conference.[11]

Thirdly, it must be realized not only that the perception was mutual but that it was reached from both sides gradually, as they both perceived a measure of convergence in their interests and values in their mutual relations. China had accepted the universal international institutions such as diplomatic conventions and forms of international law to regulate its external relations. An enduring structure of co-existence and cooperation in international politics between China and other states was gradually established by dialogue and sometimes by consent. The elements which sustained the structure were a set of recognized common rules and the structure was maintained for the common interest. In other words, China's voluntary participation in world politics and the Powers' involvement in China's foreign relations were such that a point was reached at which a member of the system had become and was recognized, or acquiesced in, as a member of the society.

There remains one seemingly insurmountable problem. China was still being denied full sovereignty. Legally, it was regarded as not yet having fully graduated to membership of the international society. Is it possible, then, that a state like China entered the international society before passing the admission test of fulfilling the European standard of 'civilization'?

The question may be approached from two different yet related perspectives. First, there is no consistency between non-European nations' entry into the international society and their fulfilment of the European standard of 'civilization'. It is true that the Europeans in the course of the nineteenth and even early twentieth centuries laid down, explicitly and implicitly, the criteria summarized under the standard of 'civilization' for non-European states to enter the originally exclusive European society of states. It is true that such non-European states as Japan and Siam were admitted into the 'charmed circle' only when they were judged by the Europeans to have fulfilled the European standard of 'civilization' in 1899 and 1939 respectively.[12] But the case of the Ottoman Empire was a contradiction. The European nations explicitly admitted the Empire into the Concert of Europe by the Treaty of Paris in 1856, but maintained their capitulations system there. Indeed, as Lord Salisbury claimed in 1895, the acceptance of the Ottoman Empire without compromising the capitulations system 'represented really a creation by the Powers'.[13] Even after World War I, they did not consider Turkey as having met their criteria to be qualified as having full international status.

Secondly, the European states did not always give up their extraterritorial rights as and when they considered that a non-European state had measured up to criteria they laid down and graduated to full membership of the international society. After World War I, the Allies sought to reimpose extraterritoriality on Turkey by the Treaty of Sèvres of 1920. They had to restore full sovereignty to Turkey in the Treaty of Lausanne in 1923, not because they judged then that Turkey had passed the test of standard of 'civilization', but because of the victory of the Turkish nationalist movement led by Kemal. In China, by 1943, only Great Britain and the United States maintained their extraterritorial system. They finally renounced it in January 1943, as an expedient to remove 'one of the obstructions to complete political equality among the United Nations'[14] rather than as a recognition that China had become a 'civilized' nation by fulfilling the European standard of 'civilization'. Elbert D. Thomas recalled, in 1951:

> I know from firsthand experience the thinking of the last two great nations of the world which maintained the extraterritorial practice, our own country and Great Britain. I know one of these two countries wanted to put off the renunciation of extraterritoriality until peace was restored and then renounce by the ordinary process of negotiation. But when we began to look forward to the meeting of Roosevelt, Churchill and Chiang Kai-shek in Cairo as Chiefs of State and after the great build-up which the nations of the West had given to their ally China as a friend in the war, thought developed to the place that to deny China an equal position in discussion seemed so illogical that extraterritoriality was of necessity abandoned.[15]

There was certain illogical absurdity in the claim that non-European states such as China and Turkey entered the global international society only at the point of the treaty Powers' reluctant renunciation of their extraterritorial jurisdiction in these countries. The standard of 'civilization' was certainly not necessarily the only test of admission of non-European states into the society of states.

The entrance of non-European states into the international society was of necessity a long process. They were invariably first incorporated into the expanding European international system. There they interlocked with the European states. At different stages, their relations with European states developed to a point where they accepted some common values and perceived some common interests as recognized among European states in conducting their regular intercourse and where, then, the system in which they were interlocked with the European states became for them also an international society. For China, this turning point is to be found in the post-war years of 1918–1920. The degree of China's voluntary involvement in world politics, its participation in the working of general international organization and its appealing to recognized international institutions for its just treatment in international relations were all unmistakable evidence. Like Japan and Siam, China was subjected to the capitulations system in its external relations with the European states when first incorporated into the European international system and tried, though probably involuntarily, to conform to the European standard of 'civilization' to win its membership in the emerging international society. Yet, unlike Japan and Siam, China entered the international society, not by meticulously fulfilling that 'standard' but by a revolt against the regime Europe introduced to regulate its relations with the non-European world. As with the Ottoman Empire, the ex-Middle Kingdom's entry into the international society did not mark the end of foreign extraterritoriality on its territory. Yet, unlike the case of the Ottoman Empire, its acceptance by the international society was not written into a formal statement but was acquiesced to in a series of actions by existing members in the peace settlement and reconstruction of a new international order after World War I.

The story of China's diplomacy in 1918–1920 was then not only a story of China's assertion for itself of a rightful place in the future international order. It was also a story of China's point of entry into the international society. It was marked by China's acceptance of European values and institutions in conducting international relations and its participation in world politics. More significantly, however, it was characterized by a revolt against the European dominance which gradually led to 'the disappearance in the present century of the distinction between full and partial membership of international society'.[16]

Notes and References

Introduction

1. See Wight, M. *Systems of States* (ed. by Bull, H.), Bull, H., *The Anarchical Society*, Bull, H. and Watson, A. eds., *The Expansion of International Society*; Northedge, F. S., *The International Political System*. See also Gong, G., *The Standard of 'Civilization' in International Society*.
2. Bull & Watson, *Expansion*, p. 1.
3. Bull, *Anarchical Society*, p. 10.
4. Bull & Watson, *Expansion*, p. 1. Compare the definition offered by Bull earlier: 'A society of states (or international society) exists when a group of states, conscious of certain common interests and common values, form a society in the sense that they conceive themselves to be bound by a common set of rules in their relations with one another, and share in the working of common institutions'. Bull, *Anarchical Society*, p. 13.

1 An Empire Contracted in a World Expanded

1. Given the ambiguity of the terms 'East ' and 'West' in their contemporary usage, it must be made clear that in this book, I mean by 'East' China and EAst Asia, and by 'West', Europe, especially the Western European nations.
2. In Adam Watson's words, 'The Renaissance turned men's minds towards classical models of independent statehood. The Reformation broke the authority of the universal church, which came to depend on the lay power of the new rulers even where it remained Catholic' (Adam Watson, 'European International Society and its Expansion', in Bull & Watson *Expansion*, p. 15).
3. For controversies about this point, see Wight, M., *Systems of States*, chs. 1, 4, 5, also Northedge, F. S., *The International Political System*, ch. 3.
4. Bryce, J,. *The Holy Roman Empire*, (2nd edn) p. 372.
5. For want of a better term, 'state' and 'nation' are also used in the description of the Eastern Family of Nations at the risk of anachronism.
6. Depuis described the medieval European order in the following words: 'Le moyen âge avait rêvé d'organiser l'Europe sur la double base de l'unité de la chretienreté et de la hiérarchie de pouvoirs. Le pape et l'empereur placés au sommet de la société internationale devaient, en théorie, maintenir l'unité, en se partageant la domination dans l'ordre spirituel et dans l'ordre temporel' (Depuis, C., *Le Principe d'Équilibre et le Concert Européen*, p. 9).
7. 'Sovereignty is supreme power over citizens and subjugated peoples and is bound by no law.' Quoted in Northedge, *International Political Systems*, p. 56.

8. See Wight, M., *Systems of States*, p. 21.
9. See Hay, D., *Europe, the Emergence of an Idea*, p. 233.
10. Gross, L., 'The Peace of Westphalia, 1648–1948', *American Journal of International Law* (hereafter, *AJIL*), vol. 42, 1948, p. 29.
11. See *Dictionnaire de la Terminologie du Droit Internationale*, p. 283.
12. Gross, L., 'Westphalia', *AJIL*, vol. 42, p. 29.
13. See Schwartz, B., 'The Chinese Perception of World Order, Past and Present'; in Fairbank, J. K. (ed.), *The Chinese World Order*, pp. 277–8.
14. Mencius explained the five relationships, saying, 'Between father and son, there should be affection; between sovereign and minister, righteousness; between husband and wife, attention to their separate functions; between old and young, a proper order; and between friends, fidelity' (Mencius, Book III, Part I, Ch. 4). He further observed, 'Of all which a filial son attain to, there is nothing greater than honouring his parents' (Mencius, Book V. Part I, Ch. 4).
15. The most challenging account is probably provided in Rossabi, M. (ed.), *China Among Equals – the Middle Kingdom and Its Neighbours, 10th–14th Centuries*.
16. Lien-sheng Yang, 'Historical Notes on the Chinese World Order', in Fairbank, J. K. (ed.), *Chinese World Order*, p. 20. See also Tao Jinsheng, *Song-Liao Guanxi Shi Yanjiu* (A Study of Relations Between Song and Liao Dynasties).
17. Tsiang, T. F., 'China and European Expansion', *Politica*, vol. II, no. 5 (1936), p. 3.
18. Ibid.
19. Vattel, E., *The Law of Nations* (tr. by Chitty, J.) p. 3.
20. Confucius, *Book of Rites*, ch. IX.
21. Quoted in Northrop, *The Meeting of East and West*, p. 325.
22. For a detailed account of what constituted *li* in relations between China and members of the Family of Nations in East Asia during the Qing Dynasty, see Fairbank, J. K. (ed.) *Chinese World Order*, pp. 10–11.
23. Ibid., p. 9.
24. Needham, J., *Within the Four Seas – the Dialogue Between East and West*, p. 11.
25. These are lines from a poem written by the Portuguese poet, Luiz de Camoes (1524–80). Quoted in Bozeman, A., *Politics and Culture in International History*, pp. 289–90.
26. Pratt, J. T., *The European Expansion into the Far East*, p. 34.
27. Ibid., p. 37.
28. See Hudson, G., *Europe and China*, pp. 134–68.
29. See Needham, J., *Science and Civilization in China*, vol. I, pp. 150, 223, 239.
30. Confucius, *Analects*, II, 3.
31. Pratt, *European Expansion*, p. 18
32. Bozeman, *Politics and Culture*, p. 389
33. Lord Macartney's mission to China in 1793 was the first attempt of Great Britain to establish diplomatic contact with China. For more about Lord Macartney and his mission, see Cramner-Byng, J. L. (ed.), *An Embassy to China: Lord Macartney's Journal*, pp. 3–38.

34. Ibid., p. x.
35. See Pratt, *European Expansion*, p. 69.
36. Cranmer-Byng, *Lord McCarthey's Journal*, p. 219.
37. Quoted in Northrop, *Meeting of East and West*, title page.
38. Bull and Watson, *Expansion*, p. 27.
39. Gentzler, J. (ed.), *Changing China*, p. 21.
40. Bull, *Anarchical Society*, p. 10.
41. Literally, 'Office in General Charge of Foreign Affairs'. It was actually a prototype Foreign Ministry.
42. Quoted in Fairbank, J. & Twitchett, D. (eds.), *Cambridge History of China* (hereafter, *CHC*), vol. 11, p. 154.
43. Fairbank, J. K. 'The Early Treaty System in the Chinese World Order', in Fairbank, J. (ed.), *Chinese World Order*, p. 259.
44. Ibid.
45. Zhong Shuhe, *Zou Xiang Shijie* (From East to West), p. 78. It is interesting to read that in 1860 Emperor Xian Feng, after reading the American Credential from the President of the United States addressed in terms of mutual equality, wrote on the margin 'Ludicrous conceit of the King of Yelang. Ridiculous!'
46. Hsu, I. *China's Entrance into the Family of Nations*, pp. 93, 97.
47. For details of these two changes, see Hsu, I., *China's Entrance* and Banno, M., *China and the West, 1858–1861: the Origins of Tsungli Yamen*.
48. Banno, M., *China and the West*, p. 1.
49. See Teng, S. Y. & Fairbank, J. K. *China's Response to the West, 1839–1923*, p. 48.
50. Zongli Yamen was meant to be a temporary office to be abolished as soon as the matters concerning the Anglo-French Expedition were all sorted out. In the memorial submitted by Prince Gong and others on January 13, 1861, it was suggested that 'As soon as the military campaigns are concluded and the affairs of the various countries are simplified, the new office will be abolished and its functions will again revert to the Grand Council for management so as to accord with the old system'. See Teng & Fairbank, *Response*, pp. 47–8.
51. For China's earlier efforts to practise and to learn international law, see Cohen, J. and Chiu, H., *People's China and International Law – A Documentary Study*, ch. I Introduction. Two interesting events have been noted. First, the Jesuit who acted as an interpreter for China in the Sino-Russian negotiations in 1689 and 1713 later claimed that those negotiations were conducted in the spirit of the law of nations. And secondly in 1840, Commissioner Lin ordered the translation of part of Vattel's *The Law of Nations*.
52. Teng & Fairbank, *Response*, p. 47.
53. Quoted in Ting-yi Kuo and Kwang-ching Lieu, 'Self-Strengthening: The Pursuit of Western Technology', *CHC*, vol. 10, pp. 492–3.
54. See Teng & Fairbank, *Response*, p. 98 and Ch'en, J., *China and the West*, p. 62.
55. For details, see Hsu, *China's Entrance*, pp. 132–48.

56. Ibid., p. 207.
57. Holland, T. E., *Studies in International Law*, p. 128.
58. Britain, France and the United States proposed, as early as 1854–1856, having mutual diplomatic missions resident in the capitals to facilitate communication between the states. But the Chinese rejected the idea on the ground that it was not compatible with Chinese institutions. To Emperor Xian Feng, their demand was 'extremely presumptuous' and must be 'sternly rebuked so that they would never think of it again'. For further details of controversies and eventual dispatch, see Hsu, *China's Entrance*, pp. 149–198.
59. Hsu, *China's Entrance*, p. 209.
60. Holland, *International Law*, p. 115.
61. Fairbank (ed.), *Chinese World Order*, p. 11. Also found in the list are Sulu, Holland and Western Ocean, which includes, as is made clear, Portugal, the Papacy and England.
62. Hsu, *China's Entrance*, p. 207.
63. Holland, T. E., *Lectures on International Law*, p.39.
64. Ch'en, J., *China and the West*, p. 59. See also Zhong Shuhe, *Zou Ziang Shjie*, p. 23.
65. Zhong Shuhe, *Zou Ziang Shjie* p. 29.
66. See Yen-p'ing Hao and Erh-min Wang, 'Changing Chinese Views of Western Relations, 1840-1895', *CHC*, vol. 11, p. 148.
67. Ibid.
68. See Cohen, P., 'Wang Tao and Incipient Chinese Nationalism', *Journal of Asian Studies*, vol. XXVI, no. 4, Aug. 1967, pp. 559–74.
69. Significantly, Wang argued that the extraterritorial jurisdiction impinged directly on national sovereignty and was only found in China, Japan and Turkey, but not among European themselves. See ibid, p. 568.
70. See Hao and Wang, 'Changing Chinese View,' p. 194.
71. See ibid, pp. 190–3 and Cohen, P., 'Wang Tao', p. 569.
72. Gentzler, *Changing China*, p. 34.
73. Quoted in Kuo and Liu, 'Self-Strengthening', *CHC*, vol. 10., p. 447.
74. Ibid, p. 534
75. Xue Fucheng, *Chou Yang Zhou Yi–Bian Fa* (Proposals Concerning Western Affairs–Reform); English translation from de Bary *et al*, (eds), *Sources of Chinese Tradition*, p. 716.
76. See Hao and Wang, 'Changing Chinese Views', *CHC*, vol. 11, p. 181.
77. Kuo T'ing-i, *Guo Songtao*, vol. II, pp. 665–6.
78. See Hao Chang, 'Intellectual Change' in *CHC*, vol. 11, p. 275.
79. Ch'en, *China and the West*, p. 272
80. See Hao Chang, 'Intellectual Change and the Reform Movement, 1890–1898', in *CHC*, vol. 11, pp. 277–82.
81. Quoted in Levenson, J., *Liang Ch'i-chao and the Mind of Modern China*, pp. 42–43.
82. Bull & Watson, *Expansion*, p. 16
83. It is important to note that, in terms of contact or interactions between members of the original regional international systems, or in other words between non-European nations, say between China and Egypt, the progress was rather limited. The existence of a core in the expanding international system was partly borne out by this fact.

84. Keylor, W. R., *The Twentieth Century World – An International History*, p. 4. He, however, refers to the process, not very convincingly, as 'Europeanization of the world'.

85. Northedge has identified seven main stages in the expansion of the European international system up to the 1960s when decolonization was virtually completed. By the end of the nineteenth century, he believes, five stages had passed which were marked by the admission into the international system of first, the United States of America in 1783, secondly, the rebellious Latin American states in 1823, thirdly, the Ottoman Empire and Romania in 1856, fourthly, Japan and fifthly, China, both in the latter half of the nineteenth century. See Northedge, *International Political Systems*, pp. 74–6.

86. Bull & Watson, *Expansion*, p. 27.

87. Wight, *Systems of States*, pp. 42–3.

88. Wight's regarding the American states as at the periphery in the third period 1763–1914 is obviously out of the calculation of their involvement in the European balance of power. In the broader perspective of an emerging universal international system, however, they were more at the core than at the periphery, for although they played a somewhat peripheral role in European politics in that period, they were full legal personalities and enjoyed full membership in the European Family of Nations.

89. Bull & Watson, *Expansion*, p. 5.

90. Keylor, *Internation History*, p. 6.

91. Gentzler, *Changing China*, p. 34.

92. For a brief and persuasive argument, see Cassese, A., *International Law in a Divided World*; pp. 40–2.

93. Watson, A., 'Hedley Bull, States Systems and International Society', *Review of International Studies*, vol. 13, no. 2, p. 151.

94. Cassese, *Divided World*, p. 55.

95. Holland, *Lectures*, pp. 39–40.

96. Hall, W., *A Treatise on International Law*, (8th ed) pp. 47–8.

97. Lorimer, J., *The Institutes of the Law of Nations*, vol. I, pp. 101–3.

98. See Oppenheim, L., *International Law*, (1st ed), vol. 1, p. 32.

99. Bull & Watson, *Expansion*, p. 6.

100. Cassese, *Divided World*, p. 39.

101. Gong in Bull & Watson, *Expansion*, p. 171

102. Bozeman, *Politics and Culture*, p. 3.

103. Lorimer, *Law of Nations*, vol. 1, p. 239.

104. Northedge, *International Political Systems*, p. 77.

105. See Gong, *The Standard of 'Civilization' in International Society*, pp. 47–93.

106. Northedge, *International Political Systems*, p. 76.

107. Quoted in Gong, *Standard*, p. 158.

108. See, for example, Teng, S-Y. & Fairbank, J. K., *China's Response to the West*, Part Six 'Reform and Revolution, 1901–1912', pp. 195–230; Hsu, I., *The Rise of Modern China*, Part IV 'Reform and Revolution 1898–1912', pp. 355–492; Wright, M., 'Introduction: The Rising Tide of Change', in Wright, M. (ed.), *China in Revolution, The First Phase 1900–1913*, pp. 1–63; and Young, E., 'Nationalism, Reform and Republican

Revolution in the Early Twentieth Century', in Crowley, J. B. (ed.), *Modern East Asia: Essays in Interpretation*, pp. 151–79.

109. Bull, H., 'The Emergence of a Universal International Society', in Bull and Watson, *Expansion*, p. 122.

110. Quoted in Teng & Fairbank, *Response*, p. 196.

111. Wright, *China in Revolution*, p. 24.

112. For more details of Imperial China's administrative reform, see 'Administrative Reform and the Central Power' in Fairbank, J. K., Reischauer, E. O. & Craig, A. M., *East Asia – The Modern Transformation*, pp. 622–5.

113. Wright, *China in Revolution*, p. 28.

114. Young, in Crowley, *Modern East Asia*, p. 162.

115. Quoted in Wright, *China in Revolution*, p. 69.

116. See Morse, H. B., *The International Relations of the Chinese Empire*, vol. III (The Period of Subjection, 1894-1911). Morse identified three periods in China's relations with the West from 1840 to 1911, the other two being the Period of Conflict, 1840–1860, and the Period of Submission, 1861–1893.

117. Young, in Crowley, *Modern East Asia*, p. 154.

118. See Willoughby, W. W., *Foreign Rights and Interests in China*.

119. Wright, *China in Revolution*, p. 55.

120. Ibid., p. 56.

121. Wilson, G., *Handbook of International Law*, (2nd edn) p. 25.

122. See MacMurray, J. V. A., *Treaties and Agreements with and Concerning China, 1894–1919*, vol. I (Manchu Period 1894–1911) pp. 682–3.

123. Bull, *Anarchical Society*, p. 13.

124. Wright, M. *China in Revolution*, pp. 3–4.

125. Liang Baochang to Koo, Feb. 20, 1961; Koo Papers, Box 1.

2 A Disappointed Nation at Paris, 1919

1. Fitzgerald, C. P., *Revolution in China*, p. 201.

2. One good illustration was the division of China into spheres of influence. According to Sun Yat-sen, at the time of World War I, the Russian sphere of influence in China constituted 42 per cent of the Chinese territory; the British, 28 per cent, the French and the Japanese, each over 5 per cent; and Germany, 1 per cent. See Ch'i, M., *China Diplomacy 1914–1918*, p. 122.

3. Millard to Bonsal, Nov. 4, 1913, in Bonsal Papers, Box 5.

4. For China's war-time diplomacy, see Ch'i, *China Diplomacy*.

5. President Xu Shichang to King George V, Nov. 13, 1918, Chinese Archives (hereafter, CA) 1039-2. Dispatches of the same content in English were sent to Wilson and the Emperor of Japan at the same time.

6. Reinsch, *An American Diplomat in China*, p. 324. The Chinese Government actually pronounced a special three-day national holiday to celebrate the victory of the Allies.

7. Ibid., p. 323. This is more significant if we remember that barely twenty years before, during the Boxer Rebellion, the Powers had to force their way into the Imperial Palace to compel the recognition by China of their

conditions and rights in their relations with China. Now they were invited as guests to celebrate the victory of a common cause.

8. *North China Herald* (hereafter, *NCH*) Dec. 7, 1918, vol. *CXXIX*, p. 749.
9. *NCH*, Nov. 18, 1918, vol. CXXIX, p. 554.
10. *NCH*, Oct. 29, 1918, vol. CXXIX, p. 328.
11. Xu to Wilson, Oct. 13, 1918; CA 1039-2.
12. *Chen Bao* (The Morning Post), Nov. 3, 1918.
13. Xu to Wilson, Nov. 13, 1918, CA 1039-2. Part of Xu's telegram sent on the same day to the French President and heads of the states of Belgium, Brazil, Italy and Portugal runs as 'Ces principes [de la justice et de l'humanité] constitueront la base essentielle de notre prochaine conférence de paix dans laquelle je serai très heureux de voir s'établir une co-operation étroite entre les délégués de nos deux pays.' Xu to the French President, Nov. 13, 1918, CA 1039-2.
14. These included (1) suspension of the Boxer Indemnity; (2) raising customs tariff to an effective 5 per cent; (3) financial assistance in the form of loans; and (4) permission for Chinese troops to enter Tianjin. On March 8, 1917, Jordan, the British Minister in Beijing, replied on behalf of Belgium, France, Great Britain, Italy, Japan, Portugal, and Russia that they agreed in principle to accord China those benefits. They also made it clear that details were to be worked out in later negotiations. Cabinet to Zhang Zongxiang, Mar. 8, 1917; *Jindaishi Ziliao* (Source Materials of Modern Chinese History), vol. 38, p. 33.
15. Alston to Balfour, Mar. 1, 1917; FO371/45940/10. See also Reinsch to Lansing, Mar. 9, 1917; *FRUS*, 1917, supp. vol., p. 428.
16. King George V to President of China, Aug. 5, 1918, CA 1039-2.
17. Wilson to Feng Guozhang, July 8, 1918, CA 1039-2.
18. Feng to Wilson, July 11, 1918, CA 1039-2.
19. See, for example, Yu Xinchun, 'Bali Hehui Yu Wusi Yundong' (The Paris Peace Conference and the May Fourth Movement) in *Lishi Yanjiu* (Historical Studies), no. 1, 1979, pp. 86–8. He claimed that China did not at all prepare itself for the Peace Conference, even as far as the Shandong problem is concerned. See also La Fargue, *China and the World War*, p. 182.
20. So far as we can find in the Chinese archives, from early April to mid-July 1918 the Preparatory Committee had 15 meetings. But the minutes of the first and the sixth meeting are missing from the archives now preserved in the Second Archive Library of China in Nanjing. See CA 1039-371-2. Koo also recalled that he was informed that 'the Ministry was establishing a committee in preparation for the Peace Conference to study the problems China should present to the Peace Conference, using as the basis for their study various reports that I sent'. Interview with Wellington Koo, V-2-8, Koo Papers, Box 1.
21. The Minutes of the Fifth Meeting of the Preparatory Committee for the Peace Conference, May 10, 1918, CA 1039-371-2.
22. The Minutes of the Ninth Meeting of the Preparatory Committee for the Peace Conference, June 10, 1918, CA 1039-371-2.
23. This is what we have found in the Library of the Chinese Foreign Ministry and the Second Archive Library of China in Nanjing which

holds most of the diplomatic archives of the period 1911–1949. There were a number of foreign advisers to the Chinese Government at the time. It is believed that the others also submitted their opinions on China's position at the peace conference.

24. He, in particular, observed that, by October, 'The objects China should aim at in connection with the forthcoming Peace Conference and the post bellum programme have already been studied and discussed by the official and private bodies as well as in the press.'

25. Printed copies of all five memoranda are still kept in the Library of the Chinese Foreign Ministry. The original copies of Willoughby's and Nagao Ariga's memoranda have also been located in CA 1039-373-2 and CA 1003-819.

26. For example, Padoux argued, 'Pour toutes ces raisons [China did not have 'une participation directe à la guerre' and 'A l'intérieur même de la Chine, la politique de combat contre l'influence allemande et contre le commerce allemand a été menée avec beaucoup moins d'activité, etc., etc.] . . . de toutes les questions qui se poseront à la conférence des belligérants une seule vous intéresse en elle-même, celle de Tsingtao, sur laquelle des arrangements sont déjà intervenus'. Willoughby also doubted the wisdom of yielding to temptation of putting all problems related to China's external relations before the peace conference.

27. Zhou Wei, 'Waijiao Jinque' (On Developing a Positive Diplomacy) in *Bali Hehui Huiqian Zhunbei Cailiao* (A Collection of Materials Related to the Preparations for the Paris Peace Conference).

28. All these memoranda, including Zhou Wei's, are found in the series *Bali Hehui Huiqian Zhunbei Cailiao* in the Library of the Chinese Foreign Ministry in Beijing. They are printed in pamphlet form. It is very likely that they were printed for limited circulation.

29. Enclosure in CA 1039-373-2.

30. Koo to Lu, Oct. 17, 1918, CA 1003-822. See also Interview with Dr. Wellington Koo IV-3-8, in Koo Papers, Box 1.

31. Chinese Minister to the Secretary of State, Nov. 25, 1918; Koo Papers, Box 1.

32. For Long's memorandum of the talk, see *FRUS*, Paris Peace Conference, 1919 (hereafter, *FRUS*, PPC), vol. II, pp. 509–10. Long, however, made a confusion of 'fiscal' with 'physical' independence! For Koo's memorandum of the talk, see CA 1039-373-2.

33. It is likely that the Chinese made these proposals with a view to enlisting American sympathy and help which the Chinese believed they would depend on at the peace conference. From what we have read in the Chinese archives, it appears that no other ministers were informed of these proposals. See also Reinsch to Lansing, Nov. 23, 1918; *FRUS*, PPC, vol. II, pp. 491–2.

34. Memorandum of an interview with the Third Assistant Secretary of State, Mr. Long, Nov. 27, 1918, CA 1039-373-2.

35. He resigned his premiership in August and was appointed the Supervisor of the War Participation Bureau. He was attending the Cabinet meeting in that capacity.

36. Cao Rulin, *Yisheng Zhi Huiyi* (Memoire of Cao Rulin), p. 188.

37. Jordan to Curzon, Nov. 25, 1918, F0 371/3693. See also Reinsch to Lansing, Nov. 24, 1918, *FRUS*, PPC, vol. II, p. 507.
38. Ibid.
39. *NCH*, Nov. 29, 1918, vol. *CXXIX*, p. 504.
40. Presidential Mandate, Nov. 30, 1918; CA 05-3-16.
41. China was at the time divided into the North and the South under two governments. The Beijing Government claimed to be the central government with its legitimacy based on the recognition of foreign Powers and on its actual rule of 17 provinces out of 22. The Canton Military Government, however, claimed its legitimacy based on interpretation of the first Constitution of the Republic of China. Its actual control was limited to five provinces in the south and southwest.
42. Presidential Mandate of Dec. 27, 1918, CA 05-3-16. The North and the South also agreed to end their armed confrontation and to convene a peace conference in Shanghai which was opened in February, 1919.
43. It was held from 2.15 to 2.30 pm. See Koo's Memorandum 'World Peace and the Far East – A Conversation at an Audience with the President of the United States, Woodrow Wilson, at the White House, Nov. 26, 1918'; Koo Papers, Box 1.
44. Hu to Cabinet, Dec. 10, 1918; CA 1039-371-2.
45. Parts of the Memorandum of a Conversation Between Mr. Robert Lansing and Mr. Hu Weide, Mr. Alfred Sze, and Mr. Wellington Koo, Dec. 18, 1918; Koo Papers, Box 1.
46. Sir Ronald Macleay was the head of the Far East Division of the Foreign Office at the time. He went to Paris as a member of the British Empire Delegation, acting as adviser on the Far Eastern affairs.
47. For example, he thought that it would be difficult for China to 'reopen these questions [Shandong and Jiaozhou] on account of its written agreements with Japan'. He 'did not think the Powers would agree to the immediate withdrawal of the Legation Guards between Beijing and Qinhuangdao'. He stated that 'the immediate total abolition [of extraterritoriality] was out of the question'. Even on the question of withdrawing the foreign post offices in China, he said that the Chinese 'post service had certainly done very well, but the Britishers in China held very strong sentiments in regard to their own post offices, so that it might be difficult to get them to agree to immediate withdrawal'. The talk was between the Chinese delegates Koo and Sze and Macleay on Jan. 21, 1919, after their dinner. See Strictly Confidential Memorandum by Alfred Sze, Jan. 22, 1919, Koo Papers, Box 1.
48. Conversation with Colonel E. M. House at Hotel Crillon, Dec. 18, 1918, Koo Papers, Box 1.
49. See *Peaking Leader*, Nov. 28, 1915.
50. Reinsch, *American Diplomat*, p. 246.
51. Hu Weide to the Foreign Ministry, Nov. 20, 1918, CA 1003-822.
52. Reinsch to Lansing, Nov. 18, 1918, *FRUS*, PPC, vol. I, p. 242.
53. See Fifield, R. H., *Woodrow Wilson and the Far East*, p. 189.
54. *NCH*, Jan. 23, 1919, vol. *CXXX*, p. 262
55. Morris to Lansing, Nov. 13, 1918, *FRUS*, PPC, vol. I, p. 489.
56. Zhang to Foreign Ministry, Oct. 12, 1918, CA 1003-822.

57. Uchida to Makino, Dec. 9, 1918; Kajima, M., *The Diplomacy of Japan, 1894–1922*, vol. III, pp. 344–7.
58. Ibid.
59. Ibid.
60. *Nihon gaikō nempyō norabini shuyō bunsho* (hereafter, *gaikō nempyō*, Chronology of Japanese Diplomacy 1875–1945 and Important Documents) vol. 1, pp. 478–9. For the English version, see Kajima, *Diplomacy of Japan*, pp. 351–2.
61. King, W., *China at the Paris Peace Conference in 1919*, p. 1.
62. There were neither Japanese nor American experts attached to the Delegation because there was a strong opposition in China to having any Japanese in its Delegation and because the Americans had declined the Chinese request to include some Americans. See Reinsch to Lansing, Nov. 16, Nov. 20 and Nov. 22, 1918; and Lansing to Reinsch, Nov. 18 and Nov. 25, 1918; *FRUS*, PPC, vol. I, pp.241–4.
63. For a complete list of members of the Chinese Delegation, see Directories of the Peace Conference – China, *FRUS*, PPC, vol. III, pp. 33–5.
64. The Chinese had believed that they would have three seats at every session. But on Jan. 13 and again on Jan. 17, 1919, just one day before the First Plenary Session of the Peace Conference, they were told that China was to have only two places. See Lu to Foreign Ministry, Jan. 15 & 17, 1919; *Miji Lucun* (hereafter *ML*, A Record of Secret Correspondence) pp. 67–8; also Interview with Wellington Koo, V-4-7, Koo Papers, Box 1.
65. Sze to Balfour, Jan. 14, 1919, FO608/209.
66. Interview with Wellington Koo, V-4-8, Koo Papers, Box 1.
67. Lu to Foreign Ministry, Jan. 17, 1919; *ML*, p. 67
68. See Lu to Foreign Ministry, Jan. 24, 1919; ibid., p. 72. China was still able to appoint five plenipotentiaries because of the panel system brought into operation at the sessions of the Peace Conference.
69. Interview with Koo, V-3-4, Koo Papers, Box 1. The actual date was, however, Jan. 27, not Jan. 26 as Koo remembered.
70. Memorandum of an Interview with Secretary Robert Lansing, Jan. 27, 1919, Koo Papers, Box 3.
71. Lu to Foreign Ministry, Jan. 27, 1919, *ML*, p. 72
72. Koo, W., *Gu Weijun Huiyi Lu* (Memoir of Wellington Koo) p. 184.
73. Memorandum of an Interview with Secretary Robert Lansing, Jan. 27, 1919, Koo Papers, Box 3.
74. Minutes of the Council of Ten, Jan. 27, 1919; *FRUS*, PPC, vol. III, pp. 735-7
75. Ibid., p. 737. Lansing, when seeing Wang and Koo before the afternoon session, also told them that at the morning session, 'other Powers wanted to exclude China from presentation, but President Wilson and I insisted on Chinese delegates being present at the discussion'. Memorandum of an Interview with Secretary Robert Lansing, Jan. 27, 1919, Koo Papers, Box 3.
76. Ibid., pp. 739–40.
77. Macleay to Muller, Feb. 21, 1919; FO608/209.
78. Minutes of the Council of Ten, Jan. 27, 1919; *FRUS*, PPC, vol. III, p. 740.

79. Lu to President, Jan. 28, 1919, CA 1003-822; see also Memorandum of an Interview with President Wilson at Murat Mansion, Jan. 27, 1919; Koo Papers, Box 3.
80. For a summary of Koo's speech, see Lu to Foreign Ministry, Jan. 30, 1919, *ML*, pp. 73–4. The English version is from *FRUS*, PPC, vol. III, pp. 755–6.
81. See Macleay to Muller, Feb. 21, 1919; FO608/209. In Macleay's words, 'Koo presented China's case in a very able speech.'
82. Yen to Wu, Jan. 29, 1919, CA 1003-823.
83. See Koo, *Gu Weijum Huiyi Lu*, p. 186–7.
84. *NCH*, Feb. 2, 1919, vol. *CXXX*, p. 326.
85. Ibid.
86. Matsui was the Japanese Ambassador to France and concurrently one of the Japanese Plenipotentiaries to the Peace Conference. On Jan. 28, he telegraphed Obata about the Chinese demands at the Council of Ten. Matsui to Obata, Jan. 28, *The Japanese Foreign Ministry Archives* (hereafter, *JFMA*), microfilmed by the Library of Congress, MT 231-22. On Feb. 1, Matsui also telegraphed Uchida, the Japanese Foreign Minister, asking him to urge the Chinese Government to instruct its delegates to be more cooperative with the Japanese at the Peace Conference.
87. Obata to Matsui, Feb. 1, 1919; ibid., p. 17.
88. Obata to Uchida, Feb. 13, 1919, *NGB*, vol. *Pari kōwa kaigi kreika gaiyō*; and Reinsch to Polk, June 6, 1919, *FRUS*, 1919, vol. I, p. 333.
89. Obata to Matsui, Feb. 17, 1919, *JFMA*, MT 231-22, pp. 63–6.
90. See for example, report by Reuter correspondent in *NCH*, Feb. 3, 1919, vol. *CXXX*, p. 319.
91. Reinsch to Polk, June 6, 1919; *FRUS*, 1919, vol. I, p. 333.
92. *NCH*, Feb. 3, 1919, vol. *CXXX*, p. 326.
93. On Feb. 6, the Cabinet told Lu that he had full power to decide whether or not to submit the secret agreements to the Conference, if asked to. Cabinet to Lu, Feb. 6, 1919, CA 05-3-33.
94. Minute by Macleay, Feb. 17, 1919; FO608/209.
95. Lu to Foreign Ministry, Feb. 10, 1919; CA 05-3-33.
96. Minutes of the Council of Ten, Jan. 27, 1919; *FRUS*, PPC, vol. III, pp. 754–5.
97. For the exchanged notes, see MacMurray, *Treaties and Agreements*, vol. II, pp. 1445–6. The Japanese troops had since their occupation of Jiaozhou been stationed along the Jiaozhou–Jinan Railway. At the time the exchange of notes was proposed, 2,000 of them were actually quartered outside the leased territory, some as far as 256 miles inland at Jinan, the capital of Shandong Province. On Oct. 1, 1917, a Japanese Imperial Ordinance (no. 175) sanctioned the establishment of civil administration in Jiaozhou. The Japanese Government proceeded then to set up Civil Administration Bureaux in Jiaozhou with branches in three other cities outside the former German leased territory. One branch of the Bureau had even asserted jurisdiction in lawsuits between Chinese citizens and had levied taxes on them. The Jiaozhou–Jinan Railway and the mines were also placed under the control of a Department of Civil

Administration under the Railway authorities. The Chinese believed and were apprehensive, not without reason, that the continued presence of the Japanese army in Shandong Province and the new move of the Japanese Government aimed at perpetual occupation of the Province. The exchange of notes on Sept. 24, 1918 was a manoeuvre, the Chinese would argue, to have the Japanese abolish their existing civil administration in Shandong and withdraw their troops to Jiaozhou. See 'The Claim of China for Direct Restitution to Herself of the Leased Territory of Kiaochao, the Tsingtao–Tsinan Railway and Other German Rights in Respect of Shantung Province', *China Year Book, 1919-1920*, p. 664.

98. Lu to Foreign Ministry, Jan. 30, 1919, CA 1003-822.
99. Sze to Wu, Feb. 7, 1919, CA 1003-823. Lloyd-George also told the Chinese that Britain was to submit its secret agreement with Japan to the Conference.
100. This is what Lloyd George said to the Council of Four to justify the agreement. See Notes of a Meeting of Heads of Governments, April 22, 1919; CAB29/37.
101. See MacMurrary, *Treaties and Agreements*, vol. II, pp. 1167–9.
102. Millard, T., *Democracy and our Eastern Question*, pp. 106–7.
103. Baker, R., *Woodrow Wilson and the World Settlement*, vol. II, p. 40.
104. Makino's secretary visited the Chinese Delegation on the afternoon of Feb. 7 and showed the Chinese the secret agreements to be submitted by the Japanese. They included (1) Japan's secret agreements of 1917 with Britain, France, Italy and Russia; (2) part of the Sino-Japanese Agreement of 1915 concerning Shandong; (3) the Sino-Japanese Agreement of Sept. 24, 1918 on the Jiaozhou–Jinan Railway; and (4) Sino-Japanese agreements on other railways in Manchuria, signed in September 1917. Lu to Foreign Ministry, Feb. 7, 1919, *ML*, p. 78.
105. Minutes of the Meetings of the Chinese Delegation at Paris (hereafter, Delegation Minutes), No. 18, CA 05-3-1. According to the minutes, from Jan. 21 to May 28, 1919, the Chinese Delegation had had 75 meetings and two secret sessions.
106. Lu to Foreign Ministry, CA 05-3-33.
107. Wilson went back to America on Feb. 14 to enlist home support for his programme for the League of Nations and to take care of his domestic scene. Clemenceau, meanwhile, was wounded in an attempted assassination on Feb. 19 and had to take to his bed for days.
108. Lu to Cabinet, Feb. 14, 1919, CA 05-3-33.
109. Cabinet to Lu, Jan. 8, 1919, Koo Papers, Box 2.
110. Delegation Minutes, No. 2, Jan. 22, 1919; CA 05-3-1.
111. Ibid., No. 4, Jan. 28, 1919. For example, the problem of foreign concessions was entrusted to two counsellors of the Foreign Ministry, Wang and Yan. Sze and Wei, two Chinese plenipotentiaries, would take on the matter of tariff autonomy and the Chinese Minister to Italy, Wang Guangxi, the matter of consular jurisdiction.
112. Ibid., No. 26, Feb. 26, 1919
113. Ibid., No. 27 and no. 28, Feb. 27 and Feb. 28, 1919.
114. Ibid., No. 33, March 3, 1919.
115. Ibid., No. 61, April 5, 1919 and no. 71, April 12, 1919.
116. Ibid., No. 67, April 10, 1919.

117. For example, in Fifield's work *Woodrow Wilson and the Far East – the Diplomacy of the Shantung Question*, probably the most detailed study so far of both Chinese and Japanese diplomacy at the Paris Peace Conference, he only mentioned in passing the Chinese presentation of the proposals.

118. During the Washington Conference, agreements were reached between China and the Powers on revision of Chinese tariff, eventual abrogation of consular jurisdiction in China, withdrawal of foreign post offices, and withdrawal of foreign troops from China. See Carnegie Endowment for International Peace, *Treaties and Agreements with and Concerning China 1919-1929*, pp. 80–100.

119. *Questions for Readjustment*, 'Introduction', April, 1919; CA 05-3-32.

120. Ibid., 'Renunciation of the Spheres of Influence or Interest'.

121. Ibid., 'Withdrawal of Foreign Troops and Police'.

122. Ibid., 'Withdrawal of Foreign Post Offices and Agencies for Wireless and Telegraphic Communications'.

123. Ibid., 'Abolition of Consular Jurisdiction'.

124. Ibid., 'Restoration of Foreign Concessions and Settlements'.

125. Ibid., 'Tariff Autonomy'.

126. Ibid., 'Conclusion'.

127. These were the Civil Code, the Criminal Code, the Commercial Code, the Code of Civil Procedure and the Code of Criminal Procedure.

128. *Questions for Readjustment*, 'Abolition of Consular Jurisdiction', CA 05-3-32.

129. *Likin* was a local tax imposed by the local authorities upon goods circulated in the interior of China.

130. The concessions proposed by China were (1) Any favourable treatment thus arranged must be reciprocal. (2) A differential scale must be established so that luxuries should pay more and raw materials less than necessaries. (3) The basis of the new conventional rate for necessaries must not be less than 12.5% in order to cover the loss of revenue resulting form the abolition of *likin* as provided for in the commercial treaties of 1902-1903. (4) At the end of a definite period to be fixed by new treaties, China must be at liberty not only to revise the basis of valuation, but also the duty rate itself. *Questions for Readjustment*, 'Tariff Autonomy', CA 05-3-32.

131. *Questions for Readjustment*, 'Conclusion'; CA 05-3-32.

132. Minute by Macleay, May 13, 1919, FO608/209.

133. See Lansing to Polk, Feb. 11, 1919, Polk Papers, Box 9. Lansing told Polk that, 'If there is one predominant ingredient of Paris atmosphere besides fog and dampness it is intrigue. Unless you are here to breathe it, you can have little conception of the schemes which are being hatched by the statesmen of the various nationalities who are assembled here to get all they can for their respective countries.'

134. Even 'the great Liberal' General Smuts, Colonel Bonsal noticed, was talking about 'more elbow room' for the British Empire after the peace negotiations. Bonsal Diary, March 1, 1919, Bonsal Papers, Box 18.

135. 'He [Makino] tells me', Colonel Bonsal recorded in his diary, 'that he and Chinda are expecting a rap over the knuckles from Tokyo. "You see," he explained, "in the days before the Tokugawa Shogun cut our sea-going

junks in half and so compelled us to stay at home we also had some
overseas colonies along the coast of Siam. Perhaps we are remiss in not
insisting upon their redemption".' Ibid.

136. Supplement to Confidential Bulletin no. 57 of the American Delegation,
March 5, 1919, White Papers, Box 47.
137. Memorandum of an Audience with President Wilson, March 24, 1919,
Koo Papers, Box 3.
138. 'An Interview with Colonel House, April 2, 1919'; 'An Interview with Mr.
Lansing at Hotel Crillon, April 4, 1919'; both memos in Koo Papers, Box
3. Koo told Lansing that 'it appeared to him highly advisable to raise the
question before the Council of the Four Chiefs of Government and urge
an early settlement'. Koo maintained on both occasions that should
China fail to redeem Jiaozhou, it might push China towards Japan, which
could not be conducive to the interests of the Occident in China.
139. 'An Interview with Mr. Lansing at Hotel Crillon, April 4, 1919', Koo
Papers, Box 3.
140. Koo to Lansing, April 8, 1919, in Koo Papers, Box 3.
141. Lu to Balfour, April 8, 1919, FO608/209.
142. Lu to Foreign Ministry, April 5, 1919, CA 05-3-33.
143. Baker, R., *Woodrow Wilson*, vol. II, p. 1.
144. Bonsal Diary, March (undated), Bonsal Papers, Box 18.
145. Private Memo, April 4, 1919, Lansing Papers, MC, AC 15,347, Reel 1.
146. Bonsal Diary, April 12, 1919, Bonsal Papers, Box 18.
147. Bliss to Nellie, Dec. 18, 1918, Bliss Papers, Box 244.
148. Bonsal Diary, April 3, 1919, Bonsal Papers, Box 18.
149. Baker, *Woodrow Wilson*, vol. III, p. 7.
150. Lansing noted Wilson's concessions on his principles and wrote on April
15 in his Private Memo, 'It is very distressing to see the way that the
President's announced principles are being honeycombed by all sorts of
compromises and concessions. It has been done gradually, a little here
and a little there, so that I do not think the President has realized what
has taken place.' Private Memorandum, Lansing Papers, MC, AC
15,347, Reel 1.
151. See *FRUS*, PPC, vol. IV, pp. 556, 571; It may be noted that the idea of
applying the principle of mandate to Jiaozhou was very much alive in the
minds of American Commissioners after the Chinese crossed words with
the Japanese at the Council of Ten in January. Henry White, in a letter to
Senator Lodge on Feb. 10, 1919, stated, 'I think we shall find that
principle [of mandate] exceedingly useful when the claims of Japan come
to be considered, which, as you foreshadowed in your memo, include
Kiaochow and the Caroline Islands. A mandate to Japan under the
League of Nations to administer the islands in question would be very
different thing from their annexation to that Empire, and the principle of
no annexation will make it less difficult to convey to Japan the idea that
China's lease of Kiaochow to Germany came to an end when those two
countries went to war with each other, and consequently that Japan has
no claim to that port and its hinterland under that lease, which I have
reason to believe is what she is likely to claim. But by termination of the
lease, Kiaochow simply reverted to China, or rather China should resume

possession thereof in the absence of any valid reason why Japan should annex it.' White to Lodge, Feb. 10, 1919, White Papers, Box 5.

152. Lu to Foreign Ministry, April 17 and 18, 1919, CA 05-3-33. Lansing's proposal was made known to the Chinese delegates by President Wilson on April 17, when four Chinese plenipotentiaries Koo, Wang, Sze and Wei met the President. He told the Chinese that it was, however, only a proposition, not a decision of the Conference.
153. Minutes of the Council of Five, April 17; *FRUS*, PPC, vol. IV, p. 556.
154. Proceedings of the Council of Heads of Governments, April 18, 1919, CAB29/37.
155. House Diary, April 19, 1919, MC, 40, Reel 4.
156. Bliss to Nellie, April 19, 1919, Bliss Papers, Box 244.
157. Proceedings of the Council of Heads of Governments, April 21, CAB29/37; See also Mantoux, P. *Les délibérations du Couseil des Quatre*, pp. 315–7.
158. See NGB, vol. *Pari kōwa kaigi*, pp. 716–20.
159. In Mantoux's notes, it was recorded as follows: 'Le President Wilson – Les Japonais m'ont dit, avec toute la politesse orientale, que si nous ne leur donnions pas raison sur cet article du traité, ils ne pourraient pas signer le reste'. Mantoux, *Délibérations*, p. 317.
160. See NGB, vol. *Pari kōwa kaigi*, pp. 723–36. According to the Japanese minutes, Lloyd George practically showed around Ambassador Greene's official letter bearing the British pledge to support Japan.
161. Proceedings of the Council of Heads of Governments, April 22, CAB29/37.
162. At one stage, he declared to the Japanese that his preoccupation was to maintain 'Open Door' in China. See Mantoux, *Délibérations*, p. 323.
163. Matsui to Uchida, April 23, 1919, *NGB*, vol. *Pari kōwa kaigi*, pp. 727–8.
164. Proceedings of the Council of Heads of Governments, April 22, CAB29/37.
165. Ibid., April 24, 1919.
166. A brief glance at the telegrams Lu sent to the Foreign Ministry after April 24 reveals that the Chinese were kept almost entirely out of touch with the development of the matter, for there was obvious lack of information and misinformation in those telegrams.
167. Lu to Foreign Ministry, April 23, 1919, *ML*, pp. 133–4.
168. Memorandum, April 23, 1919, Koo Papers, Box 3. See also Lu to Foreign Ministry, April 24, 1919; *ML*. p. 134.
169. Matsui to Uchida, April 27, 1919, *NGB*, vol. *Pari kōwa kaigi*, pp. 737–40.
170. Matsui to Uchida, April 28, 1919, *NGB*, 1919, Book 2, vol. I, pp. 261–3.
171. Baker, *Woodrow Wilson*, vol. II, pp. 260–1.
172. Kajima, *Diplomacy of Japan*, pp. 364–5.
173. NGB, vol. *Pari kōwa kaigi*, p. 748. Wilson also made a proposal, which read: 'Surrender to China of all rights of sovereignty and retention with regard to the railway and the mines only of the economic rights of the concessionaire; to retain however privilege of establishing a non-exclusive settlement at Tsingtao.' This the Japanese rejected point-blank.
174. The actual wording of the Japanese statement was as follows: 'In reply to the questions by President Wilson, the Japanese Delegates declare as

follows: The policy of Japan is to hand back the Shantung Peninsula in full sovereignty to China, retaining only the economic privileges granted to Germany and the right to establish a settlement under the usual conditions at Tsingtao. The owners of the railway will use special police only to insure security for traffic. They will be used for no other purposes. The police force will be composed of Chinese, and such Japanese instructors as the directors of the railway select will be appointed by the Chinese Government.' Matsui to Uchida, April 28, 1919, NGB, vol. *Pari kōwa kaigi*, p. 751.

175. For the text of the three articles, see MacMurray, *Treaties and Agreements*, vol. II, p. 1488.
176. Grayson Diary, April 30, 1919, Grayson Papers, Box 3.
177. Baker, *Woodrow Wilson*, vol. II, p. 266.
178. House Diary, April 28, 1919; MC, 40, Reel 4
179. Desktop Diary, April 29, 1919, Lansing Papers, MC, Ac. 15,347, Reel 2.
180. Grayson Diary, May 5, 1919, Grayson Papers, Box 3.
181. Sze to Wu, July 6, 1919, CA 1003-821.
182. See Fifield, R., 'Japanese Policy Towards the Shantung Question at the Paris Peace Conference', *Journal of Modern History*, vol. XXIII, Sept., 1951, pp. 265–72.
183. Oka, Y., *Five Political Leaders of Modern Japan*, p. 193. See also Harada, K., *Saionji ko to seikyōku*, vol. I, pp. 20–1. This is very significant not because Saionji was the head of the Japanese Delegation to the Peace Conference but because of his position as one of the surviving genrō, who had great say in Japan's foreign policy-making.
184. See Hara, K., *Hara nikki*, April 30, 1919, vol. V, p. 88.
185. Hu Shih, 'Intellectual China 1919', *Chinese Social and Political Science Review* (hereafter, *CSPSR*), vol. IV, no. 4, Dec. 1919, pp. 346–7.
186. Schwartz, B., 'Themes in Intellectual History May Fourth and after', in *CHC*, vol. 12, p. 407.
187. See, for example, Peng Ming, *Wusi Yundong* (The May Fourth Movement) and Chow Tse-tsung, *The May Fourth Movement: Intellectual Revolution in Modern China*.
188. Koo, *Gu Wejun Huiyi Lu*, p. 205.
189. See, for example, 'Beijing Students' Petition to President Xu Shichang' on May 19, 1919, reprinted in *Wusi Aiguo Yundong* (The May Fourth Patriotic Movement), p. 323.
190. See Chen, J., *The May Fourth Movement in Shanghai*, pp. 6–25, and Chow Tse-tsung, *Intellectual Revolution*, pp. 338–54.
191. See Hu Shih, 'Intellectual China', *CSPSR*, p. 347.
192. This view was held by Chen Duxiu, one of the founders of the Chinese Communist Party and its first General Secretary. See Chow, Tse-tsung, *Intellectual Revolution*, pp. 347–8.
193. See Mao Zedong, 'The May Fourth Movement', *Selected Works of Mao Zedong*, vol. II, pp. 545; 'On New Democracy', *Selected Works of Mao Zedong*, vol. IV, pp. 125–7.
194. See Meisner, M., 'Cultural Iconoclasm, Nationalism, and Internationalism in the May Fourth Movement' in Schwartz, B. (ed.), *Reflections on the May Fourth Movement: A Symposium*, pp. 15–18.

195. By this I mean the nationalist movement in May and June of 1919, demanding the Chinese Government not to sign the Versailles Treaty without reservations on the Shandong decision by the 'Big Three'.

196. *Li Dazhao Xuanji*, (Selected Works of Li Dazhao) p. 255.

197. Chow used this phrase to describe what he called the 'May Fourth Incident'. See Chow Tse-tsung, *Intellectual Revolution*, pp. 84–100.

198. It must be pointed out, however, that up to now there have been very few studies of the participation of warlords and some government officials in the populist protest during the May Fourth Movement and their role in influencing the Government's decision-making in matters of signature. This constitutes an interesting but neglected aspect of the Chinese nationalist assertion during the May Fourth period. The subject will be taken up later in the chapter.

199. The phrase 'assertive nationalism' is used here to designate an assertion by a nation of its own rights as a sovereign entity in the modern international society.

200. Kohn, H., *The Idea of Nationalism*, p. 10.

201. Snyder, L., *The New Nationalism*, p. 161.

202. Nehru, J., 'Nationalism in Asia', *International Journal*, vol. I, Winter, 1950–1951, p. 10.

203. Wright, *China in Revolution*, p. 8.

204. For a brief description of Chinese nationalism in action in the two decades before the May Fourth Movement, see Liao, K-S, *Antiforeignism and Modernization in China, 1860–1980*, ch. 4, pp. 55–80.

205. Meisner, 'Cultural Iconoclasm', in Schwartz, B. (ed.), *Reflections*, p. 17.

206. In Wright's words, 'The substratum of Chinese society shared the anti-imperialist sentiments of the upper quarters, but they were not likely to be timid if treaty rights and other things of which they knew little got in their way'. Wright, *China in Revolution*, p. 54

207. Cabinet to Lu, May 4, 1919, CA 1003-819.

208. This is another name for Jiaozhou.

209. 'Waijiao Yaodian' (Important Telegrams about Foreign Affairs), *Gongyan Bao* (Journal of Public Opinion) May 8, 1919.

210. Zhu and Tang to Lu, May 6, 1919, *Nanbei Yihe Ziliao* (Source Materials about the Peace Conference Between the North and the South in 1919) p. 154.

211. Quoted in Deng Ye, 'Bali Hehui Zhongguo Juyue Wenti Yenjiu' (On China's Refusal to Sign the Peace Treaty at the Paris Peace Conference), *Zhongguo Shehui Kexue* (The Chinese Social Sciences), no. 2, 1986, p. 135.

212. 'Dujun' was the title of the military governor in a province. They were virtually various kinds of warlords.

213. See 'Beiyang Zhengfu Dangan' (Selected Archival Materials of the Beijing Government), in *Wusi Aiguo Yundong Dangan Ziliao* (hereafter, *WAYDZ* – Archival Materials about the May Fourth Patriotic Movement) pp. 320–1.

214. Deng Ye, 'Bali Helui', p. 136.

215. *Dagong Bao* (Dagong Daily, Changsha edition), May 18, 1919.

216. *Shen Bao* (Shanghai Daily), May 27, 1919

217. This, as it turned out later, was not a problem. China, by signing the Peace Treaty with Austria, was actually recognized as one of the original members of the League of Nations. The realization of the possibility of China joining the League of Nations by signing the Austrian Peace Treaty helped the Chinese delegates in Paris to make up their minds not to sign without reservations as to the Shandong clauses. See Koo, *Gu Weijun Huiyi Lu*, p. 205.

218. For details, see 'Bali Huiyi Jiaoao Wenti Jiaoshe Jiyao' (An Outline Account of the Negotiations for the Restoration of Jiaozhou at the Peace Conference), *WAYDZ*, p. 321.

219. Lu to Cabinet, May 14, 1919, CA 05-3-33.

220. Deng Ye, 'Bali Hehui', p. 135.

221. *Chen Bao* (The Morning Post), May 15, 1919.

222. See 'Bali Huiyi Jiaoao Wenti Jiaoshe Jiyao', *WAYDZ*, pp. 325-7.

223. *Chen Bao*, May 15, 1919.

224. This is a literal translation of the Chinese phrase 'Liang Hai Qu Qing'. This policy was formulated on the basis that since either to sign or not to sign would do harm to China as a sovereign entity, it would be advisable to choose the less harmful option.

225. See *WAYDZ*, pp.325-9.

226. Wang to Cabinet, May 8, 1919, CA 1003-822.

227. Cabinet to Lu, May 21, 1919; Zhuang to Foreign Ministry, May 18, 1919, CA 05-3-33.

228. Cabinet to Lu, May 21, 1919, CA 05-3-33.

229. Cabinet to Lu, May 27, 1919, CA 1003-819.

230. Lu to Foreign Ministry, May 19, 1919, *ML*, p. 212.

231. Lu to Cabinet, May 22, 1919, Ibid., pp. 213-14.

232. This was later denied by both the two Houses and the two Speakers. See Deng Ye, 'Bali Hahui' p. 138.

233. *Dagong Bao*, May 31, 1919.

234. Chen Lu, the Acting Foreign Minister, told Lu on June 16 in a telegram that 'Duan once sent out to Dujuns and civilian governors a circular telegram advocating the signing of the Treaty and asked for their opinion. The replies received almost unanimously approved [it]'. See Chen to Lu, June 16, 1919, CA 1003-819.

235. Cabinet to Lu, May 27, 1919, CA 1003-819.

236. Cabinet to Lu, May 30, 1919, CA 1003-819.

237. Foreign Ministry to Lu, June 11, 1919, CA 05-3-34.

238. For details of the crisis in late May and June, see Chow Tse-tsung *Intellectual Revolution*, pp. 80–170.

239. *Chen Bao*, June 12, 1919.

240. Chen to Lu, May 15, 1919, CA 1003-819.

241. The caretaker Cabinet was headed by Gong Xingzhan, the Minister of Finance. He was very reluctant to take over. In a circular telegram to the provinces, he actually stated that he would act in the capacity of Premier for ten days only, while the President took time to nominate a new Premier. But, as the crisis dragged on, he had to stay all through the matter of China's signature, well into July 1919.

242. See Foreign Ministry to Lu, May 15, 1919, CA 1003-819.

243. Qin and Sun to Xu, June 20, 1919, CA 1003-819.
244. See *WAYDZ*, pp. 353–4.
245. Chen to Lu, June 16, 1919, CA 05-3-34.
246. Cabinet to Lu, May 19, 1919, CA 05-3-34.
247. Deng Ye, 'Bali Hehui', p. 142.
248. See Cabinet to Lu, June 5 and June 10, 1919, CA 1003-819.
249. Koo, *Gu Weijun Huiyi Lu*, pp. 206, 209.
250. *Shen Bao*, June 26, 1919.
251. Cabinet to Lu, June 27, 1919, CA 05-3-34. Koo suspected that it was deliberately delayed. See Koo, *Gu Weijun Huiyi Lu*, p. 210
252. Ibid., p. 199
253. As to the Chinese contention that their declaration had terminated all treaties and agreements with Germany, the Japanese argued that 'Such a treaty differs from a treaty of cession pure and simple only in that it confers for a certain period of time the exercise of the rights of sovereignty, whereas a treaty of cession pure and simple transfers it without any limitation of time. And it is universally recognized that a declaration of war does not abrogate treaties fixing frontiers and the territorial status of the belligerent powers. Moreover, in our particular case, there is no need to appeal to this juridical theory, for, if war abrogates certain treaties between belligerents, never does it abolish treaties between co-belligerents, that is to say, between allies'. See Gallagher, J., *America's Aims and Asia's Aspirations*, pp. 305–6.
254. Lu to Clemenceau, May 4, 1919, English version in Macmurray, *Treaties and Agreements*, vol. II, pp. 1494–5, see also Lu to Foreign Ministry, May 6, 1919 for a summary of the protest in Chinese, CA 05-3-33.
255. Lu to Foreign Ministry, May 6, 1919. Koo recalled that 'It had not been unexpected that the final settlement would not be very favourable but it had not even been suspected that it would be as unfavourable as it was actually.' Interview with Wellington Koo, VI-1-9, Koo Papers, Box 1.
256. Baker, R., *Woodrow Wilson*, vol. II, p. 266.
257. This was what Wei, one of the Chinese delegates, told Lansing the next day. He also said that he had handed to Kirk one copy of that informal memorandum. See Personal Memo, May 1, 1919, Lansing Papers, MC, Ac. 15,327, Reel 4. Millard, an American journalist, who happened to be with the Chinese delegates when Baker went to communicate Wilson's message, had the same story. He wrote 'I was present when the President's explanation of his action in that matter was semi-officially communicated to the Chinese Delegation in Paris, in which the President explained that political exigency (the threat of Japan to bolt the Conference and the private intimation that the British Government might, in that event, have to withdraw, too) had forced him to assent to the Shantung decision in order to save the League of Nations, and that he would see that China will get justice from the League'. Millard to Hill, July 15, 1919, Lansing Papers, vol. 44.
258. Baker, *Woodrow Wilson*, vol. II, p. 266.
259. Millard to Hill, July 19, 1919, Lansing Papers, vol. 44.
260. King, *China at the Peace Conference*, pp. 25–6.
261. Bonsal, S., *Suitors and Supplicants – The Little Nations at Versailles*, p. 239.

262. House Diary, May 1, 1919, Hist. MSS, Film 40.

263. Interview with Wellington Koo, VI-1-10, Koo Papers, Box 1.

264. There is an obvious mistake in the date of the seventy-fourth meeting of the Chinese Delegation in the minutes, copies of which are preserved in both the Chinese archives and the Japanese archives (see next footnote). The date was designated as April 31. It must be May 1, since Baker went to the Chinese Delegation only on the evening of April 30 and April does not have 31 days.

265. Delegation Minutes, no. 74, April 31 [sic], 1919, CA 05-3-1, also in *JFMA*, MT 231-4, p. 1568.

266. Lu to Foreign Ministry, May 6 and May 8, 1919, *ML*, pp. 147, 204, see also Lu to Clemenceau, May 6, 1919, FO608/209.

267. A good illustration of this is Colonel Bonsal's observation that once on May 9, 1919, Koo told House, 'If I sign the treaty even under orders I shall not have what you call in New York even a Chinaman's chance of surviving'. Bonsal Diary, May 9, 1919, Bonsal Papers, Box 18.

268. Lu to Foreign Ministry, May 20, 1919, CA 05-3-33.

269. Lu to Foreign Ministry, May 22, 1919, CA 05-3-33.

270. Lu to Foreign Ministry, May 26, 1919, CA 05-3-33.

271. The actual wording of Lu's letter runs as follows: 'Pursuant to instructions from my Government, I have the honour, therefore to inform you that the Chinese Plenipotentiaries will sign for the Republic of China the Treaty of Peace with Germany under the reservations made and recorded in the Minutes of the proceedings of the Plenary Session of the Preliminary Peace Conference on May 6, 1919.' Lu to Clemenceau, May 26, 1919, *China Yearbook, 1919–1920*, pp. 719–20. In another dispatch on the same day to the Cabinet, Lu reported that the Delegation was making it explicitly clear to the Conference that they would not sign without reservations to see how the Powers would react. They would insist on the reservations until the last moment. Lu to Foreign Ministry, May 26, 1919, CA 05-3-33.

272. Lu and Koo saw Wilson on May 27 and were practically warned that it would be highly inadvisable for the Chinese Delegation to issue any more declarations about the reservations. Lu to Foreign Ministry, May 27, 1919, CA 05-3-33.

273. He also contended that the Powers could not do any harm to China of their own will consequent to China's refusal. Germany was now too weak. America, Britain and France could divide China if they so wished and to sign the Treaty could not stop them. Japan had insatiable and unpredictable ambition in China and had to be confronted with the unity of the whole nation which the refusal to sign the Treaty could bring about.

274. Delegation Minutes, the Secret Meeting, May 28, 1919, CA 05-3-1, also in *JFMA*, MT 234-1, p. 1459. See also Lu to Foreign Ministry, May 28, 1919, CA 05-3-33, for a summary of the arguments for and against signing the Treaty even without reservations.

275. Interview with Wellington Koo, VII-1-1, Koo Papers, Box 1.

276. Interview with Wellington Koo, VII-1-2, Koo Papers, Box 1.

277. Lu to Foreign Ministry, June 25, 1919, CA 05-3-33.

278. Mantoux, *Délibérations*, vol. II, p. 516.
279. See Notes on a Meeting of the Council of Heads of the Governments, June 25, 1919, CAB29/39.
280. Wilson actually had his own considerations with regard to the reservation issue. Two days before, on June 23, he informed Tumulty in Washington that he was firmly convinced that 'the adoption of the treaty by the Senate with reservations would put the United States as clearly out of the concert of nations as a rejection'. Wilson to Tumulty, June 23, 1919, Tumulty Papers, Box 7.
281. Lu to Foreign Minister, June 25, 1919, CA 05-3-33.
282. Lu to Foreign Ministry, June 26, 1919, CA 05-3-33.
283. Italics my own.
284. The matter was decided at the Council of Four on the afternoon of June 26, with Wilson remaining silent on the issue. Clemenceau explained that he had been told by Koo that the Chinese Delegation intended to send in a letter of protest against the Shandong provisions of the Treaty. He went on with a conversation with Lloyd George:
    M. Clemenceau. – ... Faut-il que cette lettre de protestation soit écrite avant ou après la signature du traité? Quant à moi, Je préférerais qu'elle fut écrite après.
    M. Lloyd George. – Certainement.
    M. Clemenceau. – Autrement, cela pourrait encourager La Roumanie à en faire autant.
    M. Lloyd George. – Il faut même se méfier du côté des Allemands.
    See Mantoux, *Délibérations*, vol. II, p. 530.
285. Lu to Foreign Ministry, June 27, 1919, CA 05-3-33.
286. In fact, the Chinese students and other Chinese people in Paris practically surrounded both the Hotel Lutetia and St. Claude Sanitarium to stop the Chinese delegates from going to sign the Treaty the next day. Interview with Wellington Koo, VII-1-2, Koo Papers, Box 1.
287. Lu to Foreign Ministry, June 28, 1919, CA 05-3-33, see also Interview with Wellington Koo, VII-1-2, VII-1-3, Koo Papers. Box 1. Lu confessed in his memoir, published in 1943 that 'Pour la première fois dans ma carrière, je crus de mon devoir de ne pas obéir. Notre pays se devait à lui-même de ne plus consentir à se laisser jouer. Je ne voulais pas, une nouvelle fois, apposer mon nom sous des clauses injustes, et je pris sur moi seul de refuser la signature'. Lu, T. T., *Souvenirs set Pensées*, p. 82.
288. The draft of the reservations reads as follows: 'In proceeding to sign the Treaty of Peace with Germany today, the undersigned, Plenipotentiaries of the Republic of China, considering as unjust articles 156, 157, and 158 therein which purport to transfer the German rights in the Chinese Province of Shantung to Japan instead of restoring them to China, the rightful sovereign over the territory and a loyal co-partner in the war on the side of the Allied and Associated Powers, hereby declare, in the name and on behalf of their Government, that their signing of the Treaty is not to be understood as precluding China from demanding at a suitable time the reconsideration of the Shantung question, to the end that the injustice to China may be rectified in the interest of permanent peace in the Far East'. *China Yearbook, 1919–1920*, p. 720.

289. Interview with Wellington Koo, VII-1-9 and VII-1-10, Koo Papers, Box 1.
290. By noon, the Chinese Delegation received a formal note from the Secretariat General of the Conference. It stated that 'The Secretariat General of the Peace Conference has the honour to deliver herewith to His Excellency the Chinese Minister the two notes which he was good enough to deliver this morning. In returning them, it is intended to permit the Chinese Delegates to sign the treaty in the session of this afternoon, if it thinks it ought to do so without any reservation, as was indicated to the Chinese Delegation upon instructions from the Supreme Council'. *China Yearbook, 1919–1920*, p. 712.
291. Ibid.
292. King, *China at the Peace Conference*, p. 30.
293. Wang told Hornbeck on June 30 that the Government instruction was received at 5 o'clock in the afternoon, about two hours after the opening of the ceremony of signature. Hornbeck to Kirk, June 30, 1919, Lansing Papers, vol. 44.
294. Lu to President, June 28, 1919, CA 05-3-33. The English text is from *NCH*, vol. *CXXXII*, p. 85.
295. Reinsch, *American Diplomat*, p. 332.
296. At the Peace Conference, China also took part in the work of many commissions. It was elected into the Commission on League of Nations and the Commission on Ports, Waterways and Railways. Koo and Wang each represented China in the two commissions. When China was elected into the Economic Commission in March, Sze was appointed the Chinese representative. Foreign Minister Lu himself also participated in the work of the Commission on International Labour Legislation. See Lu to Foreign Ministry, Jan. 27, March 14, & April 12, *ML*, pp. 71, 108, 125.
297. Toynbee, A., *The World after the Peace Conference*, p. 25.
298. See Lu to Cabinet, June 28, 1919, CA 05-3-33.

3　Whither China in the East Asian International Order?

1. France was almost impotent in East Asia after the war, with its preoccupations in Europe. There was even a fear in the Foreign Office in London that, if France abandoned its interests in Indo-China, the Japanese would step in. See Balfour's minute on a Foreign Office Memo, 'French Indo-China and British-Japanese Perspectives: Policies after the War', no date, FO371/3190. There was talk that if the French were willing to hand over Indo-China to Britain, a compensation deal could be made in Africa. See minute by Lord Hardinge, no date, ibid.
2. Bonsal Diary, May 1, 1919, Bonsal Papers, Container 2.
3. Jordan to Tilley, Sept. 24, 1919, FO350/16.
4. What was the most revealing of the so-called 'united front' of foreign Powers *vis-à-vis* China was the existence of a Diplomatic Corps at Beijing before and during (representing the Allied and Associate Powers only) the war. The Diplomatic Corps, with the British Minister as its Dean most of the time, represented the collective interests of all treaty Powers in China and spoke in one voice to the Chinese Foreign Ministry. It

collapsed after the war only because the treaty Powers were now divided, with the defeated (Germany and former Austria–Hungary) and the defected (Russia) losing their treaty rights. It can be argued, however, that a 'united front' of a sort composed of the remaining Powers on the scene in China survived even after the Washington Conference in 1921–1922.

5. Huang Yanpei *et al.* to Alston, June 1920, Enclosure in Alston to Curzon, Aug. 7, 1920, FO228/3352.
6. Macleay to Jordan, Nov. 26, 1918, FO228/3543.
7. Ibid.
8. Jordan to Macleay, Dec. 4, 1918, FO371/3191.
9. Minute by Max Müller, Dec. 13, 1918 on Jordan to Macleay Dec. 4, 1918, FO371/3191.
10. See Jordan to Balfour, Oct. 23, 1918, FO371/3191.
11. The letter was received only on Feb. 24, 1919. For the full text of Jordan's letter, see *Documents on British Foreign Policy, 1919–1939, First Series,* (hereafter *DBFP*), vol. VI, pp. 566–83.
12. Ibid. See also minute by Max Müller on Jordan to Balfour, Dec. 23, 1918, FO371/3693.
13. Ibid.
14. Minute by Max Müller on Jordan to Balfour, Dec. 23, 1918, FO371/3693.
15. Jordan to Macleay, Dec. 4, 1918, FO371/3191.
16. Jordan to Balfour, Oct. 23, 1918, FO371/3191.
17. Jordan to Balfour, Dec. 23, 1918, *DBFP*, vol. VI, pp. 582–3.
18. The Undersecretary of State, Colonial Office to Undersecretary of State, Foreign Office, Jan. 14, 1919, FO371/3690.
19. See for example, minute by Max Müller on Jan. 18, 1919, FO371/3690.
20. Undersecretary of Foreign Secretary to Undersecretary of Colonial Office, Feb. 24, 1919, FO371/3690.
21. Jordan to FO, Feb. 11, 1919, FO371/3690.
22. Undersecretary of Foreign Office to Undersecretary of Colonial Office, Feb. 24, 1919, FO371/3690.
23. Jordan to FO, Jan. 23, 1919, FO228/3543.
24. Curzon was referring to the Hong Kong Extension.
25. Minute by Curzon, Jan. 29, 1919 on Jordan to FO, Jan. 23, 1919, FO608/209.
26. Minute by Max Müller, March 1, 1919 on Jordan to Balfour, Dec. 23, 1918, FO371/3693.
27. Minute by Macleay, Dec. 12, 1918 on Jordan to Macleay, Dec. 4, 1918, FO371/3191.
28. Minute by Müller, April 17, 1919, FO371/3693.
29. Minute by Müller, June 14, 1919 on Jordan to Curzon, June 12, 1919, FO371/3694.
30. On the April 22 session discussing China's demand on the restoration of Jiaozhou, Lloyd George simply asked 'What is the Twenty-One Demands?' He confessed that he had never heard of that before. Proceedings of the Council of Heads of Governments, April 22, 1919. For Balfour's sympathy for the Japanese, see Balfour to Curzon, May 8, 1919, commenting on the Big Three's decision on Shandong, *DBFP*, vol.

VI, p. 564. Jordan's criticism of Balfour's understanding of the Far Eastern questions was straightforward. He noted: 'The despatch of 8 May from Mr. Balfour to Lord Curzon deals with the Shantung question in a superficial way. It shows no knowledge of the question in its bearing upon political development in Corea and Manchuria during the past twenty-five years ... it fails to touch the facts as they exist and are common knowledge to students of Eastern problems'. A Note by Jordan, July 22, 1919, FO228/3543.

31. Jordan to Curzon, June 12, 1919, FO371/3694.
32. Minute by Müller, May 1, 1919, FO371/3694.
33. Minute by Macleay, March 31, 1919 on Jordan to Balfour, Dec. 23, 1918, FO608/210.
34. Alston to Curzon, June 17, 1919, FO371/3694. Alston was then the British chargé d'affaires in Tokyo.
35. Curzon to Alston, July 18, 1919, FO371/3695.
36. Ibid.
37. Ibid.
38. Curzon told Chinda that 'Viewing the circumstances in which these agreements [during the war] have been concluded, and the fact that China had not been in a position to defend herself, I could not regard them as possessing any great validity'. Ibid.
39. Curzon to Alston, July 18, 1919, FO371/3695.
40. Curzon's attitude as such can probably be accounted for partly by his experience of being the Viceroy of India, 1898–1905. Nish observed that 'his approach to diplomacy was magisterial, and to Asian countries paternalistic'. See Nish, I., *Alliance in Decline*, pp. 263–4.
41. Curzon to Alston, July 18, 1919, FO371/3695.
42. Curzon to Alston, July 22, 1919, FO371/3695.
43. Ibid.
44. FO Minute by Müller, April 17, 1919, FO371/3693.
45. Quoted in Louis, W. R., *British Strategy in the Far East*, p. 46.
46. Ibid.
47. Curzon to Alston, July 18, 1919, FO371/3695.
48. Curzon's interviews with Chinda were actually transmitted to the State Department of the United States for its consultation. See Curzon to Lindsay, July 23, 1919, *DBFP*, vol. VI, p. 639.
49. 'Foreign Office Memorandum on Effect of Anglo-Japanese Alliance upon Foreign Relationships', Feb. 28, 1920, *DBFP*, vol. VI, p. 1016. Sir Beilby Alston, the British Minister to China after Jordan, also expressed his agreement with the idea that the British and the American interests in China were almost identical. See Nish, *Alliance in Decline*, p. 308.
50. Quoted in Louis, *British Strategy*, p. 88.
51. This was, in fact, a rationale which was later repeatedly appealed to to justify the continuation of the Anglo-Japanese Alliance at the Imperial Conference in 1921. See Nish, I., *Alliance in Decline*, chs. XIX, XX and XXI, and Louis, W. R., *British Strategy*, ch. II. See also *DBFP*, vol. VI. pp. 1051–5.
52. Jordan to Curzon, June 12, 1919, FO371/3694.
53. FO Minute by Wellesley, May 31, 1920, FO371/5340. Wellesley was then the head of the Far Eastern Department of the Foreign Office.

54. Ibid.
55. Nish, *Alliance in Decline*, p. 281.
56. FO Minute by Parlett, March 27, 1920 on the Foreign Office Memo March 23, 1920, *DBFP*, vol. VI, pp. 1051–2. H. G. Parlett was Counsellor of the British Embassy in Tokyo, then on leave in London.
57. Cubitt (representing the war Office) to the Foreign Office, Feb. 14, 1920, *DBFP*, vol. VI, p. 1055.
58. Minute by Hardinge (no date) on the Foreign Office Memo, March 23, 1920, *DBFP* vol. VI, p. 1053.
59. 'Foreign Office Memorandum on Effect of Anglo-Japanese Alliance upon Foreign Relationships', Feb. 28, 1920, *DBFP*, vol. VI, p. 1022.
60. Quoted in Louis, *British Strategy*, p. 82.
61. The Committee was composed of W. Tyrrell, Assistant Under-Secretary of State for Foreign Affairs, C. Greene, former British Ambassador to Japan, J. Jordan, former British Minister to China, and V. Wellesley, Head of the Far Eastern Department. For more details about the Committee, see Nish, *Alliance in Decline*, pp. 310–13.
62. In the earlier part of the Report, it had been suggested that the Anglo-Japanese Alliance should be substituted by a Tripartite Entente between the United States, Japan and Great Britain. The closest cooperation of the United States, not that of Japan, should be relied upon for the success of British policy towards the Far East.
63. Report of the Anglo-Japanese Alliance Committee, Jan. 21, 1921, *DBFP*, vol. XIV, pp. 226–7.
64. Nish, I., 'Japan in Britain's View of the International System, 1919–37', in Nish, I. (ed.), *Anglo-Japanese Alienation, 1919–1952*, p. 32.
65. Curzon's words. Quoted in Louis, *British Strategy*, p. 46.
66. Lloyd George, in spite of his ignorance of China, exclaimed once that 'The trade of China is only one pound sterling per head of the population, whereas the trade of Japan is ten pounds sterling per head. If you have the same thing in China you would have a trade of about 4,000 millions'. See Louis, *British Strategy*, p. 74.
67. Reinsch to Lansing, Jan. 6, 1919, *FRUS*, PPC, 1919, vol. II, p. 520. Reinsch asked specifically that Polk, Acting Secretary of State, forward this dispatch of his to President Wilson in Paris.
68. Reinsch to Lansing, Nov. 23, 1918, *FRUS*, PPC, 1919, vol. II, p. 494.
69. Ibid., pp. 493–4.
70. Reinsch to Lansing, Nov. 24, 1918, *FRUS*, PPC, vol. II, p. 508.
71. 'Problems and Policy in the Far East' – a memo by Stanley Hornbeck to the American Commissioners to Negotiate Peace, no date, Bliss Papers, Box 356.
72. Reinsch to Polk, Jan. 6, 1919, *FRUS*, PPC, 1919, vol. II, p. 524.
73. Other Americans in China, notably Dr. W. W. Willoughby, an international lawyer and adviser to the Chinese Government, sent separate despatches to the State Department at approximately the same time, defining the 'Chinese question' in similar vein. See 'Précis of Second Report of W. W. Willoughby to Department of State', no date, White Papers, Box 47.
74. Reinsch to Polk, Jan. 6, 1919, *FRUS*, PPC, vol. II, pp. 522–3.
75. Ibid., pp. 524–5.

76. Ibid., p. 524.
77. Reinsch to Polk, April 11, 1919, Polk Papers, Box 12.
78. Reinsch to Polk, Jan. 6, 1919, *FRUS*, PPC, vol. II, pp. 522–5.
79. See 'Far East: Problems and Policy' – a memo by E. T. Williams and S. Hornbeck, Jan. 20, 1919, Bliss Papers, Box 356.
80. Hornbeck to Peace Commissioners (no date), Bliss Papers, Box 356. Williams, at the same time, also tried to call the Commissioners' 'particular attention to the serious importance' of this message. He warned that 'Japan must be restrained if justice is to prevail or liberty to survive in the Far East'. Williams to the Commissioners, (no date), Bliss Papers, Box 356.
81. See for example, Koo's memos on his interviews with Lansing on Nov. 15, 1918, with Wilson on Nov. 26, 1918 and with House on Dec. 18, 1918, Koo Papers, Box 1. It must be noted, however, that none of them had shown any appreciation of the so-called China problem as deep as that of Reinsch.
82. Polk to Reinsch, Feb. 28, 1919, Polk Papers, Box 12.
83. Bliss to Nellie, Dec. 18, 1918, Bliss Papers, Box 244.
84. Bonsal Diary, Dec. 6, 1918, Bonsal Papers, Box 17.
85. Memo of a Conversation with Wilson, Nov. 26, 1918, Koo Papers, Box 1.
86. Ibid.
87. This is what Clemenceau said to House on Dec. 5, 1918; see Bonsal Diary, Dec. 6, 1918, Bonsal Papers, Box 17.
88. Desktop Diary, June 9, 1919, Lansing Papers, MC, Ac 15,347, Reel 2.
89. Ibid.
90. See, for example, Polk to Ammission, Jan. 5, 1919, Bliss Papers, Box 356; Hornbeck and Williams to Lansing, Jan. 12, 1919, Lansing Papers, vol. 41; Polk to Ammission, Jan. 21 and 25, 1919, White Papers, Box 47.
91. Congressional Record. Senate, July 23, 1919, p. 3046.
92. Lansing to Reinsch, Nov. 4, 1918, *FRUS*, 1914, Supp., p. 190. Yuan Shikai, the Chinese President at the time, had a penetrating and well-known remark on this American ambivalence: 'Your words – very fine words – but after all only words'. Koo Papers, Box 3.
93. Tyler Dennett, a well-known historian of American diplomacy, had tried in 1922 to explain this ambivalence in a different light. In his words, 'The discussion of American policy in the Far East is sometimes misleading when it seizes upon the open-door policy as primary, for while that is the substance of America purpose, the play of policy is not around this doctrine, from which the American government has never receded, but around the method by which it may be made more effective, i.e. whether by isolated or by co-operative action'. See Dennett, T., 'Seward's Far Eastern Policy', *American Historical Review*, vol. XXVIII, no. 1, Oct. 1922. Almost fifty years later, Israel, J. in his book, *Progressivism and the Open Door – America and China, 1905–1921*, developed a similar framework, arguing that American policy towards China was vacillating between competition and cooperation with the other Powers to realize the Open Door doctrine. The difficulty of this approach is that it saw America's China problem only in terms of the Great Powers' relations and cannot explain the ambivalence of American attitudes in response to

the internal changes of the Chinese society, especially the emerging Chinese nationalism.

94. Nish, *Alliance in Decline*, p.280. The American support, if any, was only limited to their sympathy with the Chinese nationalist movement. In the diplomatic dispatches from the American Legation in Beijing at the time, there could be found little beyond some descriptive details of the May Fourth Movement.

95. See Cohen, W., 'America and the May Fourth Movement – the Response to Chinese Nationalism, 1917-1921', *Pacific Historical Review*, vol. XXXV, Feb. 1966, pp. 83–100.

96. Li, Tien-yi, *Woodrow Wilson's China Policy, 1913–1917*, p. 5, see also ch. I 'Academic Background', pp. 11–22.

97. See Turner, F. J., *The Frontier in American History*, pp. 311–4.

98. Wilson, a personal friend of Turner, once wrote: 'All I ever wrote on the subject [the interpretation of American history] came from him [Turner]'. Turner in 1918 was 'warmly in favour' of Wilson's Fourteen Points and the League of Nations. See Williams, W. A., 'The Frontier Thesis and the American Foreign Policy', *Pacific Historical Review*, vol. XXIV, 1955, p. 388.

99. For statistics of American investment in China: see Remer, C. F., *Foreign Investment in China*, pp. 88–89 and Ch. XV 'American Investments in China', pp. 239–338.

100. In a special memo for the American Delegates to the Washington Conference, it was frankly admitted that there was 'abandonment by the United States of Chinese interests at times'. See 'Memorandum to the American Delegates to the Washington Conference', Oct. 31, 1921, Hughes Papers, Reel 140.

101. Storry, R., *Japan and the Decline of the West in the Far East*, p. 113.

102. Joe Robinson (Senator from Arkansas) to Secretary of State, July 3, 1919, Polk Papers, Box 12.

103. Lansing to Polk, Aug. 14, 1919, Polk Papers, Box 9.

104. Lansing to Polk, Oct. 1, 1919, Polk Papers, Box 9.

105. Congressional Record, Senate, July 15, 1919, p. 2606.

106. Ibid., Aug. 26, 1919, p. 4349.

107. Ibid., Aug. 5, 1919, p. 3640.

108. Ibid., Aug. 26, 1919, p. 4345.

109. Ibid., Aug. 5, 1919, p. 3641.

110. White noted that 'the President's mind is not in a normal state and he believe [sic] that if only he can get a discussion of the Treaty into the Presidential Campaign the Senate can be compelled to accept it with no reservation'. White to Miss Pussy, April 1, 1920, White Papers, Box 6.

111. White to Lady Wemyss, April 27, 1920, White Papers, Box 6.

112. Before the Peace Conference, Bonsal had made a pertinent remark on the unpredictability of the American foreign policy. 'There is no continuity in the American foreign policy – and who can deny it? One President can cancel the work of his predecessor and an act of a new Congress can write off the slate all previous engagements.' Bonsal Diary, Dec. 7, 1918, Bonsal Papers, Box 17.

113. Statement by Hughes, Dec. 13, 1921, Hughes Papers, Reel 140.

114. Memorandum to the American Delegates to the Washington Conference [Especially Confidential], Oct. 31, 1921, Hughes Papers, Box 161.
115. John MacMurray, the chief of the Far Eastern Division of the State Department, in a memo written in April 1921, also defined the purpose of the American policy in the Far East as 'restoring the equilibrium in the Far East which has been so dangerously upset by Japan's process of aggrandizement'. SDA 811.30/131.
116. Hughes Papers, Reel 140.
117. Quoted in Hosoya, C., 'Britain and the United States in Japan's View of the International System, 1919–37', Nish, I., (ed.), *Anglo–Japanese Alienation*, p. 4.
118. Hara, K., *Hara zenshū* (Collected Works of Hara Kei), vol. II, p. 894.
119. Morris to Lansing, Nov. 13, 1918, FRUS, PPC, vol. I, p. 489. Sir Conynghame Greene, the British Ambassador to Japan, also reported that 'the news [of the Armistice] had caught the nation more or less unprepared'. Greene to Curzon, *Annual Report, Japan, 1919*, FO410/69.
120. See 'Gaikō Chōsakai kaigi hikki' (Minutes of Meetings of Advisory Council on Foreign Relations), no. 2, Nov. 13, 1918 and no. 4, Dec. 2, 1918 in *Suiusō nikki* (Suiusō Diary), pp. 281–93 and pp. 315–32.
121. Gaikō Chōsakai (Advisory Council on Foreign Relations) was organized in 1916 under the Terauchi Government 'to put 'foreign affairs' beyond the pale of domestic politics'. It was composed of important cabinet ministers and leaders of the political parties. Only Katō Takaaki, leader of the Kenseikai, refused to join. Nish called it the 'watch-dog' of Japan's foreign policy making. It is probably more than that. Gaikō Chōsakai had actually taken into its hand the Japanese foreign policy-making, as Crowley has argued that the formation of Gaikō Chōsakai 'signified the end of active leadership of the *genrō* in policy-making. Thereafter, the cabinet and the Advisory Council on Foreign Relations emerged as the primary locus of decision-making'. See Crowley J. B., 'Military Foreign Policy', in Morley, J., (ed.), *Japan's Foreign Policy, 1868–1941 – A Research Guide*, p. 34.
122. It is worth noting that the only matter for discussion on the agenda of Gaikō Chōsakai's meeting on Nov. 19, 1918 was Wilson's Fourteen Points. See *Suiusō nikki*, p. 294.
123. See 'Gaikō Chōsakai kaigi hikki', no. 3, Nov. 19, 1918 in *Suiusō nikki*, pp. 294–314. The Japanese seemed to have divided the matter touched on in the Fourteen Points into two categories: those of purely European concern and those of world-wide concern. On the matters in the former, such as Poland, Turkey and Serbia, there was little discussion before the decision was adopted to the effect that the Imperial [Japanese] Government in principle had no disagreement and could conform to them.
124. See Hosoya, C. in Nish (ed.), *Anglo–Japanese Alienation*, pp. 3–4.
125. Ibid., p. 7.
126. Morris to Polk, Jan. 7, 1919, FRUS, PPC, vol. I, p. 494, *Millard Review of the Far East*, vol. VII, No. 6, pp. 193–5, Nish (ed.), *Anglo–Japanese Alienation*, p. 77.

127. Morris, the American Ambassador to Japan, noted that 'Prince Konoye's views are shared by a number of publicists'. Morris to Polk, Jan. 7, 1919, *FRUS*, PPC, vol. I, p. 494.
128. Shiratori, R. (ed.), *Nihon no naikaku* (The Japanese Cabinets), vol. I, p. 111.
129. Greene to Curzon, *Annual Report, Japan, 1919*, FO410/69.
130. Ibid.
131. Nish, *Alliance in Decline*, p. 277.
132. Greene to Curzon, *Annual Report, Japan, 1919*, FO410/69.
133. Nish, *Alliance in Decline*, p. 281.
134. *Suiusō nikki*, pp. 326–8 and pp. 333–40.
135. Matsui to Uchida, June 17, 1919, quoted in Asada, S., 'Washinton kaigi to Nihon no taiō' (Washington Conference and Japan's Counter-measures), in Iriye, A. & Aruga, T. (eds.), *Senkanki no Nihon gaikō* (The Japanese Diplomacy Between the Wars), pp. 28–9. Almost all the communications from the Japanese Delegation at Paris to the Japanese Government in Tokyo were carried out in the name of Matsui during the Peace Conference.
136. See, for example, Hosoya, C. and Saitō, M. (eds.), *Washinton taisei to Nichi-Bei kankei* (The Washington System and the Japanese–American Relations) and Iriye, A. and Aruga, T. (eds.), *Senkanki no Nihon gaikō*.
137. Banno emphasized that there had been tussles between the Army and the Foreign Ministry on Japan's China policy all through the war. The Army had its way during the war, while after the war there began an ascendancy of the influence of the Foreign Ministry on Japan's overall foreign policy-making. See Banno, J., 'Nihon rikugun no Obeikan to Chūgoku seisaku' (Japanese Army's Attitude towards European Powers and the United States and its Policy towards China), in Banno, J., *Kindai Nihon no gaikō to seiji* (Politics and Foreign Relations in Modern Japan), pp. 77–105.
138. Kitaōka, S., *Niho rikugun to tairiku seisaku* (The Japanese Army and Japanese Policy Towards Mainland Asia), p. 229.
139. Quoted in Hosoya, C. in Nish, (ed.), *Anglo–Japanese Alienation*, p. 6.
140. Asada in Iriye & Aruga, *Senkanki no Nihon gaikō*, pp. 21–2.
141. Viscount Itō Miyoji was then a member of the Gaikō Chōsakai.
142. *Suiusō nikki*, p. 611.
143. Hara, K., *Hara nikki* (Hara Kei Diary, ed. Hara, Keiichirō), vol. III, p. 250.
144. Asada in Iriye & Aruga, *Senkanki no Nihon gaikō*, p. 31.
145. During the war, Japanese exports to the U. S. increased three times and imports from the U.S. five times. With the European countries coming back to the China market, Japan would become more dependent on the American market. Besides, Japan also depended on America for finance. See Hosoya and Saitō, (eds.), *Senkanki no Nihon gaikō*, p. 205.
146. Asada in Iriye & Aruga, *Senkanki no Nihon gaikō*, p. 31.
147. Greene to Curzon, *Annual Report, Japan, 1919*, FO410/69.
148. See *Gaikō nempyō*, vol. I, pp. 471, 487, 501–3.
149. *Hara nikki* (ed. Hara, Keiichiro), vol. IV, p. 319.
150. *Hara zenshū, p. 916.*

151. Ibid., pp. 895, 902–3.
152. Alston to Curzon, March 31, 1920, FO405/228.
153. Morley, J., *Japan's Quest for Autonomy*, p. xvi. Morley further argued that 'the identification of national security and economic prosperity with a hegemonic position in East Asia became an article of faith for the imperial government that was not compromised until the end of the Pacific war'. This was laid down in a report Yamagata submitted to the Japanese Throne in October 1906, reviewing the national defence policy of the Japanese Empire and recommending some basic guidelines of future Japanese defence policy.
154. Asada, in Iriye and Aruga (eds.), *Senkanki no Nihon gaikō*, p. 38.
155. *Suiusō nikki*, p. 634. Uchida himself put forward this notion when he first became Foreign Minister of Japan in 1912. See also Asada, in Iriye & Aruga, *Senkanki no Nihon gaikō*, p. 38.
156. *Suiusō nikki*, 'Gaikō Chōsakai kaigi hikki', no. 19, pp. 605–14, and no. 22, pp. 666–71.
157. Greene to Curzon, *Annual Report, Japan, 1919*, FO410/69.
158. *Hara nikki*, Sept. 9, 1921, vol. IX, p. 435.
159. *Gaikō nempyō*, pp. 523–4.
160. *Suiusō nikki*, p. 812.
161. Banno, J., 'Seitō seiji to Chūgoku seisaku, 1919–1926' (Party Politics and China's Policy, 1919–1926), in Banno, J. *Kindai Nihon*, pp. 152–8.
162. Alston to Curzon, July 17, 1919, FO410/67, Eliot to Curzon, Oct. 12, 1920, FO410/68. See also Banno, *Kindai Nihon*, p. 156.
163. Eliot to Curzon, *Annual Report, Japan, 1920*, May 24, 1921, FO410/69.
164. Yamane, Y., *Ronshu Kindai Chūgoku to Nihon* (Modern China and Japan), pp. 250–63, and also Andō, H., *Nihonjin no Chūgoku kan* (A Study of the Japanese View of China in Recent History), pp. 63–86.
165. Alston to Curzon, June 20, 1919, FO410/67.
166. Alston to Curzon, March 31, 1920, FO405/228.
167. Greene to Curzon, *Annual Report, Japan, 1919*, FO410/69.
168. Alston to Curzon, June 20, 1919, FO410/67.
169. FO410/68, Enclosure: 'Report of Conversation between Major Cardrew and Major-General Tanaka recording Latter's Views on Japanese Expansion'.
170. Alston to Curzon, March 31, 1920, FO405/228.
171. *Hara nikki*, vol. VIII. pp. 291–2.
172. Baron Hayashi was said to belong to 'Kokusai kyōchō ha' (faction which advocates international harmonization) and Shidehara, to 'E-Bei kyōchō ha' (faction which advocates harmonization with Britain and the United States). See Asada, in Iriye and Aruga (eds.), *Senkanki no Nihon gaikō*, pp. 25, 29.
173. Hughes Papers, Box 161.
174. Jordan to Curzon, *Annual Report, China, 1919*, Jan. 17, 1920, FO405/229.
175. Ibid.
176. For details of the Treaty, see MacMurray, *Treaties and Agreements*, vol. II, p. 1429. The extraterritoriality was granted in an appendix to the Treaty.
177. *Treaties and Agrements with and Concerning China, 1919–1929*, p. 22.

178. Pollard, R., *China's Foreign Relations, 1917–1931*, p. 97.
179. Article 2 of the Treaty spelt out specifically that the diplomatic representatives of the two High Contracting Parties 'shall be treated, in the respective countries, in the same way as the Ambassadors or Ministers Plenipotentiary of the most favoured nations, and, except in regard to rights in connection with consular jurisdiction, shall enjoy in every respect the same privileges and immunities'. And Article 4 reads 'Subjects or citizens of either of the two High Contracting Parties residing or travelling in the country of the other Party shall be subject to the jurisdiction of the other country – Persia or China as the case may be – in which they are residing or travelling, as regards legal proceedings, disputes, law-suits, or as regards crimes and offences which they may commit.' *Treaties and Agreements with and Concerning China, 1919–1929*, p. 26. For some negotiation details, see Wang (Chinese Minister to Italy) to Foreign Ministry, April 5, 1920, CA 1039-330.
180. See *NCH*, Sept. 25, 1920, vol. CXXXVI, p. 819, *NCH*, Sept. 18, 1919, vol. CXXXII, p. 728, *NCH*, July 17, 1920, vol. CXXXV, p. 146, and *Far Eastern Review*, March 1920, vol. XVI, p. 173.
181. *NCH*, April 28, 1919, vol. CXXXI, p. 269.
182. Jordan noted that this category included 'the States with which China has never been in treaty relations, those with which she has severed relations by her declaration of war, States which have broken away from their former mother States, and States which have recently been recognized as national entities by the terms of the Peace Conference'. According to Jordan's list, there were 19 countries in treaty relations with China and 24 non-treaty countries at the end of September 1919. Jordan to Curzon, Oct. 8, 1919, FO405/226.
183. Reinsch to Polk, May 9, 1919, *FRUS*, 1919, vol. I, p. 685. For a slightly different version in English, see *NCH*, April 28, 1919, vol. CXXXI, p. 269.
184. Foreign Ministry to Wang, April 9, 1920, CA 1039-330.
185. *Chen Bao*, May 27, 1920. The St. Germain Treaty was signed on Sept. 10, 1919. Foreign Minister Lu signed it on behalf of China.
186. *Chen Bao*, May 29, 1920.
187. Zhang to Foreign Ministry, Mar. 25, 1920, CA 1039-330.
188. NCH, Mar. 8, 1920, vol. CXXXIV, p. 678 and Mar. 10, 1920, p. 748.
189. See CA 1039-373,
190. *Treaties and Agreements with and Concerning China, 1919-1929*, p. 48.
191. By the treaties in the 1840s, Chinese import tariff was fixed at 5 per cent *ad valorem*. By the most-favoured-nation clause, this privilege extended to all countries later entering treaty relations with China. In commercial treaties signed with China in 1902 and 1903, Britain and other Powers agreed that the Chinese import tariff increase eventually to 12½ per cent *ad valorem*. This, however, was not put into effect until after the Washington Conference.
192. Jordan to Curzon, Oct. 8, 1919, Enclosure 1, Memorandum respecting Chinese General Tariff and Certificates of Origin, FO405/226.
193. Ibid., Enclosure 2, Wai-chiao Pu (Foreign Ministry) to Jordan, July 23, 1919 .

194. Jordan to Curzon, Oct. 8, 1919, FO405/226.
195. Ibid., Enclosure 1. See also Enclosure 3, British Chamber of Commerce, Shanghai to Commercial Counsellor, Aug. 29, 1919.
196. Wai-chiao Pu (Foreign Ministry) to Legation, Dec. 22, 1919, Enclosure 1 in Clive to Curzon, Sept. 24, 1920, FO405/228.
197. *NCH*, Sept. 20, 1919, vol. CXXXII, p. 725.
198. For Chinese nationalism and the 'rights-recovery movement' in the first decade of the century, see Wright, M., 'Introduction: The Rising Tide of Change' in Wright, M. (ed.), *China in Revolution, The First Phase, 1900–1913*, pp. 11–19.
199. See Political Intelligence Department to Foreign Office, no date, FO608/209.
200. Jordan to Curzon, *Annual Report, 1919, China*, FO405/229.
201. *NCH*, June 12, 1920, vol. CXXXV, p. 642.
202. *China Yearbook, 1919–1920*, p. 741.
203. See Clive to Curzon, June 30, 1920, FO405/228. Alston frankly admitted later in his annual report of 1920 that 'while the Alliance had not saved her [China] from the twenty-one demands, it had enabled Japan to tie our [the British] hands over the Shantung question'. Alston to Curzon, *Annual Report, 1920, China*, Feb. 4, 1921, FO405/229.
204. Clive to Curzon, June 30, 1920, Enclosure 'A Friendly Word to Mr. Alston Regarding the Anglo-Japanese Alliance', Extract from the *Wei I Jih Pao* of June 12, 1920, FO405/228.
205. Huang was vice-President of the Educational Association of the Jiangsu Province at the time.
206. Alston to FO, Aug. 7, 1920, Enclosure, FO228/3352.
207. Ibid.
208. Clive to Curzon, June 30, 1920, Enclosure, FO405/228.
209. *NCH*, June 12, 1920, vol. CXXXV, p. 642.
210. Alston to Curzon, Feb. 4, 1921, *Annual Report, 1920*, China, FO405/229.
211. *Treaties and Agreements with and Concerning China, 1919–1929*, p. 29.
212. *NCH*, June 18, 1921, vol. CXXXIX, p. 791.
213. See Fifield, *Woodrow Wilson and the Far East*, pp. 215–16.
214. Wilson, G., *Handbook*, p. 25.
215. Ibid., p. 18.
216. Curzon to Clive, Dec. 22, 1920, FO228/3338.

4 Russia Breakthrough

1. The two good examples are Allen Whiting's pioneering study, *Soviet Policies in China 1917–1924* and Wang Yujun's *Zhong Su Waijiao de Xumu* (The First Period of the Sino-Soviet Diplomacy) .
2. See, for example, Xiang Qing, *Gongcan Guoji Yu Zhongguo Geming De Lishi Gaishu* (An Outline Account of the Relations Between the Comitern and the Chinese Revolution).
3. Carr, E. H., *The Bolshevik Revolution, 1917–1923*, vol. III, p. 490.
4. This was part of the Trans-Siberian Railway built on the Chinese territory under a protocol attached to the Russo-Chinese Treaty of 1896. Other concessions along the railway line were acquire at the same time.

The railway authorities were entitled to acquired Chinese government land free of charge and private land by lease or purchase. It was estimated that they had appropriated 1,300 km^2 along the railway. this was the so-called CER Zone. At the time of the Bolshevik Revolution, there were about 70,000 Russians living in the CER Zone.

5. Reinsch to Lansing, Nov. 19, 1917, *FRUS*, 1918, Russia, vol. II, p. 4. For more detailed accounts of the situation in Harbin, see Moser (American Consul in Harbin) to Reinsch, Nov. 17, 1917, ibid., pp. 2–4, *NCH*, Jan. 5, 1918, 'Affairs at Harbin', pp. 22–3, and Leong, S. T., *Sino-Soviet Diplomatic Relations, 1917-1926*, pp. 16–20.

6. Foreign Ministry to Meng Enyuan and Guo Zhongxi, Dec. 5, 1917, *Zhong E Guanxi Shiliao – Zhongdong Tielu* (hereafter, *ZEGS – ZT*, Archive Materials on Sino-Russian Relations – the Chinese Eastern Railway) 1917–1919, vol. I, p. 3.

7. Ibid.

8. Reinsch to Lansing, Dec. 6, 1917, *FRUS*, 1918, Russia, vol. II, p. 5.

9. Foreign Ministry to Zhang Zuolin and Bao Guiqing, Dec. 7, 1917, *ZEGS – ZT* 1917–1919, vol. I, p. 7.

10. Foreign Ministry to Cabinet Secretariat, Dec. 7, 1917, ibid.

11. Reinsch to Lansing, Nov. 19, 1917, *FRUS*, 1918, Russia, vol. II, p. 4.

12. Scalapino, R. A. & Yu, G. T., *Modern China and its Revolutionary Process – Recurrent Challenges to the Traditional Order, 1850–1920*, p. 590.

13. Shi Shaochang to Foreign Ministry, Nov. 26, 1917, *ZEGS – ZT* 1917–1919, vol. I, p. 2.

14. Foreign Ministry to Meng Enyuan and Guo Zhongxi, Dec. 6, 1917, ibid., p. 5.

15. Foreign Ministry to Meng Enyuan and Guo Zhongxi, Dec. 7, 1917, ibid, p. 6.

16. Meng to Foreign Ministry, Dec. 20, 1917, ibid., p. 14.

17. Meng to Foreign Ministry, Dec. 27, 1917, Meng to Foreign Ministry, Dec. 30, 1917, Bao to Foreign Ministry, Dec. 30, 1917, and He Zhonglian and Zhang Zhongchang to Foreign Ministry, ibid., p. 27 and pp. 34–5. See also *NCH*, Jan. 12, 1918, vol. CXXVI, pp. 70–1.

18. See Meng to Foreign Ministry, Dec. 18, 1917, ibid., pp. 11–2, Meng and Guo to Foreign Ministry, Dec. 17, 1917, p. 12, Meng, Zhang and Bao to Foreign Ministry, Dec. 20, 1917, p. 17, and Cabinet to Meng, Dec. 22, 1917, p. 25.

19. Cabinet to Meng, Dec. 22, 1917, ibid., p. 25.

20. Cabinet to Foreign Ministry, Dec. 30, 1917, ibid., p. 35.

21. *Millard Review*, Jan. 5, 1918, p. 161.

22. Cabinet to Guo, Jan. 7, 1918, *ZEGS – ZT* 1917–1919, vol. I, p. 48.

23. Meng and Guo to Foreign Ministry, Jan. 13, 1918, ibid., pp. 57–8.

24. Ibid.

25. Abstract from Memo by Russian Minister Prince Kudachev, Jan. 24, 1918, ibid., p. 77.

26. Cabinet to Foreign Ministry, Jan. 24, 1918, ibid., p. 75.

27. Liu Jingren to Foreign Ministry, Jan. 19, 1918, *ZEGS – E Zhenbian Yu Yiban Jiaoshe* (hereafter, ZEGS – EZYYJ, The Russian Revolution and General Contact) 1917–1919, vol. I, pp. 244–5.

28. Ibid.
29. Wang Yujun, *Zhong Su Waijiao De Xumu* (The First Period of Sino-Soviet Diplomacy), pp. 24–5.
30. Liu Jingren to Foreign Ministry, Jan. 19, 1918, ZEGS – EZYYJ, 1917-1919, vol. I, pp. 244–5.
31. The last official contact between Narkomindel and the Chinese Legation was probably Voznesensky's meeting with Li Shizhong on Feb. 4. The former made the same proposal and the latter gave the same reply as they did on Jan. 19. See Liu Jingren (Chinese Minister to Russia) to Foreign Ministry, Feb. 5, 1918; ZEGS – ZT 1917–1919, p. 98. After the withdrawal of the Legation, Li remained in Petrograd as the caretaker of the Legation.
32. See Leong, *Sino–Soviet Relations*, ch. 5, 'China's Recovery of Outer Mongolia', pp. 70–92 and ch. 6, 'Decolonization of North Manchuria', pp. 93–115.
33. *NCH*, Nov. 29, 1919, vol. CXXXIII, p. 551. For text of the two treaties, see MacMurray, *Treaties and Agreements*, pp. 992–6, 1239–1244. See also Pollard, *China's Foreign Relations*, pp. 120–1 for China's official note addressed to Kudachev and the latter's protest.
34. Bao to Cabinet, Feb. 4, 1920; *ZEGS – ZT* 1920, p. 35.
35. He was given a job in Beijing as an adviser to the Ministry of Communication.
36. Carnegie Endowment for International Peace, *Treaties and Agreements, 1919–1929*, p. 30.
37. Ibid., p. 31.
38. For example, Chen Lu, the acting Foreign Minister, told Boppe, the French Minister in Beijing, in April 1919 that he regarded as invalid the Sino-Russian treaties concluded with the Imperial Russian Government because of the political disorganization and anarchy in Russia. He dismissed Kudachev's protest against China's dispatching troops to Outer Mongolia as 'an unnecessary move' because of Kudachev's ignorance of the situation. Memo of Chen–Boppe Interview, April 14, 1919; *ZEGS – EZYYJ* 1917–1919, vol. II, p. 149.
39. Office of Army Chief of Staff to Foreign Ministry, April 19, 1919, ibid., p. 204. See also Yu Yixi to Office of Army Chief of Staff, no date, CA 1016-54;
40. Foreign Ministry to Wang Guanxi, May 24, 1919, *ZEGS – EZYYJ*, 1917–1919, vol. II, p. 268.
41. Cabinet to Shanghai National Peace Association, June 13, 1919, Cabinet to Foreign Ministry, June 16, 1919, *ZEGS – EZYYJ* 1917–1919, vol. II p. 329, 327.
42. Xinjiang ceased to be a possession and became a Chinese province in 1884.
43. For a brief and interesting account of Anglo-Russian conflict in Xinjiang, see Lattimore, O., *Pivot of Asia*, ch. II 'Anglo-Russian Rivalry over Sinkiang, 1800–1917', pp. 24–44.
44. Russian interests had been diverted from its land frontiers in Central Asia to the Pacific after its acquisition of the Maritime Province. This seemed to have allayed the British apprehension of a Russian threat to India. Consequently, there was a sort of entente between Britain and Russia in Xinjiang.

45. See Yang, R., 'Sinkiang Under the Administration of Governor Yang Tseng-hsin, 1911-1928', *Central Asiatic Journal*, vol. VI, no. 4, Dec. 1961, pp. 270–316.
46. Lattimore, *Pivot of Asia*, p. 17.
47. Cabinet to Foreign Ministry, Nov. 14, 1919, *ZEGS – EZYYJ* 1917–1919, vol. II, p. 578.
48. Presidential Secretariat to Foreign Ministry, Dec. 10, 1919, ibid., p. 633.
49. Foreign Ministry to Ministry of War, Dec. 31, 1919, ibid., pp. 668–9.
50. Lampson to Curzon, April 9, 1920, FO371/5341.
51. Foreign Ministry to Yang, April 3, 1918, *ZEGS – Xinjiang Bianfang* (hereafter *ZEGS – XB*, Xinjiang Frontier Defence) 1917–1919, p. 25.
52. Yang to Cabinet, May 25, 1918, ibid., p. 50. The Foreign Ministry in Beijing at the same time received the same dispatch by Chicherin from Li Shizhong, who remained in Petrograd after the withdrawal of the Chinese Legation. Li to Foreign Ministry, April 15, 1918, ibid., p. 26.
53. Yang to Cabinet and Foreign Ministry, May 25, 1918, ibid., pp. 50–1.
54. Yang to Cabinet and Foreign Ministry, June 9, 1918, Foreign Ministry to Cabinet Secretariat, June 19, 1918, ibid., pp. 57–9.
55. See Scalapino & Yu, *Modern China*, pp. 592–3.
56. It was estimated that in total about 150,000 Chinese labourers were recruited by the Russian Government for the war effort on the European front. Following the Armistice, however, most of them were stranded in various parts of Russia because of the Russian civil war.
57. Yang to Cabinet and Foreign Ministry, May 25, 1918 and June 9, 1918, Yang to Foreign Ministry, Aug. 25, 1918, *ZEGS – XB* 1917–1919, pp.50–1, 57–8, 102–3.
58. Yang to Cabinet and Foreign Ministry, Feb. 12, 1920, ibid., pp. 80–1.
59. Yang reported to Beijing on Jan. 31, 1920 that the Commander of the Yili Garrison had been recently approached by the Bolsheviks who demanded first, repatriation of White Russian soldiers fleeing into Yili and of members of the Russian consulate in Yili, second, dispatch of a Russian commercial agent resident in Yili, third, restoration of telegraphic communication between Qihe and Yili, and fourth, repatriation of the Russian refugees in Yili. He had sent Xiao Chang, Director of the Bureau of Foreign Affairs to open talks with them. Yang to President, Jan. 31, 1920, CA 1016-107.
60. See Wang Tieya, (ed.) *Zhongwai Jiuyue Huibian* (A Collection of Sino-Foreign Treaties and Agreements), vol. 1, pp. 381–5.
61. Yang estimated that calculated on the treaty tariff basis, in more than thirty years after 1881, China had lost 40–50 million taels of revenue on the Russian import into China. This did not include the loss suffered by China from imports via Xinjiang by merchants of other nationalities claiming protection of the British Consulate in Kashgar. See Yang to Cabinet, Apr. 1, 1920 and Yang to Foreign Ministry, Sept. 23, 1920, *ZEGS – Yiban Jiaoshe* (hereafter, *ZEGS – YJ*, General Contact) 1920, pp. 291, 289.
62. Yang to Foreign Ministry, Dec. 3, 1919, ibid., p. 5.
63. See Beijing Chamber of Commerce to Foreign Ministry, Jan. 20, 1920 and Ministry of Agriculture and Commerce to Foreign Ministry, Jan. 20, 1920, ibid., pp. 7–8, 14.

64. Minute by Chen Lu on Ministry of Agriculture and Commerce to Foreign Ministry, Jan. 20, 1920, ibid., p. 14.
65. See Xu Guozeng to Yang, Apr. 4, 1920, ibid., pp. 292–5.
66. Yang to Cabinet, Apr. 1, 1920, ibid., pp. 291–2.
67. Yang to Foreign Ministry, Sept. 7, 1920, ibid., pp. 236–7.
68. Foreign Ministry and Finance Ministry to Yang, May 2, 1920, ibid., p. 295.
69. Owing to technical problems of applying the general tariff to imports along the land frontiers in Xinjiang, Yang later decided to levy taxes on the Russian goods according to the 'Xinjiang Combined Tax Regulations'. See Xu to Yang, May 14, 1920 and Yang to Xu, May 16, 1920, ibid., p. 297.
70. Yang to Xu, May 18, 1920, ibid., pp. 297–8.
71. Cabinet to Foreign Ministry, May 21, 1920, ibid., pp. 141–2.
72. Cabinet to Foreign Ministry, May 18, 1920, ibid., p. 131.
73. Cabinet to Foreign Ministry, May 24, 1920, Presidential Secretariat to Cabinet, May 24, 1920, and Foreign Ministry to Yang, May 25, 1920, Frontier Defence Bureau to Yang, May 26, 1920, ibid., pp. 145, 146–7, 302.
74. Xu to Yang, May 19, 1920, ibid., p. 298.
75. The English translation is from *Treaties Concerning China, 1919-1929*, p. 24. For the Chinese text, see *ZEGS – YJ* 1920, pp. 304–6.
76. Yang to Foreign Ministry, Sept. 7, 1920, *ZEGS – YJ* 1920, pp. 235–6.
77. Ministry of Finance to Foreign Ministry, June 14, 1920, ibid., p. 168.
78. Xu to Yang, July 4, 1920 and Yang to Foreign Ministry, Sept. 23, 1920, ibid., pp. 310, 290.
79. Memo of an Interview between Alston and Chen Lu, June 3, 1920, Memo on an Interview between Chen Lu and Boppe, June 3, 1920, ibid., pp. 159, 160.
80. Wang, Y., *Zhong Su Waijiao*, p. 532.
81. Zhang Silin to Frontier Defence Bureau, July 21, 1920, CA 1016–81.
82. For the itinerary of Zhang's mission in Russia, see *ZEGS – E Dui Hua Waijiao Shitan* (hereafter, *ZEGS – EDHWS*, Preliminary Soviet Diplomatic Feelers to China), 1920, Appendix I, '1917–1923 Dashi Nianbiao' (Chronicle of Principal Events, 1917–1923), pp. 522–43.
83. See for example, Wang, *Zhong Su Waijiao*, p. 532 and Leong, *Sino–Soviet Relations*, pp. 148–9.
84. For example, President Xu, in his memorandum to the Cabinet on Dec. 10, 1919, suggested that an agreement with the Soviet Government would not only bind both parties against mutual aggression and ensure China's border security but also 'have the effect of countering Japanese aggression' which he believed 'requires our closest attention now'. Presidential Secretariat to Foreign Ministry, Dec. 10, 1919, *ZEGS – EZYYJ* 1917–1919, vol. II, p. 633.
85. The Chinese Government intention was even known to the British Consul-General in the remote area of Kashgar as early as Nov. 1918. Major Etherton wrote in his diary entry of Nov. 15, 1918 that 'the Taoyin [Intendant] told me that it was the intention of the Central Government after the War to revise existing treaties with Russia'. Kashgar Diary, Oct. 1918–Sept. 1919, FO371/3698.

86. See Zhang Silin to Frontier Defence Bureau, Sept. 18, 1919, CA 1016-54 and Frontier Defence Bureau to Foreign Ministry, Sept. 23, 1919, *ZEGS – EZYYJ* 1917–1919, vol. II, p. 506.

87. Cabinet to Foreign Ministry, Dec. 12, 1919, ibid., p. 640.

88. For China's contact with the Bolsheviks in Vladivostok, see Li Jiaoao to Foreign Ministry, March 30, 1920, *ZEGS – YJ* 1920, p. 123.

89. Cao Yunxiang to Foreign Ministry, Apr. 19, 1920, ibid., p. 102.

90. Shao Hengrui to Foreign Ministry, Apr. 2, 1920, *ZEGS – EDHWS* 1920, pp. 13–4.

91. Cabinet to Foreign Ministry, May 18, 1920, *ZEGS – YJ* 1920, p. 203.

92. In June, the French Minister Boppe had been to the Foreign Ministry twice to tell Chen Lu that he had been instructed by Paris that 'if China only negotiate with the Bolsheviks on trade relations, it is acting in concert with the Allies. If, however, the negotiations are on international relations, China is obviously acting contrary to the Allied policies'. Wang, *Zhong Su Waijiao*, p. 117.

93. The Chinese Government's anxiety to find out the actual situation in Russia could be seen in the fact, that in June 1920, it sent out to Siberia a fact-finding mission consisting of three foreign advisors to the Chinese Government: J. Ferguson, C. Padoux and B. Simpson. See Wang, *Zhong Su Waijiao*, pp. 106–7.

94. Zhang to Foreign Ministry, Oct. 26, 1920, *ZEGS – YJ* 1920, pp. 331–2.

95. War Participation Bureau to Foreign Ministry, Apr. 5, 1919, *ZEGS – EZYYJ* 1917–1919, p. 139.

96. One significant fact was that, while Zhang was in Harbin in March 1920, involved in resolving problems of the CER strike, a copy of the Karakhan Manifesto was officially yet secretly handed to him by a Soviet-despatched agent across the border. Zhang was actually one of the channels through which the Chinese Government was officially handed the Karakhan Manifesto. See Cabinet to Foreign Ministry, Apr. 2, 1920, *ZEGS – EDHWS* 1920, pp. 15–6.

97. There was an unconfirmed report that Zhang had been in Petrograd University in 1918 as an assistant professor of Chinese, and while there he had acted as an intermediary between the Soviet government and the Chinese in the Red Army. See Military Attaché in Beijing to Director of Military Intelligence, Oct. 8, 1920, FO371/5344.

98. According to Zhang, both in Verkhne Udinsk, the capital of the Far Eastern Republic, and in Moscow, he was able to win the confidence of both governments because of his former contacts with the Bolsheviks. See Zhang to Frontier Defence Bureau, July 21, 1920, CA 1016-81 and Zhang to Foreign Ministry, Oct. 26, 1920, *ZEGS – YJ* 1920, pp. 331–2.

99. See FO minute on the despatch by Acting Military Attaché in Peking, Dec. 16, 1920, FO371/5344 and Military Attaché in Peking to director of Military Intelligence, Oct. 8, 1920, FO371/5344. The so-called Anfu [Anhui and Fujian] Clique was a warlord faction headed by ex-Premier Duan Qirui.

100. Zhang to Frontier Defence Bureau, July 22, 1920, CA 1016-81.

101. Zhang to Frontier Defence Bureau, July 21, 1920, CA 1016-81.

102. Frontier Defence Bureau to Foreign Ministry, July 24, 1920, *ZEGS – EDHWS* 1920, p. 64.

103. Zhang to Frontier Defence Bureau, July 22, 1920, CA 1016-81.
104. Zhang to Frontier Defence Bureau, July 23, 1920, CA 1016-81.
105. Office of Army's Chief of Staff to Foreign Ministry, Sept. 24, 1920, *ZEGS – YJ* 1920, pp. 252–3.
106. Ibid.
107. Zhang to Frontier Defence Bureau, July 23, 1920, CA 1016-81.
108. Office of Army's Chief of Staff to Foreign Ministry, Sept. 24, 1920, *ZEGS – YJ* 1920, p. 253.
109. Ibid.
110. Frontier Defence Bureau to Foreign Ministry, July 24, 1920, *ZEGS – EDHWS* 1920, p. 64.
111. Office of Army's Chief of Staff to Ministry of War and Foreign Ministry, Sept. 24, 1920, and Ministry of War to Foreign Ministry, Sept. 28, 1920, *ZEGS – YJ* 1920, pp. 248, 258. The Ministry of War actually pressed the Foreign Ministry for a quick decision because it believed that the matter was of international significance.
112. Zhang to Frontier Defence Bureau, July 22, 1920, CA 1016-81. Zhang asked the Bureau to refer the matter to the Foreign Ministry.
113. Military Attaché in Peking to Director of Military Intelligence, Oct. 8, 1920, FO371/5344.
114. Cabinet to Foreign Ministry, Sept. 20, 1920, *ZEGS – EDHWS* 1920, pp. 100–1.
115. Ibid.
116. Ibid.
117. The allusion was made to Japan.
118. Zhang and Zhu to Foreign Ministry, Sept. 18, 1920, *ZEGS – EDHWS* 1920, p. 99.
119. Cabinet to Foreign Ministry, Sept. 20, 1920, ibid., pp. 100–1.
120. Military Attaché in Peking to Director of Military Intelligence, Oct. 8, 1920, FO371/5344. See also Foreign Ministry to Zhu and Zhang, Sept. 23, 1920, *ZEGS – YJ* 1920, p. 247.
121. That is the so-called 'Second Karakhan Manifesto' which was officially addressed to Zhang and handed to him on Oct. 2, 1920.
122. Zhang to Foreign Ministry, Oct. 6, 1920, *ZEGS–EDHWS* 1920, pp. 114–15.
123. Zhang to Foreign Ministry, Oct. 9, 1920, ibid., pp. 115–16.
124. Zhang to Foreign Ministry, Oct. 3, 1920, and Zhang to Foreign Ministry, Oct. 6, 1920, ibid., pp. 109–13, 114–15.
125. The Chinese Government seemed to have formally acknowledged its receipt first on Nov. 23, 1920. Its reply ran in part as follows: 'The contents of this communication have received the attention of the Chinese Government, particularly the principle of international equality and reciprocity. By virtue of the many thousands of miles of common frontier, the relations between China and Russia naturally should be of the closest nature . . . The Chinese Government is therefore anxiously awaiting the earliest opportunity of opening direct negotiations with Russia along the lines indicated in the communication now under reply.' *NCH*, Dec. 1, 1923, vol. CXLIX, p. 591.
126. Zhang to Foreign Ministry, Oct. 9, 1920, *ZEGS – EDHWS* 1920, pp. 115–16. See also an extract from *Izvestia*, Oct. 22, 1920 in Admiral de

Robeck (British High Commissioner in Constantinople) to Curzon, Nov. 13, 1920, Enclosure, FO371/5444.
127. Wang, *Zhong Su Waijiao*, p. 540.
128. FO minute Nov. 19, 1920, FO371/5444, FO minute Dec. 16, 1920, FO371/5344.
129. Memo of a Conversation Between Dr. Yen and Mr. Boppe, Oct. 21, 1920, also Foreign Ministry to Si, Oct. 12, 1920, *ZEGS – YJ* 1920, pp. 282, 271.
130. Pollard, *China's Foreign Relations*, p. 135.
131. Pasvolsky, L., *Russia in the Far East*, p. 88.
132. See Foreign Ministry to Lu, Apr. 24, 1919, War Participation Bureau to Foreign Ministry, Apr. 29, 1919, War Participation Bureau to Foreign Ministry, May 19, 1919, Foreign Ministry to Chinese Ministers in Britain, France and the United States, Dec. 31, 1919, Cabinet to Foreign Ministry, May 18, 1920, Cabinet to Foreign Ministry, June 30, 1920, *ZEGS – YJ* 1920, pp, 196–7, 204, pp. 258-9, 669, 131, 183-184
133. Wang, *Zhong Su Waijiao*, p. 113.
134. It might be argued, however, this was a clever diplomatic manoeuvre to preempt any possible diplomatic representations by treaty Powers to protest against the Chinese move.
135. Zhang to Foreign Ministry, Nov. 26, 1920, *ZEGS – YJ* 1920, p. 332.
136. See Whiting, *Soviet Policies in China*, pp. 28–35.
137. Alston to Curzon, Feb. 11, 1921, FO405/231.
138. Crane to Colby, Sept. 17, 1920, *FRUS* 1920, vol. I, p. 762.
139. *China Yearbook, 1921–1922*, p. 624.
140. Leong, *Sino-Soviet Relations*, p. 29.
141. For example, it protested against the initial informal contact between the Chinese Legation in Petrograd and the Narkomindel. In May 1919, Kudachev even solicited the assistance of the Allied Governments in protecting his authorities as head of the Russian Legation.
142. Kashgar Diary, Jan. 21, 1919, FO371/3698.
143. Memo of Russian Embassy to State Department, May 17, 1919, SDA 761.93/126.
144. Memo on Chen–Boppe Interview, Apr. 14, 1919, *ZEGS – EZYYJ* 1917-1919, vol. II, p. 149.
145. See Cabinet to Foreign Ministry, Jan. 23, 1920, *ZEGS – YJ* 1920, pp. 29–30 and Cabinet to Foreign Ministry, Feb. 26, 1920, p. 46 The other Simpson proposals were (1) to arrange for the supervision of the CER, (2) to dispatch police and military forces to two border towns: Manzhouli and Suifenhe, (3) to set up courts to hear cases involving foreigners from non-treaty nations, (4) to follow closely activities of the Soviet Government in Europe and to get prepared to open negotiations with it as soon as a European nation (e.g. Italy) had diplomatic relations with the Soviet Government.
146. Memo on Boppe–Chen Conversation, Apr. 3, 1920, *ZEGS – Tingzhi E Shiling Daiyu* (hereafter, *ZEGS – TESD*, Discontinuation of Recognition of Russian Minister and Consuls) 1920, p. 1.
147. Finance Ministry to Foreign Ministry, May 22, 1920, *ZEGS – YJ* 1920, pp. 145–6.
148. Clive to Curzon, July 23, 1920, Enclosure 1, FO405/228.

149. Alston told Curzon that 'the French and the Japanese Government had brought considerable pressure to induce the Chinese Government to continue payment of the Russian Boxer Indemnity'. Alston to Curzon, Feb. 4, 1920, *Annual Report, China, 1920*.
150. Clive to Curzon, July 23, 1920, FO405/228, Curzon to Clive, Sept. 18, 1920, *DBFP*, vol. XIV, p. 120.
151. The Chinese Government first proposed to discontinue payment of the Russian share of indemnity money early in 1918. The collective representations by the Diplomatic Corps in Beijing that they were in favour of continued payment seemed to have turned China around. China agreed to continue to pay the indemnity instalment in full to the Russo-Asiatic Bank under the guarantee of the Russian Minister that as soon as there was a government of the whole of Russia recognized by China, those sums should be forwarded to such a government, remaining until then on deposit with the Bank. Prince Kudachev, however, had made private arrangement with the Bank for using the money to finance the Russian diplomatic and consular establishments in the Far East. See ibid.
153. Whiting, A., *Soviet Policies in China*, p. 142.
154. Foreign Ministry to Chinese Ministers to Britain, France, America, Italy, Belgium, Holland, Aug. 19, 1920, *ZEGS – TESD*, 1920, p. 1.
155. Memo on Yen–Kudachev Conversation, Aug. 24, 1920, ibid., p. 6.
156. Presidential Secretariat to Foreign Ministry, Aug. 22, 1920, *ZEGS – TESD* 1920, p. 250.
157. Ivan Kalmykov fled into China early in 1920, charged by the Soviets with absconding with Russian State gold. He was then arrested by the Chinese authorities in Jilin. On one of his visits to the Russian Consulate in July, he disappeared and was later found living in the consulate premises. The complicity of the Russian consul in Jilin provided a good excuse for the Chinese Government to start its withdrawal of recognition of the Russian Legation and consulates in China.
158. Minutes of the Sixth Meeting of the Committee for the Study of Russian Treaties, Aug. 24, 1920, and Minutes of a Meeting of Councillors and Department Heads on the Status of Russian Minister and Consuls, Aug. 30, 1920, *ZEGS – TESD* 1920, pp. 2–4, 7–11.
159. Memo on Foreign Ministry Propositions on the Treatment of the Russian Minister and Consular Officials, Sept. 2, 1920, ibid., p. 13.
160. Take the five great Powers for example. The reports from the Chinese Legations showed that Britain, France and Italy had all discarded the Tsarist diplomats. America still recognized the Russian Ambassador there, who was sent, however, by Kerensky's Provisional Government. Only Japan treated the Tsarist Ambassador as before. See ibid., pp. 5–6, 12, 14, pp. 15–6.
161. Foreign Ministry to Zhang Zuolin, Bao Guiqing, Sun Liecheng and Yang Zengxin, Sept. 1, 1920, ibid., p. 12.
162. Zhang to Foreign Ministry, Sept. 3, 1920, Bao to Foreign Ministry, Sept. 3, 1920, Sun to Foreign Ministry, Sept. 10, 1920, ibid., pp. 14, 17.
163. Clive to Curzon, Sept. 10, 1920, *DBFP*, vol. XIV, p. 118, Crane to Colby, Sept. 10, 1920, *FRUS*, 1920, vol. I, pp. 761–2, Kudachev to Yen, Sept. 18, 1920, *ZEGS – TESD* 1920, pp. 34–5,

164. Memo of Yen–Clive Interview, Sept. 15, 1920, ibid., pp. 32–4, French Ambassador to FO, Sept. 17, 1920, FO Minute on Clive to Curzon, Sept. 10, 1920, FO371/5344, Crane to Colby, Sept. 17, 1920, FRUS, 1920, vol. I, p. 762.
165. Kudachev to Yen, Sept. 18, 1920, ZEGS – TESD 1920, pp. 34–5.
166. Foreign Ministry to President, Sept. 23, 1920, ibid., p. 39.
167. Presidential Mandate, Sept. 23, 1920, ibid., pp. 39–40. For English versions, see Crane to Colby, Sept. 24, 1920, FRUS, 1920, vol. I, pp. 764–5 and Clive to Curzon, Sept. 24, 1920, FO371/5344.
168. See, FRUS, 1920, vol. I, p. 765.
169. Foreign Ministry to Provincial Military and Civil Governors, Sept. 23, 1920, ZEGS – TESD 1920, p. 40.
170. Foreign Ministry to Provincial Special Commissioners and Commissioners of Foreign Affairs, Sept. 24, 1920, ibid., p. 44.
171. Foreign Ministry to Cao Rui and Sun Zhenjia, Sept. 23, 1920, and Foreign Ministry to Sun Liecheng, Zhang Zuolin and Bao Guiqing, Sept. 23, 1920, ibid., pp. 42, 40–1.
172. Huang Rongliang to Foreign Ministry, Sept. 25, 1920, ibid., p. 45, and Kerr to Clive, Oct. 1, 1920, FO228/3563.
173. Porter to Clive, Sept. 30, 1920, FO228/3563.
174. Porter to Clive, Sept. 29, 1920, and Porter to Clive, Oct. 1, 1920, FO228/3563.
175. See *China Yearbook, 1921–1922*, p. 627. Two Russian consulates were located in areas beyond Chinese authorities: the Russian Consulate in Shanghai in the International Settlement and the Russian Consulate in Canton on the island of Shameen. The Russian Consulate in Canton was soon sealed by the British Consul, while the Russian Consulate in Shanghai was permitted to continue its function for some time. Also beyond the Chinese authorities was the Russian Legation in Beijing which was taken over by the Diplomatic Corps. See Dean of Diplomatic Corps to Foreign Ministry, Oct. 4, 1920, ZEGS – TESD 1920, p. 76.
176. Yen to Crane, Oct. 12, 1920, FRUS, 1920, vol. I, p. 775.
177. Colby to Crane, Sept. 21, 1920, ibid., p. 763.
178. Extracts from a Letter from Peking, Sept. 20, 1920, Enclosure, FO371/5344.
179. Colby to Crane, Sept. 21, 1920, FRUS, 1920, vol. I, p. 763.
180. Crane to Colby, Sept. 24, 1920, ibid., pp. 765–6, Clive to Curzon, Sept. 24, 1920, DBFP. vol. XIV, p. 124.
181. Crane to Colby, Sept. 30, 1920, FRUS, 1920, vol. I, p. 768.
182. Crane to Colby, Sept. 25, 1920, ibid.
183. Curzon to Clive, Sept. 25, 1920, DBFP, vol. XIV, p. 125.
184. Memo on Yen–Clive Interview, Sept. 29, 1920, ZEGS – TESD 1920, pp. 76–7, Clive to Kerr, Oct. 3, 1920, FO228/3563. See also Clive to Curzon, Oct. 2, 1920, DBFP, vol. XIV, pp. 147–8.
185. Porter to Clive, Oct. 12, 1920, FO228/3563.
186. Clive to Curzon, Sept. 24, 1920, DBFP, vol. XIV, p. 124.
187. Yen argued that international guardianship of the Russian interests did not have any sound legal justification because (1) China did not break its relations with Russia, and (2) Russian interests concerned were entirely

located in Chinese territory. Memo on Yen-Crane Interview, Sept. 24, 1920, *ZEGS – TESD* 1920, pp. 57–9.

188. Colby to Crane, Oct. 2, 1920, *FRUS*, 1920, vol. I, p. 769.
189. Ibid.
190. On Sept. 24, the Foreign Ministry cabled all Chinese legations and consulates-general that China's withdrawal of its recognition of the Russian Legation was not a rupture of diplomatic relations like that with Germany and Austrian–Hungary but an interregnum in view of the inability of the old regime to function. On Oct. 7, the Chinese Minister Koo in Washington was further instructed that, '(1) The Mandate of September 23rd does not put an end to treaty relations between China and Russia, which are merely suspended for the time being, (2) The above-mentioned mandate does not terminate the treaties between China and Russia, or such rights as are derived from the treaties.' See Foreign Ministry to Chinese Legations and Consulates-General, Sept. 24, 1920, *ZEGS – TESD* 1920, p. 44 and Chinese Foreign Office to Chinese Legation, Oct. 7, 1920, SDA 761.93/146.
191. Extracts from *Central China Post*, Sept. 18, 1920, FO228/3563.
192. Weekly Report of the Chinese Legation in Paris, Sept. 28, 1920, *ZEGS – TESD* 1920, pp. 147–8.
193. Koo to Foreign Ministry, Oct. 1, 1920, (two telegrams), *ZEGS – TESD* 1920, p. 71, 73–74.
194. Colby to Crane, Oct. 2, 1920, *FRUS*, 1920, vol. I, p. 769
195. Dean of Diplomatic Corps to Yen, Oct. 11, 1920, *ZEGS – TESD* 1920, p. 94.
196. Yen to Dean of Diplomatic Corps, Oct. 22, 1920, ibid., p. 130.
197. Appendix to Minutes of the Sixth Meeting of the Committee for the Study of Russian Treaties, Aug. 24, 1920, ibid., pp. 5–6.
198. Extracts from a Letter from Peking, Sept. 20, 1920, Enclosure, FO371/5344.
199. *China Year Book, 1921–1922*, pp. 644–5. Foreign Minister Yen later defended his Government's action to bring the Russians under Chinese jurisdiction, arguing that in consequence of the withdrawal of recognition, no one was capable of fulfilling duties of the Russian consuls and 'China cannot do otherwise than assume provisionally the performance of the duties connected with the examination of civil and criminal cases involving Russians in China. This measure is also a practical solution, natural in the situation which has arisen'. As for Russian courts in the CER Zone, Yen stated, their establishment was at the time an arbitrary act on the part of the Russians. In his words, 'such a contravention of treaty stipulations constituted an act infringing the sovereign rights of China' and 'a decision was already reached in this question a long time ago and the present measure was in no way a result of the suspension of recognition'. See Yen to Dean of Diplomatic Corps, Nov. 29, 1920, *FRUS* 1920, vol. I, pp. 779–80.
200. Fishel, W. R., *The End of Extraterritoriality in China*, p. 35.
201. Clive to Curzon, Dec. 6, 1920, FO371/5344.

Conclusion

1. Hsu, *China's Entrance*, p. 209
2. In 1899, all treaty Powers renounced their extraterritoriality in Japan. See Gong, *Standard of 'Civilization'*, p. 195.
3. Wilson, G., *Handbook*, p. 25.
4. Bull, *Anarchical Society*, p. 9.
5. The Treaty of Sèvres was an exception. China did not sign the treaty only because it felt it was unjustifiable to reimpose on Turkey the system of extraterritorial jurisdiction.
6. *NCH*, April 15, 1919, vol. CXXXI, p. 37.
7. Wright, *China in Revolution*, p. 4.
8. Watson, 'Hedley Bull', p. 151.
9. Ibid.
10. Whereas membership of the League of Nations was unsatisfactory as general criterion for membership in the emerging international society, as Watson argued (Ibid., p. 149), it must be pointed out that membership for China did signify the degree of its being accepted by the international society.
11. The acceptance of China into the emerging international society was more clearly manifest in the Washington Conference when China was invited and recognized as one of the nine Powers which signed the so-called the Nine Power Treaty on the Far East and the Pacific.
12. See, Gong, *Standard of 'Civilization'*, pp. 195, 234–7. For more details on the entry of Japan and of Siam into the international society, see ibid., chs VI and VII, pp. 165–237.
13. Holland, *Lectures*, p. 39.
14. Fishel, *Extraterritoriality*, p. 1.
15. See Thomas, E. D., 'Foreword', ibid., p. vi. He was then American High Commissioner in the Trust Territory of the Pacific Islands.
16. Bull, H., 'Foreword, in Gong, *Standard of 'Civilization'*, p. ix.

Glossary

pinyin	*Chinese characters*
Anfu	安福
Anhui	安徽
Bao Guiqing	鲍贵卿
Beiyang Zhengfu	北洋政府
Cao Rulin	曹汝霖
Cao Yunxiang	曹云祥
Chen Duxiu	陈独秀
Chen Lu	陈籙
Da Qing Huidian	大清汇典
Dao Guang	道光
Duan Qirui	段祺瑞
dujun	督军
Fa Bu	法部
Feng Guozhang	冯国璋
Fujian	福建
Gu Weijun	顾维钧
Guo Zongxi	郭宗熙
Hai Guo Tu Zhi	海国图志
Hankou	汉口
Heilongjiang	黑龙江
Hu Weide	胡惟德

Huai Ren Tang	怀仁堂
Huang Yanpei	黄炎培
Hunan	湖南
Jiangsu	江苏
Jiangxi	江西
Jiaozhou	胶洲
Jilin	吉林
Jinan	济南
Li Hongzhang	李鸿章
Li Yuanhong	黎元洪
liang hai qu qin	两害取轻
Liang Qichao	梁启超
Liang Ruhao	梁如浩
Liu Jinren	刘静仁
Lu Zhengxiang	陆征祥
Meng Enyuan	孟恩远
Najing	南京
Niu Binwen	牛炳文
Qian Long	乾隆
Qihe	七河
Qingdao	青岛
Qinhuangdao	秦皇岛
Shandong	山东
shang zhan	商战
shouhui liquan	收回利权

shuyuan	书院
Si Zhou Zhi	四洲志
Suifenhe	绥芬河
Tang Shaoyi	唐绍仪
Tian Xia	天下
Tian Xia Yi Jia	天下一家
Tianjin	天津
Tizhi	体制
waijiao	外交
Waijiao Bu	外交部
Wang Guangxi	王广析
Wang Tao	王韬
Weihaiwei	威海卫
Wu Peifu	吴佩孚
Xi Yang Ren	西洋人
Xian Feng	咸丰
Xiemi	斜米
Xing Bu	刑部
Xinjiang	新疆
Xu Guozeng	许国祯
Xu Shichang	徐世昌
Xue Fucheng	薛福成
Yan Huiqing	颜惠庆
Yang Zengxin	杨增新
Yang Ren	洋人

Yangwu	洋务
yi	夷
Yili	伊犁
Yining	伊宁
Yuan Shikai	袁世凯
Zeng Guofan	曾国藩
Zhang Silin	张斯麐
Zhang Zongxiang	章宗祥
Zhi Fang Wai Ji	职方外记
Zhili	直隶
Zhu Qiyin	朱启吟
Zhu Shaoyang	朱绍阳
Zongli Yamen	总理衙门

Bibliography

PRIMARY SOURCES

Chinese (unpublished)

1. Chinese diplomatic records deposited in the Second National Archive Library in Nanjing, China:

CA 05-3-1, *Zhongguo Daibiaotuan Neibu Huiyi Jilu* (Minutes of the Meetings of the Chinese Delegation at Paris).

CA 05-3-16, *Huiquian Zhunbei Cailiao He Shuotie* (Materials and Memos Prepared for the Peace Conference).

CA 05-3-32, *Zhongguo Daibiaotuan De Jianyi He Yaoqiu* (Proposals and Demands made by the Chinese Delegation at Paris).

CA 05-3-33, 34, 37 & 38, *Yu Waijiaobu Laiwangdian* (Telegrams Sent to and Received from the Foreign Ministry by the Chinese Delegation at Paris).

CA 05-3-45, *Yu Geguo Daibiaotuan Jiaohuan Yijian De Jilu* (Memos on Interviews and Talks with Other Delegations).

CA 1003-819, 821, 822 & 823, *Guanyu Bali Hehui De Laiwang Dian* (Telegrams about the Paris Peace Conference Sent and Received).

CA 1014-171-2, *Sulian Laonong Zhengfu Waijiao Buzhang Kanakang Xiang Zhongguo Nanbei Zhengfu Shengming* (Soviet Foreign Minister Karakhan Manifesto to the Northern and the Southern Governments of China).

CA 1014-172-2, *Yang Zengxin Bao Youguan Yu Sulian Jiaoshe Shi Laiwang Dian* (Yang Zengxin's Reports on Contact with Soviet Russia).

CA 1014-176-2, *Hedu Sun Liecheng Baogao Su Chita Jiaotong Zongzhang Qiatan Huifu Bianjie Tongshang Qinxing Youguan Dian* (Helongjiang Military Governor Sun Liecheng's Reports on Talks with Minister of Communication from Chita on Restoration of Border Trade).

CA 1016-54, *Lianleyuan Zhang Silin Baogao Sulian Zhengfu Zuzhi Ji Youguan Neiwai Zhengce Dian* (Liaison Officer Zhang Silin's Reports on the Organization of the Soviet Government and Its Internal and External Policies).

CA 1016-63-2, *Guanyu Balihehui Shiqian Zhunbei Yu Lu An Jiaoshe* (Materials Related to Preparations Before the Paris Peace Conference and Presentation of the Shandong Question).

CA 1016-74 & 78, *Zhang Silin Lai Dian* (Telegrams Received from Zhang Silin).

CA 1016-81, *Zhang Silin Mosike Zhi Xing* (Zhang Silin's Mission to Moscow).

CA 1016-107-2, *Xindu Yang Zengxin Qingshi Guanyu Sulian Yaoqiu Yingdu Beie Ji Paiqian Shangwu Zhuanyuan Ge Shi Laidian* (Telegrams Received from Xinjiang Military Governor Yang Zengxin, Seeking Instructions on Soviet Russia's Demands on Repatriation of White Russians and on Dispatch of Trade Commissioners).

CA 1039-2, *Guo Dian Huicun* (A Collection of Important Telegrams Sent and Received by the President and the Government).

CA 1039-329 & 330, *Shou Fa Dian Chaolu* (Copies of Telegrams Sent and Received).

CA 1039-373-2, *Zhongde Xuanzhan Jinyaowen Ji Yihe Choubeichu Diyi Zhi Dishiwu Ci Huiyi Jilu* (Important Documents on China's Declaration of War with Germany and Minutes of Meetings of the Preparatory Committee for the Peace Conference).

2. Documents deposited in the Library of the Chinese Foreign Ministry, Beijing, China:

Bali Hehui Huiqian Zhunbei Cailiao (A Collection of Materials Related to the Preparation for the Paris Peace Conference).

3. Documents deposited in Box 2 and Box 3 of Wellington Koo Papers in Butler Library of Columbia University in New York:

Yu Bali Hehui Daibiaotuan Laiwang Dian (Telegrams sent and received by the Chinese Delegation in Paris).

Chinese (published)

1. *Jindai Shi Ziliao* (38) (Source Materials of Modern Chinese History, no. 38) ed. by The Institute of Modern History, Chinese Academy of Social Sciences (Zhonghua Publishing House, Beijing, 1979).

2. *Miji Lucun* (A Record of Secret Correspondence) ed. by Tianjin Museum of History and The Institute of Modern History, Chinese Academy of Social Sciences (China Social Sciences Press, Beijing, 1984).

3. *Waijiao Gongbao*, 1919 (Foreign Affairs Bulletin, 1919) nos. 3, 7 & 8; ed. by the Chinese Ministry of Foreign Affairs, 1919.

4. *Wusi Aiguo Yundong Dangan Ziliao* (Archival Materials about the May Fourth Patriotic Movement) ed. by The Institute of Modern History, Chinese Academy of Social Sciences and the Second National Archive Library (China Social Sciences Press, Beijing, 1980).

5. *1919 Nian Naibei Yihe Ziliao* (Source Materials about the Peace Conference Between the North and the South in 1919) ed. by Institute of Modern History, Chinese Academy of Sciences (Zhonghua Publishing House, Beijing, 1962).

6. *Zhong E Guanxi Shiliao* (Archival Materials on Sino-Russian Relations) ed. by the Institute of Modern History, Academia Sinica, Taipei, 1959–1970, of which the following volumes have been consulted:

   E Zhengbian Yu Yiban Jiaoshe, 1917–1919 (Russian Revolution and General Contact, 1917-1919) 2 vols.

   Xinjiang Bianfang, 1919 (Xinjiang Frontier Defence, 1919).

   Zhongdong Tielu, 1917–1919 (Chinese Eastern Railway, 1917–1919) 2 vols.

   E Dui Hua Waijiao Shitan, 1920 (Preliminary Soviet Diplomatic Feelers to China, 1920).

   E Zhengbian, 1920 (Russian Revolution, 1920).

Tingzhi E Shiling Daiyu, 1920 (Discontinuation of Recognition of Russian Minister and Consuls, 1920).
Xinjiang Bianfang, 1920 (Xinjiang Frontier Defence, 1920).
Yiban Jiaoshe, 1920 (General Contact, 1920).
Zhongdong Tielu Yu Dongbei Bianfang, 1920 (Chinese Eastern Railway and the Northeast Frontier Defence, 1920).

7. *Zhonghua Minguo Shi Ziliao Conggao – Dashi Ji* (A Collection of Historical Materials of the Republic of China – Chronicle of Events) vol. 5 (1919) and vol. 6 (1920) ed. by Institute of Modern History, Chinese Academy of Social Sciences, Beijing, 1978–1979
8. *Zhonghua Minguo Waijiao Shi Ziliao Xuanbian, 1919–1931* (A Collection of Selected Documents on Chinese Diplomacy, 1919–1931) ed. by Chen Daode et al. (Beijing University Press, Beijing, 1985).
9. *Zhong Wai Jiuyue Huibian* (A Collection of Pre-1919 Sino-Foreign Treaties and Agreements) 2 vols, ed. by Wang Tieya (Sanlian Press, Beijing, 1982).

English (unpublished)

1. Deposited in the Public Record Office, Kew
CAB29/28, British Empire Delegation at the Paris Peace Conference.
CAB29/37, 38, 39; Proceedings of the Council of Heads of Governments.
FO228/3338, 3352, 3511, 3543, 3544, 3545, 3546, 3563, Embassy and Consular Archives, China.
FO350, Jordan Papers.
FO371/3191, General Correspondence, Political, China, (1918), 3683, 3690, 3693, 3694, 3695, 3696, 3697, 3698 (1919), 5318, 5340, 5341, 5342, 5343, 5344 (1920).
FO405/226, Confidential Print, China (1919), 228 (1920), 229 (Annual Report, 1914–1920), 231 (1921).
FO410/67, Confidential Print, Japan (1919), 68 (1920), 69 (Annual Report, 1914–1920).
FO608/209, Peace Conference of 1919–1920, Correspondence, Political Relations with Japan.
FO608/210, Peace Conference of 1919–1920, Correspondence, Political Relations with the Allies.

2. Deposited in the British Library:
Balfour Papers

3. In America (private papers):
Ray S. Baker Papers (Princeton University); General Tasker H. Bliss Papers (Library of Congress); Colonel Stephen Bonsal Papers (Library of Congress); Colonel Edward M. House Papers (Yale University); Charles E. Hughes Papers (Library of Congress); Wellington Koo Papers (Columbia University); Robert Lansing Papers (Library of Congress and Princeton University); Frank L. Polk Papers (Library of Congress and Yale University); Henry White Papers (Library of Congress and Columbia University).

4. State Department Archives (National Archives):
SDA 711.93, 711.933; SDA 741.9411; SDA 761.93; SDA 861.77; SDA 811.30
and SDA 893.00, 893.041, 893.51.

English (published)

1. Woodward, E. L. & Butler, R. (eds.), *Documents on British Foreign Policy, 1919–1939 (DBFP)*, first series, vols. III & VI (Her Majesty's Stationery Office, London, 1956).
2. Butler, R. & Bury, J. P. T. (eds), *Documents on British Foreign Policy, 1919–1939 (DBFP)*, first series, vol. XIV (Her Majesty's Stationery Office, London, 1966).
3. *Papers Relating to the Foreign Relations of the United States (FRUS)* (United States Government Printing Office, Washington, 1935–1948).

   1918, vol. I; 1918, Russia, vol. II
   1919, vol. I
   1919, PPC, vols. I, II, III, IV, V, VI and XI
   1920, vol. I; 1920, Russia, vols I and II

4. *Congressional Record–Proceedings and Debates of the First and the Second Sessions of the Sixty-sixth Congress of the United States, 1919-1920.*
5. *The Papers of Woodrow Wilson*, vols. 53 & 54, ed. by Link, A. S. (Princeton University Press, Princeton, New Jersey, 1986).
6. *Treaties and Agreements with and Concerning China, 1894–1919*, 2 vols., ed. by J. V. A. MacMurray (Macmillan Company, New York, 1920).
7. *Treaties and Agreements with and Concerning China, 1919–1929*, ed. by Carnegie Endowment for International Peace, New York, 1931.

Japanese (unpublished)

1. *Japanese Foreign Ministry Archives (JFMA)* 1868–1945, microfilmed by the Library of Congress:
   MT 1.6.3.24-4, Policy of Japan and of other nations with regards to the USSR.
   MT 2.3.1-1-1, The Paris Peace Conference, the attitudes and political conditions of various countries.
   MT 2.3.1-4, The Paris Peace Conference, the Shangtung problem.
   MT 2.3.1-7, The Paris Peace Conference, policies regarding the peace settlement.
   MT 2.3.1-22, Sino-Japanese relations.

Japanese (published)

1. *Nihon gaikō nempyō narabini shuyō bunshō, 1840–1945* (Chronology of Japanese Diplomacy and Major Diplomatic Documents, 1840–1945) vol. I, ed. by Gaimushō (Nihon Kokusai Rengō Kyokai, Tokyo, 1955).
2. *Nihon gaikō bunshō* (Documents on Japanese Foreign Policy) 1919, vol. 2, Part II, vol. 3, Part I, vol. *Pari kōwa kaigi keika gaiyō* (Summaries of the

Proceedings of the Paris Peace Conference) ed. by Gaimushō (Nihon Kokusai Rengō Kyokai, Tokyo, 1960).
3. Hara, K., *Hara Kei nikki* (Diary of Hara Kei) vols. 8 & 9 (Kengen-sha, Tokyo, 1950–1951).
4. Hara, K., *Hara Kei zenshū* (Collected Works of Hara Kei) 2 vols, Hara Shobō, Tokyo, 1969).
5. Kobayashi., T. (ed.), *Suiusō nikki: Rinji gaikō chōsa iinkai hu kaigi hikki tō–Itō-ke monjō* (The Diary of Itō Miyoji and Selected Documents Relating to Japan's Foreign Policy in the Early Taishō Peirod) (Hara Shobō, Tokyo, 1966).

SECONDARY SOURCES

Newspapers and Periodicals

Chinese
Chen Bao (Morning Post) 1918–1920.
Shen Bao (Shanghai Daily) 1918–1920.
Dongfan Zazhi (Eastern Miscellanea) 1918–1921.
English
North China Herald, 1918–1920.
Millard Review, 1918–1921.
Chinese Social and Political Science Review, 1917–1921.

Articles

Chinese
Deng Ye, 'Bali Hehui Juyue Wenti Yanjiu' (A Study of China's Refusal to Sign the Versailles Treaty), *Zhongguo Shehui Kexue* (China Social Sciences), no. 2. 1984.
Han Xueru, 'Wusi Yundong Yu Maliezhuyi Zai Zhongguo De Chuanbo' (The May Fourth Movement and the Dissemination of Marxism and Leninism in China), *Lishi Yanjiu* (Historical Studies), no. 2, 1965.
Pang Pu, 'Wenhua Jiegou Yu Jindai Zhongguo' (Changing Culture and Modern China), *Zhongguo Shehui Kexue* (China Social Sciences), no. 1, 1985.
Yu Xinchun, 'Bali Hehui Yu Wusi Yundong' (The Paris Peace Conference and the May Fourth Movement), *Lishi Yanjiu* (Historical Studies), no. 1, 1979.

English
Chang, H., 'Liang Ch'ichao and Intellectual Changes in the Late Nineteenth Century', *Journal of Asian Studies*, vol. XXIX, no. 1, Nov. 1969
Cohen, P., 'Wang Tao and the Incipient Chinese Nationalism', *Journal of Asian Studies*, vol. XXIV, No. 4, Aug. 1967.
Cohen, W., 'America and the May Fourth Movement – The Response to Chinese Nationalism, 1917–1921', *Pacific Historical Review*, vol. XXXV, Feb. 1966.

Dennet, T., 'Seward's Far Eastern Policy', *American Historical Review*, vol. XXVIII, no. 1, Oct. 1922.

Hoffman, S., 'Hedley Bull and His Contribution to International Relations', *International Affairs*, vol. 62, no. 2, Spring, 1986.

Kennedy, D., 'The Expansion of Europe', *Journal of Modern History*, vol. 59, no. 6, June 1987.

Langer, W. L., 'The Well-spring of Our Discontents', *Journal of Contemporary History*, vol. 3, no. 4, Oct. 1968.

Schrecker, J., 'The Reform Movement, Nationalism, and China's Foreign Policy', *Journal of Asian Studies*, vol. XXIX, no. 1, Nov. 1969.

Tsiang, T. F., 'China and the European Expansion', *Politica*, vol. II, no. 5, 1936.

Watson, A., 'Hedley Bull, States Systems and International Society', *Review of International Studies*, vol. 13, no. 2, April, 1987.

Williams, W. A., 'The Frontier Thesis and the American Foreign Policy', *Pacific Historical Review*, vol. XXIV, no. 2, 1955.

Wright, A. F., 'The Study of Chinese Civilization', *Journal of History of Ideas*, vol. XXI, no. 1960.

Yang, R., 'Sinkiang Under the Administration of Governor Yang Tseng-hsin, 1911–1928', *Central Asiatic Journal*, vol. VI, no. 4, Dec. 1961.

Yost, D. S., 'New Perspectives on Historical States-Systems', *World Politics*, vol. XXXII, no. 1, Oct. 1979.

Books

Chinese

Cai Xiaozhou & Yang Lianggong (eds.), *Wusi* (The May Fourth), reprint (Zhuanji Wenxue Press, Taipei, 1982).

Cao Rulin, *Yisheng Zhi Huiyi* (Memoir of Cao Rulin) (Chunqiu Publishing House, Hong Kong, 1967).

Chen Gongbo, *The Communist Movement in China* (Social Sciences Press, Beijing, 1982).

Ding Minlan *et al.*, *Diguozhuyi Qing Hua Shi* (A History of Imperialist Aggression of China) vol. 2 (People's Press, Beijing, 1986).

History Department, Fudan University (ed.), *Jindai Zhongguo Zican Jieji Yanjiu* (A Study of Modern Chinese Bourgeoisie) (Fudan University Press, Shanghai, 1984).

Koo, W., *Gu Weijun Huiyilu* (Memoir of Wellington Koo, tr. by Institute of Modern Chinese History) vol. I (Zhonghua Publishing House, Beijing, 1983).

Li Guoqi *et al.*, *Minzu Zhuyi* (Nationalism) (Shibao Press Ltd., Taipei, 1985).

Liu Yan, *Zhongguo Waijiao Shi* (A Diplomatic History of China) (Sanmin Publishing House, Taipei, 1962).

Peng Ming, *Wusi Yundong* (The May Fourth Movement) (Beijing People's Publishing House, Beijing, 1980).

Wang Kefeng, *Wusi Yundong He Zhongguo Gongchandang De Dansheng* (The May Fourth Movement and the Birth of the Chinese Communist Party) (Jiangsu People's Press, Nanjing, 1958).

Wang Yujun, *Zhong Su Waijiao De Xumu* (The First Period of Sino-Soviet Diplomacy) (Institute of Modern History, Academia Sinica, Taipei, 1963).

Wang Yunsheng, *Liushi Nian Lai Zhongguo Yu Riben* (China and Japan in the Last Sixty Years) vols VI and VII (Sanlian Press, Beijing, 1981).

Xiang Qing, *Gongchanguoji He Zhongguo Geming Guanxi De Lishi Gaishu* (An Outline History of the Relations Between the Comintern and the Chinese Revolution) (Guangdong People's Press, Guangzhou, 1983).

Yang Yunruo, *Gongchanguoji He Zhongguo Geming Guanxi Jishi* (A Chronological Record of the Relations Between the Comintern and the Chinese Revolution) (Social Sciences Press, Beijing, 1983).

Zhang Jin (ed.), *Zhongguo Waijiao Lianjian, 1933* (Yearbook of China's Foreign Relations, 1933) (Shenhuo Press, Shanghai, 1934).

Zhang Zhongfu, *Zhonghua Minguo Waijiaoshi* (A Diplomatic History of the Republic of China) vol. I (Zhengzhong Press, Taipei, 1961).

Zhong Shuhe, *Zouxiang Shijie* (From East to West) (Zhonghua Publishing House, Beijing, 1985).

English

Baker, R. S., *Woodrow Wilson and the World Settlement*, 3 vols (Double-Day, Page & Co., New York, 1923).

Bell, H. T. M. & Woodhead, M. J. I. (eds.), *China Yearbook, 1919–1920* (George Routledge & Sons Ltd., London, 1921).

Bonsal, S., *Suitors and Supplicants – The Little Nations at Versailles* (Cromwell Books, New York, 1946).

Bozeman, A., *Politics and Culture in International History* (Princeton University Press, New Jersey, 1960).

Bull, H., *The Anarchical Society* (Macmillan, London, 1977).

Bull, H. & Watson, A. (eds), *The Expansion of International Society* (Clarendon Press, Oxford, 1984).

Carr, E. H., *International Relations Between the Two World Wars* (Macmillan, London, 1947).

———, *The Bolshevik Revolution, 1917–1923*, 3 vols (Macmillan, London, 1950–1953).

———, *Nationalism and After* (Macmillan, London, 1945).

Cassese, A., *International Law in a Divided World* (Clarendon Press, Oxford, 1987).

Chan, G. (ed.), *Nationalism in East Asia: An Annotated Bibliography of Selected Works* (Garland Publishing Inc., New York, 1981).

Ch'en, J., *China and the West – Society and Culture 1815-1937* (Hutchinson, London, 1979).

Ch'i, M., *China Diplomacy, 1914–1918* (Harvard University Press, Cambridge, Massachusetts, 1970).

Chow Tse-tsung, *The May Fourth Movement – Intellectual Revolution in Modern China* (Harvard University Press, Cambridge Massachussetts, 1964).

Chu Pao-chin, *V. K. Wellington Koo – A Case Study of China's Diplomat and Diplomacy of Nationalism, 1912–1966* (The Chinese University Press, Hongkong, 1981).

Clubb, O. E., *Twentieth Century China* (Columbia University Press, New York, 1964).

Cobban, A., *The Nation-state and National Self-Determination*, rev. ed., (Collins, London, 1969).

Crowley, J. B. (ed.), *Modern East Asia – Essays in Interpetation* (Harcourt, Brace and World Inc., New York, 1970).

Cranmer-Byng, J. L. (ed.), *An Embassy to China: Lord Macartney's Journal* (Longman, London, 1962).

Emerson, R., *From Empire to Nations: The Rise of Self-assertion of Asian and African Peoples* (Harvard University Press, Cambridge, Massachussetts, 1960).

Fairbank, J. K. (ed.), *The Chinese World Order – Traditional China's Foreign Relations* (Harvard University Press, Cambridge, Massachussetts, 1968).

Fairbank, J. K., Reischauer, E. O. & Craig, A. M., *East Asia – The Modern Transformation* (George Allen & Unwin, Ltd., London, 1965).

Fairbank, J. K. & Twitchett, D. (eds), *Cambridge History of China*, vols. 11 and 12 (Cambridge University Press, London, 1980 & 1983).

Feuerwerker, W., Murphey, R. & Wright, M. (eds.), *Approaches to Modern Chinese History* (University of California Press, Berkeley, 1967).

Fifield, R. H., *Woodrow Wilson and the Far East – The Diplomacy of the Shantung Question* (Archon Books, Hamden, Connecticut, 1965).

Fishel, W. R., *The End of Extraterritoriality in China* (University of California Press, Berkeley, 1952).

Fitzgerald, C. P., *Revolution in China* (Cresset Press, London, 1952).

——, *The Chinese View of Their Place in the World* (Oxford University Press, London, 1969).

Fung Yulan, *A Short History of Chinese Philosophy* (tr. by Bodde, D.) (Macmillan Company, New York, 1948).

Gentzler, J. (ed.), *Changing China – Readings in the History of China from the Opium War to the Present* (Praeger Publishers, New York, 1977).

Gong, G., *The Standard of 'Civilization' in International Society* (Clarendon Press, Oxford, 1984).

Grayson, T. C., *Woodrow Wilson: An Intimate Memoir* (Holt, Rinehart and Winston, New York, 1960).

Griswold, A. W., *The Far Eastern Policy of the United States* (Yale University Press, New Haven, 1962).

Hackett, R. F., *Yamagata Aritomo in the Rise of Modern Japan, 1838–1922* (Harvard University Press, Cambridge, Massachussetts, 1971).

Hankey, M., *The Supreme Control* (George Allen & Unwin Ltd., London, 1963).

Higgins, A. P. (ed.), *Hall's International Law*, 8th ed (Clarendon Press, Oxford, 1924).

Hoffmann, S. (ed.), *Contemporary Theory in International Relations* (Prentice-Hall, Inc. New Jersey, 1960).

Holland, T. E., *Studies in International Law* (Clarendon Press, Oxford, 1898).

——, *Lectures on International Law* (ed. by Walker, T. A. & Walker, W. L.) (Sweet & Maxwell Ltd., London, 1933).

Hsu, I., *China's Entrance into the Family of Nations – the Diplomatic Phase, 1860–1880* (Harvard University Press, Cambridge, Massachussetts, 1960).

Hudson, G., *Europe and China – A Survey of their Relations from the Earliest Times to 1800* (Edward Arnold Ltd., London, 1961) (reprint).

Iriye, A., *After Imperialism: the Search for a New Order in the Far East, 1921–1931* (Harvard University Press, Cambridge, Massachussetts, 1965).
——, *The Origins of the Second World War in Asia and the Pacific* (Longman, New York, 1987).
Israel, J., *Progressivism and the Open Door – America and China, 1905–1921* (University of Pittsburgh Press, Pittsburgh, 1971).
Iyer, R. ed., *The Glass Curtain Between Asia and Europe* (Oxford University Press, London, 1965).
Kajima, M., *The Diplomacy of Japan, 1894–1922*, vol. III (The Kajima Institute of International Peace, Tokyo, 1980).
Keylor, W. R., *The Twentieth Century World – An International History* (Oxford University Press, New York, 1984).
King, W., *China at the Paris Peace Conference in 1919* (St. John's University Press, New York, 1961).
——, *V. K. Wellington's Foreign Policy – Some Selected Documents* (Commercial Press, Shanghai, 1931).
Lansing, R., *The Peace Negotiation – A Personal Narrative* (Constable and Company Ltd., London, 1921).
Lattimore, O., *The Pivot of Asia* (Little Brown and Company, Boston, 1950).
Latourette, K. S., *A History of Modern China* (Penguin Books, London, 1954).
Leong, S.-T., *Sino-Soviet Diplomatic Relations, 1917–1926* (Australian University Press, Canberra, 1976).
Levenson, J., *Liang Ch'i-chao and the Mind of Modern China* (Harvard University Press, Cambridge, Massachussetts, 1953).
Li Tien-yi, *Woodrow Wilson's China Policy, 1913–1917* (University of Kansas City Press/Twayne Publishers, New York, 1952).
Lloyd George, D., *The Truth about the Peace Treaties*, 2 vols (Victor Gollancz Ltd., London, 1938).
Lorimer, J., *The Institutes of the Law of Nations*, 2 vols (William Blackwood & Sons, London, 1883).
Louis, W. R., *British Strategy in the Far East* (Clarendon Press, Oxford, 1974).
Lowe, P., *Britain in the Far East – A Survey from 1819 to the Present* (Longman, London, 1981).
Mantoux, P., *Minutes of the Council of Four – Proceedings of the Council of Four, March 24 to April 18* (tr. by Whiton, J. B.) (Librairie Droz, Geneva, 1964).
Millard, T., *Democracy and the Eastern Question* (Kelly & Welsh Ltd., Shanghai, 1931).
Morley, J. W. (ed.), *Japan's Foreign Policy, 1868–1941 – A Research Guide* (Columbia University Press, New York, 1974).
Morse, H. B., *International Relations of the Chinese Empire*, 3 vols (Longmans, Green & Co., London, 1910–1918).
Morton, W. F., *Tanaka Giichi and Japan's China Policy* (Wm Dawson & Sons Ltd., Kent, 1980).
Needham, J., *Within the Four Seas – The Dialogue Between East and West* (George Allen & Unwin, Ltd., London, 1969).
Nicolson, H., *Peacemaking, 1919*, revised edn (Methuen, London, 1964).
Nish, I., *Alliance in Decline: A Study of Anglo-Japanese Relations, 1908–23* (The Athlone Press, University of London, London, 1972).

——, *Japanese Foreign Policy, 1868–1942* (Routledge & Kegan Paul, London, 1977).

—— (ed.), *Anglo-Japanese Alienation, 1919–1952* (Cambridge University Press, London, 1982).

Northedge, F. S., *The International Political System* (Faber and Faber, London, 1976).

Northrop, F. S. C., *The Meeting of East and West: An Inquiry Concerning World Understanding* (Macmillan Company, New York, 1946).

Oka, Y., (tr. by Fraser, A. & Murray, D.) *Five Political Leaders of Modern Japan* (University of Tokyo Press, 1986).

Pasvolsky, L., *Russia in the Far East* (Macmillan Company, London, 1922).

Pollard, R. R., *China's Foreign Relations, 1917–1931* (Macmillan Company, New York, 1933).

Pratt, J. T., *War and Politics in China* (Janathan Cape Ltd., London, 1943).

——, *The European Expansion into the Far East* (Macmillan, London, 1948).

Reinsch, P., *An American Diplomat in China* (William Heinemann, London, 1922).

RIIA, *Nationalism* (Oxford University Press, London, 1939)

——, *The Impact of the Russian Revolution, 1917–1967* (Oxford University Press, London, 1967).

Scalapino, R. A. & Yu, G. T., *Modern China and its Revolutionary Process* (University of California Press, Berkeley, 1985).

Schwartz, B. (ed.), *Reflections on the May Fourth Movement–A Symposium* (Harvard University Press, Cambridge, Massachussetts, 1972).

Snyder, L., *The New Nationalism* (Cornell University Press, Ithaca, NY, 1968).

Storry, R., *Japan and the Decline of the West* (Macmillan, London, 1979).

Takeuchi, T., *War and Diplomacy in the Japanese Empire* (George Allen & Unwin, London, 1936).

Temperley, H. W. V. (ed.), *A History of the Peace Conference of Paris*, 6 vols, (Henry Frowde & Hodder & Stoughton, London, 1924).

Teng Ssu-Yu & Fairbank, J. K. (eds.), *China's Response to the West – A Documentary Survey 1839–1923* (Harvard University Press, Cambridge, Massachussetts, 1954).

Thorne, C., *The Limits of Foreign Policy* (Hamish Hamilton, London, 1972).

Toynbee, A. *The World after the Peace Conference* (Oxford University Press, London, 1925).

Turner, F. J., *The Frontier in American History* (Henry Holt & Co., New York, 1920).

Tyau, M. T. Z., *China Awakened* (Macmillan Company, New York, 1922).

Vinacke, H., *A History of the Far East in Modern Times* (George Allen & Unwin Ltd., London, 1964).

Walworth, A., *Woodrow Wilson and His Peace Makers: American Diplomacy at the Paris Peace Conference, 1919* (W. W. Norton & Co., New York, 1986).

Whiting, A., *Soviet Policies in China, 1917–1924* (Columbia University Press, New York, 1954).

Whyte, Sir Frederick, *China and Foreign Powers – An Historical Review of Their Relations* (RIIA, London, 1928).

Wight, M., *Systems of States* (ed. Bull, H.) (Leicester University Press, Leicester, 1977).

Williams, E. T., *China Yesterday and Today*, 5th ed (Thomas Y. Cromwell, New York, 1932).

Wilson, G., *Handbook of International Law*, 2nd ed (West Publishing Company, Minnesota, 1927).

Wood, G. Z., *The Shantung Question* (Fleming H. Revell Company, New York, 1922).

Woodhead, H. G. W. (ed.), *China Yearbook, 1921–1922* (Tientsin Press Ltd., Tientsin, 1921).

Wright, M. (ed.), *China in Revolution: The First Phase, 1900–1913* (Yale University Press, New Haven, 1968).

French

Lu Tseng-tsiang, *Souvenirs et Pensées* (5th ed. Pruges, Brussels, 1946).

Mantoux, P., *Les délibérations du Conseil des Quatre* (Éditions de la Recherche Scientifique, Paris, 1955).

Nagao Ariga, *La Chine et La Grande Guerre Européenne* (A. Pedoue, Éditeur, Paris, 1920).

Renouvin, P., *La Question d'Extrême-Orient, 1840–1940* (Librairie Hechette Paris, 1946).

Yong, D. T. A., *Chine et Japon à la Conférence de la Paix* (Brurges, Abbey de Saint-André, 1934)

Japanese

Andō, H., *Nihonjin no Chūgoku-kan* (A Study of the Japanese View of China in Recent History) (Keisō Shōbō, Tokyo, 1971).

Banno, J., *Kindai Nihon no gaikō to seiji* (Politics and Foreign Relations in Modern Japan) (Kenkyū Shuppan, Tokyo, 1985).

Hosoya, C. & Saitō, M. (eds.), *Washinton taisei to Nichi-Bei kankei* (The Washington System and the Japanese–American Relations) (Tokyo Daigaku shupaan-kai, Tokyo, 1978).

Iriye, A. & Aruga, T. (eds.), *Senkanki no Nihon gaikō* (The Japanese Diplomacy Between the Wars) (Tokyo Daigaku Shuppan-kai, Tokyo, 1983).

Kajima, M. (ed.), *Nihon gaikōshi* (The Diplomatic History of Japan), vols. 11 & 12 (Kajima Kenkyujō Shuppansha, Tokyo, 1973 & 1971).

Kitaōka, S., *Nihon rikugun to tairiku seisaku* (The Japanese Army and Japanese Policy Towards Mainland Asia, 1906–1918) (Tokyo Daigaku Shuppan-kai, Tokyo, 1978).

Shiratori, R. (ed.), *Nihon no naikaku* (The Japanese Cabinets), vol. I (Shinhyō ron, Tokyo, 1981).

Usui, K., *Nihon to Chūgoku* (Sino-Japanese relations in the Taisho Era) (Hara Shobo, Tokyo, 1982).

Yamane, Y., *Ronshu kindai Chūgoku to Nihon* (Modern China and Japan) (Yamakawa Shuppansha, Tokyo, 1979).

Index

Acculturation 26
Aleni, Julio 21
Alston 108, 136, 145, 165, 175
Anfu Clique 168, 171, 173
Anfu-Zhili War 178
Anglo-French Expedition 17
Anglo-Japanese Alliance 98, 110,
    112–13, 190
  American view of 112, 125
  and China 143–6
  and the United States 112, 113
Annam 20
Armistice 41, 100
  China's enthusiasm over 41–2
  Japan's reserved attitude
    towards 49, 128
Austria 97, 140, 187
  end of treaty relations with
    China 140
Austria-Hungary 60, 97, 101, 102

Baker
  sent by Wilson to Chinese
    Delegation 89
Balance of power 8, 11
  in East Asia 39, 101
  pre-war 100
  Shandong and, 62
Balfour 55, 71, 72, 107
Bao Guiqing, General 167
Bismarck 32
Bliss, General 68, 119
Bolsheviks 148, 156, 158, 159, 166,
    177, 178
  and China's break with Imperial
    Russian Legation 184
  and equality among nations 162
  China's intention to
    approach 157
  diplomacy of 148
  military victory of 158, 161
Bonsal, Colonel 90
Boppe 165, 176

Borah 123
Boxer Indemnity 177
  payment of Russian share
    suspended 177–8
Boxer Rebellion 36, 37
Brest-Litovsk Treaty 155
Britain 19, 100, 107, 110, 146, 191
  concern over Japan's expansion in
    China 114–15
  cooperation with America in East
    Asia 111–14
  formula of powers relations in
    China 112
  interests in China 107–8
  renunciation of extraterritorial
    system in China 195
  staging a come-back to East
    Asia 101
British Chamber of Commerce 142
Bruce, Frederick 17
Burma 20

Canning, George 27
Capitulations 27, 30, 31, 36
Carr, E. H. 149
Cecil 146
CER (Chinese Eastern Railway)
  Zone 150, 151, 152, 153, 167,
    181
  Chinese taking control of 152–3
  tariff in 153
Chen Lu 56, 82, 87, 176
Chevony 168, 169
Chicherin 165, 166, 171, 172, 174
China 27, 30, 33, 64, 150
  a disappointed nation 95–6
  a nation-state 33
  and American ideal 122, 123
  and equality of nations 16, 17,
    138
  and international law 16, 17,
    18–19

China (*cont.*)
  as a candidate to the Family of
    Nations 20
  assault on the Russian treaty rights
    and privileges 5, 187, 190,
    192
  at international conferences 21,
    36–7, 188
  at margin of international
    system 5, 21, 37, 187
  break with the Russian
    Legation 178–81
  cultural crisis of 24–6
  cultural superiority of 15, 23
  diplomacy of 2, 187, 189, 191,
    192, 196
  dispatch of diplomatic missions
    abroad 19–20,
  imperial reforms 34–6
  loss of vassal-states 16, 20,
  no war aims 43
  optimism over Peace
    Conference 41–2
  Petrograd contacts with Soviet
    Russia, 153–5
  ratification of the Hague
    conventions 36–7
  Republican revolution of 34
  resistance to imperialism 38
  review of Russian policy 166,
    176–7
  treaty with Bolivia 139
  treaty with Persia 139
  treaty with Switzerland 139
China and Europe
  communication problem
    between 12–15
  incompatibility between 13
China problem 1, 101, 138
Chinda 68, 137, 146
  meetings with Curzon 108–11
  under express instruction not to
    sign 69
Chinese Delegation 56, 66
  composition of 51
  efforts to make
    reservations 90–4
  formal protest of 91
  organization of 47

preparations for 'Questions for
  Readjustment' 60–1
refuses to sign 94–5
secret meeting of May 28 92
signature in the hands of 93
Chinese Communist Party 148
Chinese demands
  abrogation of consular
    jurisdiction 63
  on tariff autonomy 64
  relinquishment of leased
    territories 63
  renunciation of the spheres of
    influence 62
  restoration of concessions and
    settlements 63–4
  withdrawal of foreign post
    offices 62–3
  withdrawal of foreign troops and
    police 62
Chinese Eastern Railway *see* CER
  Zone
Chinese Government
  crisis of 86
  dilemma of 83
  final instruction to Chinese
    Delegation 87–8, 95
  issue of signature unexpected
    for 78
  sending troops to CER Zone 151
Chinese nationalism 1, 26, 37–8, 75,
  76, 143
  concern of 77–8
  incipient 23
  Mary Wright on 37–8, 76
  not an ideological movement 76
  official vs populist 74, 76, 77–8,
    191
  rise of 76, 98
Chinese Parliament
  attitude towards signature 79
Chinese world order 5, 9, 11
  as moral order 9, 11
  collapse of 33, 39
Clemenceau 54, 55, 57, 69, 90, 93
  on France bound by secret
    agreements 58
Clive 144, 182, 183
Colby 182, 184

Comintern 148
Confucius 13, 24
doctrines of 9
Conventional tariff 139, 141
and non-treaty countries 141–2
Council of Five 68
Council of Four 66, 67, 71, 90, 94,
120
China's submission to 71
Jiaozhou question at 68–72
passim
sessions of April 22 69–70
Council of Ten 52, 59, 66
Crane 182, 184
Curzon 106, 108, 109, 111, 146, 177,
182
on Japanese policy in
China 108–10

Dao Guang, Emperor 17
Diplomatic Corps 140, 142, 143,
150, 176, 185
Duan Qirui 44, 85, 171
caution on Chinese demands at
Peace Conference 45
Dujuns 79, 85
consensus on signature 80

Europe 6, 26, 191 (*see also* China
and Europe)
and the universal international
system 30–1
assuming cultural
implications 28
cultural superiority of 14–15
domination of 29
European expansion 3
and universal international
system 26
becoming a civilizing mission 29
four phases of 28
three stages of 27
European-dominated international
system 27–30, 188–9
composed of two distinguishable
groups of states 27–8
Extraterritoriality 139, 187, 191,
195
and judicial reforms 35

Family of Nations 6, 51
all-inclusive 26
China's acceptance in 2, 20–1,
147, 193
Chinese 7, 8, 11
European 6, 8, 16, 31
European vs Chinese 11–2
exclusiveness of 30–1
Far Eastern Republic 165, 166, 168,
174, 186
Zhang mission at 168–170
Fashoda crisis, 1898 32
Fauchille 8
Feng Guozhang 43
Four Power Banking
Consortium 134, 136
France 19, 32, 39, 147
impotent in East Asia 101
Franco-Prussian War, 1870–1 32

Gaikō Chōsakai 128, 131, 132, 134
reaction to Wilson's Fourteen
Points 128
Gaimusho 131
policy difference with the Army
131, 134–5
Germany 219, 40, 51, 60, 88, 101,
102, 112, 125, 187
Gong, Prince 18, 19
Grayson, Admiral 72
Greece 13, 146
Greene, Sir Conyghame 130
Guo Songtao 19, 23, 24
Guo Zongxi 151, 152

Hague Peace Conferences 5
and China 36–7, 188
Hall, W. 30
Han Dynasty 9
Hara, K. 128, 132, 133, 137
China policy of 133–4
cooperation with the United
States 132
instruction to Japanese
Delegation 73
on alliance with Great
Britain 133
vision of international order 132

Harbin   150, 151, 153, 168
  -Soviet   151
  crisis in   149–50
Harding Administration, China
    policy of   125–7
Hardinge, Lord   113
Hayashi, Baron   137
Holland, T. E.   30, 31
  on China's observation of
    international law   19
Hong Kong Extension   105, 106
Hornbeck, S.   118, 121
Horvath, General   150, 151, 154, 167
  removed from CER   156
House, Colonel   48, 65, 66, 72, 90
  advice to Wilson   68
Hu Weide   47
  supports signing Versailles
    Treaty   83
Huang Yanpei   145
Hughes, Charles Evans   126, 127

Industrial Revolution   29
Internal Peace Conference at
    Shanghai   78
International law   8, 11, 18–19, 30,
    43, 147, 184, 185, 188, 192
International order, post-war
  American vision of   119
  and China problem   101–2
  China's rejection of   96
  Japanese view of   127–8
  of East Asian   100
  reconstruction of   137
International society   1, 97 195, 196
  acquiescence of China's equality
    in   147
  China's entry into   5–6, 34, 37–8,
    188, 193–4
  definition of   4
  entry of non-European nations   3,
    195–6
International system   6, 193
  and Soviet Russia   148
  and the European expansion   6
  British vision of   114
  China's place in   34, 96, 100, 147
  core-periphery divide of   28,
    32–3

cultural confrontation in   33
  definition of   3
  democratization of   40–1, 190
  dislocation of China in   75
  domination of the 'core'   33
  impact of Chinese nationalism
    on   76
  Japanese view of   129, 132
  most idiosyncratic trait of   30
  resistance and revolt at the
    'periphery' of   32–3
Italy   91, 95, 170

Japan   20, 27, 39, 66, 73, 127–37,
    passim, 190, 194, 196
  and international
    cooperation   133
  bluff of   73
  China policy of   130, 131
  conditions for peace of   50
  declaration of war against
    Germany   40
  new diplomacy of   131, 132
  predominance in China   101
  special relations with China   129
  war aims of   49
Japanese expansion   40
  and Manchuria and
    Mongolia   134, 135
  British view of   107–8, 110
Japanese foreign policy
  and the Army   134–5
  transition of   131
Japanese Delegation
  and change of Wilson's
    attitude   69–70
Jean Bodin   7
Jiaozhou   40, 44, 53, 54, 65, 68–70,
    74, 97, 191
  Japanese statement about   68, 72,
    82
Jordan, Sir John   102, 115, 151
  and Harbin crisis   150
  radical proposals of   103–5
  views of Japanese expansion in
    China   104

Kalmykov case   179
Kang Youwei   25

Karakhan 165, 171, 174
  Manifestos of 161, 164, 165, 166,
    169, 172, 177
  talks with Zhang 170
Kato, Viscount 135, 136
  on legitimacy of Japanese
    expansion in China 137
Kolchak 158, 160, 168
Konoe Fumimaro
  against Anglo-American
    peace 128–9
Koo 45, 47, 52, 66, 67, 93, 94, 119,
  184
  and decision not to sign Versailles
    Treaty 94–5
  approaches to the State
    Department 44–5
  interviews with Wilson 47, 66
  speech at the Council of
    Ten 54–55
Korea 20
Kotow
  abolished in Sino-foreign
    relations 23
Kudachev, Prince 183, 187, 190,
  205, 211, 216
  meeting with Yen Huiqing 219
  official note refused by
    Chinese 217
  position anomalous 190, 215

Lansing, R. 44–5, 52–3, 55, 66, 67,
  71, 72, 91, 120, 121
  non-committal on Chinese
    questions 47–8
  proposals at the Council of
    Five 68
Lansing-Ishii Agreement 121, 129,
  144
League of Nations 41, 44, 59, 63,
  73, 89, 119, 120, 129, 163, 189,
  193
  and renewal of Anglo-Japanese
    Alliance 146
  and Soviet Russia 163
  China's election into the Council
    of 147, 187
  China's membership in 1, 80, 93,
    97, 145

Wilson's faith in 119
Lenin 41, 165, 172
li 8, 11, 18
  and international law 11
Li Hongzhang 23
Li Yuanhong 43
Liang Qichao 25
Liang Ruhao 38
Lin Zexu 22
Litvinov, Maxim, 166
Liu Jingren 158
Liz de Camoes 14
Lloyd George 55, 68, 69, 70, 93, 107
  on Britain bound by secret
    agreements 58
  pledges to stand by the British
    commitment 69
Lodge, Henry Cabot 124
Lorimer, J. 30–1
Lu Zhengxiang 51, 59, 78, 91, 92,
  94
  China's conditions for
    peace 45–6
  on Allied war-time assurances 52
  on China's signature 81–2

Macartney, Lord, 15
Macleay 48, 91, 102, 103, 106, 108
  on Obata Incident 57
Makino, Baron 49, 65, 69, 93
  and Japanese demands at Council
    of Ten 53–4
  at April 22 session of Council of
    Four 69
  on Japan's new diplomacy 131
Manchuria 62, 134, 136, 149, 150,
  156, 157, 158
  Japan's special position in 134
Marco Polo 13
Martin, W. A. P. 19
Matteo Ricci 21
Matsui 56, 131
May Fourth Movement 1, 2, 74–7,
  80, 121
  American response to 121
  and China's decision-making on
    signature 77–8
  as climax of Chinese
    nationalism 77

May Fourth Movement (*cont*).
  how to define   75
  uniqueness of   76
Meng Enyuan   151, 152
Middle East
  as 'curtain' between China and
    Europe   12–13
Ming Dynasty   6, 10, 22
Mo Zi   15
Mongols   13, 156
Morrison, Dr.   90
Müller   106, 107

Narkomindel   147, 153, 165, 170,
    172
  and Soviet consuls in Xinjiang
    159
National self-determination   40,
    101, 121, 192
Nationalism   76, 188, 189   (*see also*
    Chinese nationalism)
Needham, J.   12, 13
New Culture Movement   2, 75
Nehru   76

Obata   56–7, 136, 183
  Incident   56, 59
October Revolution   153, 175
Okuma   130
Open Door   105, 108, 121, 125
Opium War   1
Oppenheim, L.   31
Ottoman Empire   27, 32, 147, 194,
    196
Outer Mongolia   156, 158, 164

Palmerston, Viscount   17
Paris Peace conference   2, 5, 41, 50,
    129, 139, 146
  China
    allocated only two seats   52
    fear of being represented by
      Japan   48–9
    preparations for   43–6
  Japan
    preparations for   49–50
Pax Tartarica   13
Persia   30
Peru   19

Pichon   48, 84, 94
  refuses China demands to make
    reservations   91
Polivanov   154, 176
Polk   120, 121
Pufendorf   7

Qian Long, Emperor   15
Qingdao   79, 80, 83
Qing Dynasty   6, 10, 19, 34

Reinsch, P.   41, 46, 118, 121
  defining China question   115–18
  view of Japan's expansion in
    China   116
Republic of China   33, 34
Rights recovery   143, 152, 158, 162,
    163, 175, 186
  and Karakhan Manifestos   167
  and nationalism   166
Rivier   8
Rodriguez, Jean   22
Rome   13, 139
Rousseau   7
Russia   19, 39, 100, 125, 147
  an imperialist power in East
    Asia,   148
Russian civil war   160
  China's neutrality in   160, 179
Russo-Asiatic Bank   156
Russo-China Bank   156

Saionji, Marquis   73, 128
St. Germain Treaty   97, 146, 187
  China's ratification of   140
Salisbury, Lord   195
Self-Strengthening Movement   1, 23
Shandong   2, 49, 52, 59, 66, 71, 107
  and Sino-Japanese secret
    agreements   57
  disposal of   70
  in American Senate   123–5
  Sino-Japanese controversy
    over   65, 68
Shandong decision
  Chinese official reaction to   79
  Chinese resentment of   89–90
Shao Chaolin   19
Shidehara, Baron   137

Siam 20, 30, 194, 196
Sino-Japanese secret
  agreements 56–8, 109
  and Treaty of London 109
  submitted by both China and
    Japan 59
Sino-Japanese War, 1895 20, 24
Sino-Russian Agreement, 1909 150,
  151
Sino-Russian treaties
  China's view of 177
Sino-Russian Treaty, 1881 150, 161
  Chinese demanding revision
    of 162–3
Sino-Soviet Friendship Treaty,
  1924 164, 187
Sinocentrism 15, 21, 33
  as resistance to European
    expansion 15
  conceptual 21, 22
  disintegration of 16, 22–3, 26
Song Dynasty 10
Soviet Russia 161, 162, 190
  Chinese policy towards 163–4,
    166, 173
  contact with Chinese Legation at
    Petrograd 153–155
  offer to renounce Russian treaty
    rights 154
  treated as non-treaty nation 177
Spain 19
Standard of 'civilization' 5, 32, 138,
  194, 195, 196
  and China 65
Sun Yat-sen 34

Taishō Democracy 135
Tanaka, General 136
  on Japanese expansion 137
Tang Dynasty 10
Tang Shaoyi 79
Tian Xia 8
  called into question 22
Treaty of Lausanne, 1923 195
Treaty of Nanjing, 1842
  as a *modus vivendi* 17
Treaty of Paris, 1856 27, 147, 195
Treaty of Sèvres, 1920 195
Treaty of Tianjin, 1861 17, 22

Treaty system 20, 195
  China's revolt against 5
Tribute system 10, 20, 22
  Chinese 11
  disappearance of 20
Trotsky 175
Turkey 195
Turner, F. J. 122
  and frontier thesis in American
    history 122
Turkestan Soviet Republic 160, 162
Twenty-One Demands 40, 135

Uchida, 49, 134
  and Japanese statement on
    Jiaozhou 84
Ugaki, General 131
United Nations 195
United States 19, 39, 58, 100, 130,
  190
  ambivalence in China
    policy 120–3, 183
  British view of cooperation
    with 111, 112
  China policy of 118–19, 125
  interest in China 122–3
  renunciation of extraterritorial
    system in China 195
  view of Japanese policy in
    China 116–17

Vasco da Gama 12
Vattel 10
Versailles Treaty 99, 161, 189
  American rejection of 124
  China's signing of 74, 77, 78–87
    passim
  favourable provisions for China
    in 81
Voltaire 7
Von Borch 141
Voznesensky, A. N. 154

Wang, T. 52, 54, 112
  against signing Versailles
    Treaty 92
Wang Chonghui 146
Wang Tao 23
Warlord politics 2, 171

Washington Conference 2, 61, 99, 100, 115, 138, 190, 194
Washington System 115, 190
Wei Yuan 22
Weihaiwei 105
Western culture, impact of 24
Westphalia 6, 7
Wheaton, Henry 19
White, Henry 125
Williams, E. T. 52, 100, 118, 121
Wilson, W. 41, 42, 53, 68, 71, 119, 124, 128
  absence of from Peace Conference 59
  advice on China's presentation 54
  and American public opinion 71
  approaches to China problem 122
  at April 22 session of Council of Four 69–70
  changing attitude of 69–70
  China policy of 119
  Chinese reservations unacceptable 94
  faith in the League 73, 119
  on Shandong settlement 72, 89
  view of secret treaties 70
  weakened position of 67
World War I 2, 40, 190, 195
  outbreak of and China 40
Wu Peifu, General 86, 87

Xian Feng, Emperor 17
Xinjiang 62, 156, 157–65, *passim*
  and future Sino-Russian relations, 159
  end of consular jurisdiction and conventional tariff in 164
  Soviet démarche in 159, 161, 162

Xu Shichang 42, 85–6, 87, 210, 217
  and Chinese policy towards the Bolsheviks 194
  final instruction on China's demands at peace conference 73
  on China's aspirations after the War 51
  resignation of 85–6
Xue Fucheng 24

Yamagata Aritomo 127
Yan Huiqing, Dr. 171, 178, 182
Yang Zengxin 158–64 *passim*
  and proposed Soviet consuls in Xinjiang, 159–60
  as Governor of Xinjiang 158
  proposal of revising Sino-Russian Treaty, 1881 161
Yangwu 26, 27
Yili 160, 162, 163
  Customs office of 164
  Sino-Soviet talks in 163
Yili Protocol 157, 164
  and tariff autonomy 164
Yining 164
  Soviet trade agency in 160
Yuan Dynasty 12
Yurin 165, 168, 178
  interview with Dr. Yan 186

Zeng Guofan 23
Zhang Silin 165–75 *passim*
  chosen as head of the mission 168
  connection with Bolsheviks 168
  mission of 165–6, 167
  controversies over 173–5
  problem of credentials 168, 170
  talks with Karakhan 170
Zhu Qiyin 79
Zongli Yamen 16, 18, 24
  replaced by Foreign Ministry 35